RECENT DEVELOPMENTS
IN PSYCHOANALYSIS

Recent Developments in Psychoanalysis

A CRITICAL EVALUATION

Morris N. Eagle

McGRAW-HILL BOOK COMPANY

New York • St. Louis • San Francisco
Auckland • Bogotá • Johannesburg • London • Madrid • Mexico
Montreal • New Delhi • Panama • Paris • São Paulo • Singapore
Sydney • Tokyo • Toronto

Thomas H. Quinn and Michael Hennelly were the editors of this book. Christopher Simon was the designer. Teresa F. Leaden supervised the production. It was set in Caledonia by Achorn Graphics.

Printed and bound by R. R. Donnelley & Sons, Inc.

Library of Congress Cataloging in Publication Data

Eagle, Morris N.
  Recent developments in psychoanalysis.

  Bibliography: p.
  Includes index.
  1. Psychoanalysis. 2. Interpersonal relations.
3. Self. I. Title.
BF173.E16 1984   150.19′5   83-23887
ISBN 0-07-018597-2

  2 3 4 5 6 7 8 9 DOC/DOC 8 9 8 7 6 5

ISBN 0-07-018597-2

To Rita and David

CONTENTS

Acknowledgments

I want to express my gratitude and appreciation to my wife Rita Simon Eagle, not only for her personal encouragement, but for her helpful advice and thoughtful comments. I can no longer think of anything I write as completed unless it has gone through her critical reading. I am also grateful to Robert R. Holt who read and critically assessed the manuscript with his typical thoroughness, from pointing out grammatical and spelling errors to raising basic problems and issues. Whatever is clear about the current version of the manuscript owes a good deal to him. Finally, I want to express my appreciation to Jim Blight whose enthusiasm and understanding of what I was trying to say was very helpful and encouraging.

A CRITICAL EVALUATION OF RECENT DEVELOPMENTS IN PSYCHOANALYTIC THEORY

1

INTRODUCTION

There is a great deal of ferment within psychoanalysis these days. One major aspect of this ferment is the intense focus on object relations and the concept of self. Such interest is, in part, related to the current concern with borderline conditions and narcissistic personality disorders (e.g., Kernberg, 1975; 1976; Kohut, 1971; 1977), but has, of course, a longer history. It was also stimulated by the pioneer studies of Spitz (1945; 1946a; 1946b) on the effects of maternal deprivation, the work of Melanie Klein (e.g., 1932; 1948; 1957) and the British object-relations theorists (e.g., Fairbairn, 1952; Guntrip, 1969; Winnicott, 1958; 1965), the formulations of Mahler and her colleagues (1968; 1975) on symbiosis and separation–individuation, the work of Bowlby (1969; 1973) on attachment and separation, and simply general dissatisfaction with certain aspects of psychoanalytic theory (e.g., Klein, 1976). Also, by now findings from diverse areas of investigation have accumulated which throw into question certain basic assumptions of traditional Freudian theory (Eagle, 1981; 1982a).

In the last number of years the very face of psychoanalytic theory has changed radically. Some of what were once thought to be the very foundational propositions of psychoanalysis have been markedly reformulated. It is not at all certain that all these alterations are consistent with classic psychoanalytic theory as developed by Freud and his early followers. Indeed, when one takes a comprehensive look at the range of reformulations one is not at all clear as to what remains of traditional psychoanalytic theory. And yet, these reformulations and

3

alterations are often presented as if they were merely extensions of earlier ideas or merely complementary sets of formulations without regard to the question of whether they are logically consistent with pre-existing traditional theory. Such reformulations often also incorporate persistent and especially cogent past criticisms of psychoanalytic theory but without explicit acknowledgment that such criticisms were made, are now being recognized, and indeed are being dealt with. Thus the attempted correction of a deficiency in traditional psychoanalytic theory, long noted by critics, is too often hailed as a theoretical advance, even breakthrough—often without any scholarly recognition or citation of the earlier criticism. And finally, too often, these reformulations, some radical in nature, are ostensibly shown to be anticipated in *some* of Freud's writings and to be consistent with and an extension of *some* of Freud's ideas, with little or no regard for the question of whether these reformulations are logically consistent with the core ideas of psychoanalysis as a theoretically coherent system.[1]

Recent formulations and findings, mainly in the areas of object relations and the development of self, entail severe challenges to certain basic Freudian propositions and concepts regarding the nature of personality development and of psychopathology. I will argue that many of these more recent formulations and findings, however they may have been originally presented, are, in fact, inconsistent with some central Freudian propositions and concepts. In short, a good deal of recent psychoanalytic work, even if not always presented in this light, in fact constitutes a radical overhaul of traditional psychoanalytic theory in certain important respects.

Modell (1975) has noted that "this new dimension of object relations . . . has yet to be integrated within Freud's model of *The Ego and the Id*," and has further acknowledged that "if object relations theory cannot be integrated within *The Ego and the Id*, this latter itself will not survive as the central paradigm of psychoanalysis" (p. 58). Although Modell concludes that *The Ego and the Id* can remain as the central paradigm of psychoanalysis, I do not believe that this is so in any simple way, and will try to present the basis for this conclusion.

I believe it is important to take a systematic look at the rush of recent ideas and conceptualizations and to make explicit how psychoanalytic theory has been overhauled, what remains of traditional theory, and what shape the new psychoanalytic conceptions of personality development, of psychopathology, and of the human condition have taken. I strongly endorse the recent suggestion by Gedo (1979) that "the time has finally come to stop the 40-year effort to make

do with the theoretical legacy of Freud through piecemeal patching"
(p. 9). This work, then, is intended as a systematic overview of recent
ideas with the aim of providing a coherent account of the current
status of psychoanalytic theory.

In discussing recent developments in psychoanalysis, I did not in-
tend to be comprehensive and to cover all significant and recent con-
tributors to psychoanalytic theory. I want to explain why some obvious and important figures were omitted. For example, Erikson has
obviously made enormously important contributions to psychoanalysis. However, these contributions were made some time ago and have
been somewhat absorbed in psychoanalytic theory and widely discussed in the general intellectual community. It is more difficult to
explain why I did not include a chapter on Kernberg. Although I refer
to Kernberg in the manuscript and although Kernberg has obviously
made contribution to psychoanalysis (e.g., his descriptions and explanations of borderline conditions), I could not identify an organized set
of coherent theoretical formulations which I could understand well
enough to present and to evaluate critically. Finally, I want to explain
especially why I did not include a chapter on Benjamin B. Rubinstein,
whose writings represent, in my view, some of the most clearheaded
and precise thinking in the current psychoanalytic literature. For one
thing, in contrast to the other material I have included in the manuscript, Rubinstein's writings do not present clinical and theoretical
modifications of psychoanalysis so much as conceptual analyses and
clarifications of basic psychoanalytic concepts. Secondly, at the time I
was completing this manuscript, I agreed to write a chapter on
Rubinstein's contributions for a book on psychoanalysis edited by J.
Reppen. Hence, I knew I would have an opportunity to write about
the important work carried out by Rubinstein during the last number
of years.

2

OBJECT RELATIONS AND FREUDIAN INSTINCT THEORY

Most divergences from traditional psychoanalytic theory have taken as their starting point a rejection or, at least, a reformulation of Freudian instinct theory. While the positing of the dynamic unconscious and the principles of psychic determinism and overdetermination are the most familiar central features of Freudian theory, I believe that Bowlby (1969) is correct in observing that Freud's instinct or drive theory is at the heart of his metapsychology. While the former principles are acceptable to an analyst of almost any persuasion, it is drive theory that is distinctly Freudian and constitutes the groundwork for many other psychoanalytic concepts—for example, anxiety, defense, primary process functioning. It is no wonder that historically, acceptance or rejection of instinct theory has served as the main criterion for defining apostasy from Freudian psychoanalysis. Criticism of instinct theory was, and still is, taken by many to constitute a rejection of the biological, of man's instinctual heritage, of that which, more than anything else, differentiated Freudian from the presumably more superficial neo-Freudian interpersonal and cultural schools of psychoanalysis. I will try to show that this view is mistaken. I will also try to show that traditional Freudian theory, in particular instinct theory, does not deal adequately with object relations.

It will be useful first to remind ourselves of the manner in which the issue of object relations is dealt with in traditional theory. Freudian instinct theory is one of those all-embracing motivational theories of human behavior in which *all* behavior—the cognitive, interpersonal,

6

social, etc.—is seen to be, directly or indirectly, in the service of and an expression of presumably basic or primary drives. In such theories, all behavior either serves to gratify these primary drives or other drives which have secondarily developed in association with the so-called primary drives.

I think it can be shown that this formulation derives directly from the quasi-Darwinist assumption that behavior is to be understood in terms of its survival function. This is more apparent in early Freud when he posited essentially self-preservative (e.g., hunger) and species preservative (e.g., sex) instincts. Although later Freud spoke mainly of sexual and aggressive instincts, the essence of the early evolutionary idea was never relinquished.[2]

Since for Freud, drive gratification and discharge of excitation are essentially synonymous, another way of stating the proposition that all behavior is in the service of drive gratification is to say that the basic tendency of the organism is immediate discharge of excitation. That Freud viewed this tendency as having survival value is made apparent with his assumption that excitation, if left undischarged or permitted to reach an excessively high level, can damage the organism. Indeed, excessive excitation is viewed as the basic psychic danger facing the organism—an idea formulated in the "Project" and never relinquished by Freud (1887–1902)—and various means of avoiding this danger comprise much human behavior.[3] While external stimulation can contribute to excessive excitation, it is mainly instinctual tensions which constitute the major source of such danger. This is so because in contrast to external stimulation, one cannot physically flee from internally generated tensions. In any case, the natural tendency of the organism is to seek immediate discharge. What makes this impossible are essentially physical reality and social reality, that is, civilization.

That immediate discharge is not possible has enormous consequences for personality development and behavior. According to Freudian theory, the impossibility of immediate discharge "forces" the development of thinking and other ego functions, and generates commerce with and interest in objects in the world. That is, were one to live in a science fiction world in which wishing would, indeed, make it so, one would never develop functions other than wishing nor would one develop object relations. Consider as an example of this view Freud's (1900) speculation that the young infant, after receiving gratification of its hunger, attempts to establish wish fulfillment through hallucination of the breast when experiencing hunger once again ("the establishment of a perceptual identity along the short path of regression"). Freud observes that it is only because this pathway does not remove the tensions of hunger that it must yield to more realistic, albeit more delayed and indirect, means of discharge. Stated very clearly in Freud's writings is the proposition that were it not for the imposed delays and frustrations of reality, thinking and other ego functions mediating reality would never develop. For Freud, thinking is only a detour or roundabout means to drive gratification made necessary by the nature of reality. As he puts it, despite hallucinatory activity, "satisfaction does not follow; the need persists" and hence, this forces the psychic apparatus "to seek out other patterns which lead eventually to the desired perceptual identity being established from the direction of the external world" (p. 605). However, Freud reminds us, "all the complicated thought-activity which is spun out from the mnemic image to the moment at which the perceptual identity is established by the external world—all this activity of thought merely constitutes a roundabout path to wish-fulfillment which has been made necessary by experience. Thought is after all nothing but a substitute for a hallucinating wish . . . ." (pp. 605–606). And even after reality testing and thoughts develop, it continues to be true, according to Freud, that nothing but a wish can set our mental apparatus at work.[4]

What can be said of thinking can also be said of an interest in objects and of object relations in general. Were drive gratification possible without objects (that is, were hallucination of the breast and its equivalents successful in achieving satisfaction), one would develop neither an interest in objects nor object relations. But given the nature of reality, one is *forced* to overcome what Freud calls the "primal hatred" of objects and look to them for drive gratification. Hence, their significance lies mainly in their role as "the thing in regard to which or through which the instinct is able to achieve its aim" (Freud, 1915a, p. 122).

Freud's (1914) discussion of narcissism also makes clear his belief that we only reluctantly cathect objects. Thus, according to Freud, there is "an original libidinal cathexis of the ego, part of which cathexis is later yielded up to objects, but which fundamentally persists and is related to the object-cathexes much as the body of a protoplasmic animalcule is related to the pseudopodia which it puts out" (p. 58). Later in the same essay, Freud speaks of the neurotic's ego as being depleted by "excessive object-cathexes." In other words, the original narcissistic reluctance to cathect objects is fundamental and persists throughout life; and further, object investment always entails the potential danger of ego depletion.

The Freudian account of the formation of interpersonal attachments follows directly from the general conception of the role and function of objects. The essential nature and origin of the interpersonal or of object relations is also to be understood in terms of Freud's instinct theory. A child's attachment to his mother (and, by implication, our later attachment to each other) is explained primarily in terms of the latter's role in providing experiences of instinctual gratification. As Freud (1940a) puts it, "love has its origins in attachment to the satisfied need for nourishment" (p. 188). On a more general level, the bases for the child's attachment to mother lie primarily in her role in preventing excessive stimulation that would accrue from the build-up of instinctual drive tensions and, as a corollary of this role, as exciter of erotogenic zones (or, to use one of Freud's more dramatic terms, as "seducer"). Although, as Bowlby (1969) points out, one can find passages in Freud's writings which point to the primary, autonomous nature of early infant-mother object relations, his general writings and the logic of his instinct theory explain the child's attachment to mother in terms of the latter's role in providing instinctual gratifications.

To the extent that interpersonal attachment is seen as deriving its force from its association with instinctual gratification, the former is given a secondary, derived status in Freudian theory which thereby serves as an example of what Bowlby (1969) calls a "secondary drive" theory of mother-child attachment. In such theories, the instinctual (or, in traditional learning theory, the so-called "primary drives") is seen as primary, the biological core of personality, while the interpersonal and social are seen as the secondary, derived, overlain aspects of personality.

This conception of the object relational as derived from and secondary to the basic instincts is exemplified, for example, by Spitz's (1960) explanation of his findings on maternal deprivation. Because these findings have been so frequently cited to show the devastating developmental effects of lack of early mothering, even when the more obvious bodily needs (hunger, thirst, shelter) are met, it is easy to overlook the fact that Spitz's own interpretations of his findings were formulated rather strictly within the terms of Freudian instinct theory. That is, Spitz attributes part of the effects of maternal separation to the fact that the loss of the love object interrupts the discharge of both the libidinal and aggressive drives. He states specifically: ". . . I have to stress once again that in the emotional interchanges with the love object *both* the libidinal *and* the aggressive drives find their discharge. The loss of the love object interrupts the discharge of both drives" (p. 90). In other words, it is not the loss of the love object *per se* that is so harmful, but the fact that the loss takes away opportunities for discharge of libidinal and aggressive drives. Clearly implied in this formulation is the idea that the damming up of libidinal and aggressive drive energies is the primary mechanism responsible for the extreme effects on development attendant upon maternal separation. This is as clear-cut a hydraulic model as one is likely to come upon in recent psychoanalytic formulations. It is also illustrative of how the data on early object relations are interpreted from the point of view of Freudian instinct theory. From this perspective, objects and object relations are important primarily as means and vehicles for discharge of libidinal and aggressive drives. In this regard, the former, indeed, have a secondary and derived status.

In summary then, according to Freudian theory, we would develop neither an interest in objects nor object relations nor reality-testing ego functions were objects not necessary for drive gratification and were immediate gratification possible (as exemplified, for example, in hallucination of the breast). But, given the nature of reality, immediate gratification is not possible and objects *are* necessary, as are planning and detour methods of gratification.[5] Hence, we are forced to have commerce with objects. But the nature of that commerce—of object relations—is one in which our interest in and relationship with objects continues to be directly or indirectly linked to their use in and relevance for drive gratification.

There is now a great deal of evidence indicating that Freud's "anaclitic" model of infant-mother attachment and the general conception of the basis for object relations offered by traditional theory is incorrect. The most well known such evidence is provided by Harlow's (1958) studies on "the nature of love."

The dissatisfaction with "secondary drive" explanations (which it should be noted, includes the "anaclitic" model) of the interpersonal led to the now classic Harlow (1958) studies which showed rather decisively that the infant monkey's attachment to its surrogate mother was not derived from or secondary to the latter's association with reduction of so-called primary drives (i.e., hunger, thirst). Rather such attachment seemed to be based on the autonomous need for what Harlow called "contact comfort." Infant monkeys were taken from their natural mothers at birth and were raised by artificial wire and terrycloth surrogate mothers. Harlow reasoned that if the infant monkey's attachment to its mother were secondarily derived from the association of mother with reduction of "primary" drives, then the infant monkey would become attached to whichever surrogate mother reduced the primary drives of hunger and thirst. Instead the infant monkey developed an attachment to the (terrycloth) surrogate mother providing "contact comfort" even when a different surrogate (wire) mother satisfied its so-called "primary" drives.

It is important to keep in mind that the surrogate mothers to whom the infant monkeys became attached did not simply serve the function of dispensing "contact comfort" analogously to the surrogate mothers who dispensed milk, but were also clung to and provided a security base in situations of novelty and experienced danger. In other words, while the infant monkeys would go to the milk-dispensing wire mothers when they were hungry, they showed *a generalized attachment* to the terrycloth mother and clung to "her" when they needed comforting and security.[6]

These findings present serious challenges to "homeostatic drive reduction" models of attachment and, if one can generalize from infant monkeys to infant humans, they also present serious challenges to the traditional "anaclitic" model of attachment.[7] If attachment to an object is derived from its role in drive gratification, why didn't the infant monkeys become attached to the milk-dispensing mother who provided gratification more closely fitting a drive discharge model than the "contact comfort" gratification provided by the terrycloth mother?

The fact that the infant becomes attached to the provider of "contact comfort" rather than to the provider of milk reveals something important about the nature of attachment. It suggests that infants are genetically predisposed to become attached to an entity with certain characteristics, prominent among which is the capacity to provide "contact comfort." It is likely that this early need for "contact comfort" and predisposition to become attached to the provider of "contact comfort" forms the basis for and is a precursor to later contact and object relational needs which become increasingly psychological in nature—for example, the need for empathic responses from the mothering figure. In short, rather than being secondary or "anaclitic," there is an independent genetic basis for the development of attachment and object relations.

Of course, in the natural environment, the feeding, caring, and "contact comfort" functions are carried out together by one and the same person or animal, and indeed, much "contact comfort" is provided through and during feeding and caring. Undoubtedly, this strengthens the infant's attachment to mother and thus has survival value.[7A] What the Harlow study shows, however, through an experimental separation of these functions, is that the main "carrier" of attachment is the "contact comfort" rather than the feeding function. Some thought suggests that this too is highly adaptive. For the capacity to provide "contact comfort" is a quality integral to and shared by all members of the species, thus virtually guaranteeing attachment to *some* member of the species. This becomes increasingly important beyond infancy when peer relationships and mating considerations become relevant. "Contact comfort" as a primary vehicle for attachment constitutes a wider base for and guarantees a wider range of attachments than does feeding. Insofar as the wider base and wider range of attachment facilitate peer relationhips and mating, they have obvious adaptive and selective value for the species. (For example, animals incapable of establishing peer affectional attachments are less likely to pass on their genes).

It is important to note that monkeys raised without mother, but with peers, do not seem to show any of the major developmental disturbances shown by monkeys raised by artificial surrogate mothers (i.e., wire and terrycloth mothers) or in isolation. By contrast, monkeys reared with their biological mothers, but denied any contact with age mates, are markedly inadequate in their social repertoires (Alexander and Harlow, 1965).

Monkeys raised with peers but without mothers exhibit intense attachment to one another (Harlow, 1969)—a pattern which strikingly parallels the description of six children who had been thrown together in concentration camps at ages ranging from a few months to one year. At the time they became known to Freud and Dann (1951) they had been together continuously in a variety of concentration camps for over two years. They had formed intense attachments to one another, showed great sensitivity to one another's attitudes and feelings, and shared all possessions. They displayed a strong in-group feeling and initially responded to adult caretakers with either disregard or verbal and physical attacks. Most important in the present context, these children did not show the degree and kind of gross pathology which, according to most current psychodynamic theories, an absence of maternal rearing should inevitably produce. Freud and Dann observe that these children "were neither deficient, delinquent nor psychotic" (p. 514).

The importance of the peer affectional system in development and its possible limited substitutability for the maternal relationship highlights, in still another way, the autonomous basis for object relations and casts further doubt on the assumption that interpersonal attachments are secondarily derived from the gratification of so-called primary drives. If early attachment were primarily a function of gratification of the hunger drive, one would be hard put to account for the strength of the peer affectional system. Quite obviously, the young rely on peers, not for feeding, but for object relational needs which are quite independent of feeding.

All the evidence, from research and observations on humans and infra-human behavior, overwhelmingly supports the idea of a primary and autonomous attachment instinctual system relatively independent of the hunger drive and of sex and aggression. As described by Bowlby (1969) and others, it is a system comprising such behavioral components as smiling, vocalizing, sucking, soothability, a readiness to respond to objects with certain specific features, and, as the work of Harlow (1958) shows, a need for "contact comfort." In all species in which attachment between infant and mother develops, the mother exhibits caretaking behavior reciprocal to the infant's attachment responses (Bowlby, 1969). There is no evidence at all that these attachment responses are wholly dependent upon or entirely built up from the gratification of other needs (although, of course, attachment to mother can be strengthened by these gratifications).

Elements of the infant's attachment behavioral repertoire (that is, components of the attachment behavioral system) appear at birth across practically all members of the species. They all facilitate the "predictable outcome" of proximity to and contact with the caregiver either through signaling responses (e.g., crying, smiling) which elicit complementary responses from the caregiver or through active behaviors (e.g., sucking, clasping) which directly accomplish proximity and contact.

Stern (1980), a prominent researcher in the field of infant-mother interactions, concludes that there is now sufficient evidence indicating "that powerful relationships are not forged by feeding in comparison to experiential sharing and complementing. It is perhaps time to suggest that the experience of being hungry, getting fed, and going blissfully to sleep, even when associated with a particular person, does not lead to subjective intimacy with the feeding person unless accompanied by subject-object complementing and state sharing" (p. 37). This position can be contrasted with the classical psychoanalytic one which assumes "a first 'anaclitic' relation to the mother, i.e., a phase in which the pleasurable sensations derived from the gratification of major needs are instrumental in determining which person in the external world is selected for libidinal cathexis" (A. Freud, 1960, p. 55). (This contrast is particularly clear when one considers that in classical theory "major needs" do not include what Stern refers to as "subject-object complementing" and "pleasurable sensations" as defined in the context of a drive discharge model).

That the proper model for attachment is not the "anaclitic" one proposed by Freud is also indicated by the effects of object (primarily maternal) deprivation. Thus, that the infant mortality rate of monkeys is influenced by presence or absence of a piece of cheesecloth in the otherwise bare cage can hardly be accounted for in terms of feeding or nutrition (Harlow, 1958). Also, it has been shown that even if visual, auditory, and olfactory interactions are maintained, the prevention of physical contact between infant and mother leads to abnormal development in monkeys (Harlow and Zimmerman, 1959; Hinde and Spencer-Booth, 1971; Harlow and Harlow, 1965). There is similar evidence in children that despite adequate nutrition and medical care, inadequate maternal attention is associated with abnormal development (e.g., Powell *et al.*, 1967 a, b; Silver and Finkelstein, 1967) and a high mortality rate (Bakwin, 1949; Patton and Gardner, 1963). Chronic maternal deprivation is also associated with permanent decreases in body size, a development referred to as "psychosocial dwarfism" (e.g., Thoman and Arnold, 1968). Also, Goldschmidt (1975) has reported that although Sebei children are demand fed and weaned at a relatively late age, there is a remarkable lack of fondling and eye contact, and mothers are remote, disengaged, and detached. The result is that as adults the Sebei tend to relate to each other mainly in terms of instrumental use, show little empathy for suffering of others, and are relatively affectless.

In an attempt to develop an animal model of human "psychosocial dwarfism," Schanberg and Kuhn (1980) have presented striking evidence that maternal deprivation is a primary factor rather than secondary to other variables. First, they have shown that maternal deprivation of preweaning rat pups results in a decrease in the activity of brain, heart, and liver ornithine decarboxylase (ODC)—a biochemical index of tissue maturation—and that returning the pups to mother increases ODC activity. That the decline in ODC activity is unrelated to food deprivation was conclusively shown by the *absence* of such a decline when the pups were placed with a lactating female rat whose nipples had been tied off, and the *presence* of a decline when deprived pups were fed Sustacal through an intragastric cannula or when pups were placed with lactating females whose active maternal behavior had been prevented by the anesthetizing effects of urethane (an intervention which did not affect milk production,. ejection, or suckling by the pups).

That the denial of tactile stimulation is a critical aspect in the effects of maternal deprivation is shown by the finding that maternally deprived pups who were stroked vigorously on the back and head for two hours with a moist camel hair brush (which is similar to the mother's grooming) did *not* show the usual decline in ODC activity. Shanberg and Kuhn relate these findings to the report that tactile stimulation of premature babies increased their weight gain significantly over controls (White and La Barba, 1976).

The ideas that an interest in objects must overcome a fundamental narcissistic tendency and "primal hatred," that it is an outcome of the failure of primary process attempts at direct discharge (as in hallucination of the breast), and that it is generally dependent on the vicissitudes of instinctual gratification are also refuted by the growing evidence that infants are stimulus-seeking organisms and that their selective preferences for certain stimulus configurations are autonomous, inborn, natural propensities which appear at birth or shortly after birth.

It has been demonstrated that infants will even interrupt feeding in order to look at a novel or interesting stimulus (Emde and Robinson, 1979). The young infant is capable of orienting visually to the source of a sound. Among other abilities, he can recognize in one modality (vision) an object he has experienced in another modality (tactile). He can match events showing the same temporal structure and can match intensities of a stimulus experienced in two different modalities.

The research evidence has also established that very young infants show perceptual discrimination and/or selective preferences for novel visual and auditory stimuli (e.g., Friedman, Bruno, and Vietze, 1974); for one set of geometric features over another (e.g., McCall and Nelson, 1970; Ruff and Birch, 1974); for one set of patterns over another (e.g., Frantz, 1958; 1965) for number and size of stimulus elements (e.g., Fantz and Fagan, 1975); for intermediate brightness (Hershenson, 1964); for colors (Cohen and Gelber, 1975; Cohen *et al.*, 1971) and for an optimal level of discrepancy from pre-existing stimuli (e.g., Kinney and Kagan, 1976). It is to be noted that insofar as these studies deal with selective preferences (as determined, for example, by visual fixation) the concept of an *interest* in objects seems particularly appropriate to the phenomena in question.

To summarize the main point, all the evidence taken together indicates that an interest in objects as well as the development of affectional bonds is not simply a derivative or outgrowth of libidinal energies and aims or a consequence of gratification of other needs, but is a critical independent aspect of development which expresses inborn propensities to establish cognitive and affective links to objects in the world. Apparently, tactile stimulation (and, as other evidence which I have not cited suggests, kinesthetic stimulation) is, early on, an especially critical dimension of objects to which the infant responds. The research evidence also supports the clinical intuitions and formulations of Balint (1937), who argued that "primary object love" more accurately describes the infants' early propensities than Freud's concept of primary narcissism; and those of Fairbairn (1952), who proposed that "libido is primarily object-seeking rather than pleasure-seeking."[8]

Ego Psychology

The above findings represent challenges from without to traditional psychoanalytic theory. The last number of years, however, have also witnessed challenges from within.

Within traditional psychoanalytic theory, the idea that all behavior and all psychic functions are derived from and secondary to the basic instincts was first seriously questioned in regard to ego functions. This theme is explicit in the developments of psychoanalytic ego psychology and is most closely associated with the work of Hartmann (1958; 1964). He opened the door to the possibility of considering aspects of behavior, development, and psychic functioning as relatively autonomous from instinctual drive. While important for the development of psychoanalytic theory, this was hardly an empirical discovery; as a substantive statement, it amounted merely to acknowledging and admitting into psychoanalytic theory the phenomena and facts of biological *maturation* as applied to cognitive functions—phenomena and facts with which biologists, pediatricians, experimental and developmental psychologists were long familiar. After all, isn't the proposition that in an "average expectable environment" certain ego functions will develop relatively independent of conflict and other drive vicissitudes essentially a statement, in psychoanalytic terms, of the phenomenon of maturation? In this sense Hartmann's contribution can be viewed as essentially a politico-theoretical one, for it permitted psychoanalytic theorists who still considered themselves Freudian analysts to view cognitive-ego functions at least somewhat autonomously of instinct gratification and instinct theory.[9] And I say *somewhat* autonomously because in some of his writings Hartmann has noted that while ego apparatuses may develop along the lines of biological maturation, they nevertheless require the driving force of instincts in order to function and lead to action. This contention will be taken up in a later separate discussion.

However incomplete, what was accomplished in the area of ego functions—the freedom to view them relatively independent of the context of instinct theory—was not accomplished for other areas of behavior and psychic functioning, in particular for the areas of object relations and self. Because cognitive development was not a central point of contention between neo-Freudian and Freudian theorists, it was more "neutral" ground and hence, more susceptible to modification and reformulation. The interpersonal, social and cultural, however, was precisely the battleground between Freudian and neo-Freudian theories and hence, more emotionally charged and more likely to become a central ideological issue. In addition, while a good deal of work had already been done on maturational processes in cognitive development, parallel work on the biological roots of interpersonal and social aspects of behavior came later or, at least, was slower to make a major impact on psychoanalytic thinking. For example, it was not until 1969 that Bowlby's first major work appeared which tried to incorporate into psychoanalytic theory the important findings from ethological studies and other systematic research attesting to the primary biological roots of the interpersonal and social. It was not until 1958 that Harlow reported his classic experiment described above, in which he tried to show that the infant's attachment to its mother was not secondarily derived from so-called primary drives such as hunger and feeding. And only recently has systematic research on infant-mother interaction been carried out.

It is an interesting historical note that paralleling the emergence of psychoanalytic ego psychology were similar developments within academic psychology. Indeed, Harlow's classic experiment was designed to counter the idea that all behavior serves to gratify so-called primary drives or satisfy motives and aims which have been secondarily derived from these drives, a basic assumption not only of Freudian theory, but of learning theory as formulated by Hull (1943) and later by Dollard and Miller (1950).[10] Similar to Freudian theory, Hullian learning theory was also one of those all-embracing motivational theories, ostensibly derived from evolutionary theory, in which all behavior is held to be motivated by drive-reduction. This view, which dominated American learning theory, came under challenge at about the same time as the emergence of ego psychology and, although concerned mainly with animal behavior, on grounds similar to those presented by the ego psychologists. Animals were shown to exhibit, for example, curiosity and exploratory behavior—the animal version of ego functions—quite independently of the so-called primary drives (e.g., Barnett, 1958; Berlyne, 1960; Butler, 1965).

An Overview of Recent Developments in Psychoanalysis

As I will elaborate on later, whatever the modifications in traditional psychoanalytic theory represented by ego psychology, they were and were intended to be entirely consistent with the basic id-ego structural model of Freudian theory. In this sense, they did not constitute a critical challenge to the basic assumptions of traditional theory. The same, however, cannot be said of more recent findings and formulations which, as Modell (1975) has noted, raise basic difficulties for some core aspects of Freudian theory. The core of these challenges is that certain critical issues and features of personality development and of psychopathology, having to do with object relations and self, do not easily fit the basic id-ego model of traditional theory. For example, the descriptions of psychological development which have appeared most meaningful to many recent clinicians and theorists are not those having to do with psychosexual development, but accounts that focus on such dimensions as self-other differentiation, the move from symbiosis to separation-individuation, and degree of self-cohesiveness. The increasing interest in these dimensions has been prompted, not only by observations of children and of mother-child interactions, but also by a recent preoccupation with certain classes of pathology— mainly, borderline conditions, narcissistic personality disorders, and schizoid personalities[11]—which do not seem to center on the usual intrapsychic id-ego oedipal conflicts, but on pre-oedipal problems of self-cohesiveness and of separation-individuation.

The next few chapters will take up these challenges from within. Broadly speaking, they fall into one of four different categories. In the first category, the response consists mainly of an attempt to preserve traditional instinct theory and combine it with a recognition of the importance of object relations and of self. This approach is exemplified by the work of Mahler (1968; 1975). (It is also represented by Kernberg [1975; 1976] and Jacobson [1964], whose work will not be covered here). In this approach, while greater recognition is given to issues of object relations and of self, the assumption continues to be made that development in these areas is somehow linked with and contingent upon the vicissitudes of instinctual unfolding and gratification.

The second category can be called a two-factor theory and is exemplified by the early writings of Kohut (1971) and the work of Modell. Psychoanalytic theorists who represent this point of view seem to accept both instinct theory and a psychology of object relations and self, with each theoretical perspective presumably appropriate to a different set of phenomena (e.g., narcissistic personality disorders versus neurotic "structural conflicts").

A third response entails an outright rejection of Freudian instinct theory and a thoroughgoing replacement of it by a psychology of object relations and of self. This approach is exemplified by Fairbairn (1952), Guntrip (1969) and, I believe, G. S. Klein (1976). It is also represented by Kohut's (1977) later writings and that of his followers.

A residual fourth category is reserved for Gedo's (1979) epigenetic hierarchical theory which bears certain similarities to both Kohut's and Klein's formulations.

Finally, I will take up the work of Weiss, Sampson and their colleagues (Horowitz *et al.*, 1975; Sampson, 1982; Sampson *et al.*, 1972; Sampson *et al.*, 1976; Sampson, and Weiss, 1977; Sampson, H., Weiss, and Gassner, 1977; Weiss, 1952; 1971; 1982; Weiss *et al.*, 1977; Weiss *et al.*, 1980) which does not fit any of the above categories, but which is sufficiently challenging to traditional ideas and of sufficient interest to warrant inclusion. As will be seen, the approach of this group can be characterized as an updated and sophisticated ego psychology.

3

OBJECT RELATIONS AND SELF AS AN OUTGROWTH OF INSTINCTUAL VICISSITUDES:
The Work of Mahler

The formulations of Mahler and her colleagues (Mahler, 1968; Mahler *et al.*, 1975) on psychic development are presented mainly in terms of symbiosis and separation–individuation. Mahler's focus is on that dimension of psychological development which traces the growth of the infant from a state of non-differentiation between "I" and "not-I" to an eventual phase of separation-individuation. According to Mahler *et al.* (1975), "the biological birth of the human infant and the psychological birth of the individual are not coincident in time" (p. 3). The latter is referred to as the separation-individuation process. Separation refers to "the child's emergence from a symbiotic fusion with the mother" while "individuation consists of those achievements marking the child's assumption of his own individual characteristics" (Mahler *et al.*, 1975, p. 4). In other words, the interest of Mahler and her co-workers is in that line of development which culminates in one having a sense of one's own separate bodily and psychological identity, in functioning separately and autonomously in the world, and in experiencing one's own individual characteristics (e.g., in the areas of perception, thinking, and memory) in the course of that autonomous functioning.

According to Mahler, development proceeds from a stage of "normal autism" to a symbiotic period to the four sequentially unfolding sub-phases of the separation-individuation process. Although these steps and sequences are part of a normally unfolding maturational process, as we shall see, each step is strongly influenced by the infant-

20

mother interaction, in particular by such factors as early symbiotic gratification and the emotional availability of the mother. Although most people in the field are familiar with the stages in development posited by Mahler, it nevertheless might be useful to review them briefly here.

During the first few weeks of life the infant is, according to Mahler (1968), in a state of *normal autism* in which experiences are limited to "deposits of memory traces of the two primordial qualities (pleasurable-good versus painful-bad) of stimuli occur" (p. 8). Freud's (1911) use of the bird egg as a model of a closed system is invoked to describe this state. The infant at this stage is presumably shut off from and unresponsive to external stimuli and is essentially a physiological creature who "seems to be in a state of primitive hallucinatory disorientation in which need satisfaction seems to belong to his own 'unconditional', omnipotent, *autistic* orbit (cf. Freneczi, 1913)" (p. 42).

The stage of normal autism is followed from the second month on by the *symbiotic phase*, which is marked by a dim awareness of the need-satisfying object. In this stage, the infant is in a "state of undifferentiation, of fusion with mother, in which the 'I' is not differentiated from the 'not I'. . . ." (Mahler, 1968, p. 9). "The essential feature of symbiosis," according to Mahler, "is hallucinatory or delusional, somato-psychic *omnipotent* fusion with the representation of the mother and, in particular, the delusion of a common boundary. . . ." (Mahler *et al.*, 1975, p. 45).

At about four or five months of age, the first subphase—*differentiation*—of the separation-individuation makes its appearance. During this subphase, "infants take their first tentative steps toward breaking away, in a bodily sense, from their hitherto completely passive. . . . stage of dual unity with the mother" (Mahler *et al.*, 1975, p. 55). In infants who experience "safe anchorage within the symbiotic orbit" and for whom symbiotic gratification has been optimal, one observes the infant's great pleasure in sensory perception, his curiosity and wonderment (rather than stranger anxiety) in the inspection of strangers, and a pattern of "checking back to mother," a sort of comparative scanning of mother and others. Transitional phenomena (Winnicott, 1958) also make their appearance during this subphase.

From about nine months on (and lasting to about 15–18 months), the second sub-phase, referred to as *practicing* by Mahler, makes its appearance. The most obvious behavioral characteristic of this period is the active practice of locomotion, including crawling, paddling, and climbing and, of course, eventually culminating in free, upright locomotion. According to Mahler (1968), at this stage the child "appears to be at the peak point of his belief in his own magic omnipotence, which is still to a considerable extent derived from his sense of sharing in his mother's magic powers" (p. 20). Mahler refers to Greenacre's (1957) description of the infant at this stage as having a "love affair with the world." The infant's exploration of and love affair with the world is, however, exquisitely linked to mother's availability. This is seen in a number of ways. During exploration, the infant maintains an optimal distance from mother, looks to her as a "home base," and periodically returns for what Furer termed "emotional refueling." Also, the degree of freedom of exploration of the world varies as a function of the prior history and nature of relationship between infant and mother.

The third sub-phase—*rapprochement*—follows practicing at about 15–18 months of age (and lasts until about 24 months of age). This stage is characterized by the toddler's greater awareness of separateness, greater separation anxiety, and, in consequence, an increased need and wish to be with mother, to know her whereabouts, to share his new skills with her, and to have her love. According to Mahler *et al.* (1975), at this age the child shows two characteristic patterns of incessant "shadowing" of the mother and darting away from her, which are interpreted as expressing "both his wish for reunion with the love object and his fear of engulfment by it" (p. 77). The growth in the child's cognitive abilities makes possible increased verbal communication and the beginning of "representational intelligence" (Piaget, 1936). One can also observe the beginning establishment of a cohesive self and of gender identity. According to Mahler and her colleagues, how the rapprochement phase is handled is extremely important for the future development of the child. It is at this stage that the mother must combine continued emotional availability with an emotional willingness to let go and to provide a "gentle push" toward independence. Because of their own difficulties, some mothers are unable to let go and become the "shadowers" rather than the "shadowed," while other mothers are not sufficiently available and abruptly and prematurely push toward independence. Such failures often bring in their wake increased separation anxiety, desperate clinging to mother, and difficulty in investing interest in one's surroundings and in pleasure and confidence in one's own functioning.

At about the beginning of the third year of life, the fourth subphase appears and is referred to by Mahler *et al.* (1975) as "consolidation of individuality and the beginnings of emotional object constancy" (p.

109). The main developmental tasks during this subphase are achievement of a lifelong, definite individuality and the attainment of a certain degree of object constancy. The main achievements during this phase include the establishment of affective object constancy, which implies the earlier "cognitive acquisition of the symbolic inner representation of the permanent object" (Mahler *et al.*, 1975, p. 110); the internalization of parental demands (superego formation); the increased consolidation of gender identity; and the unifying of "good" and "bad" representations into one integrated representation. In contrast to earlier subphases, this phase is open-ended and includes tasks that are continued in the course of further development.

In a recent paper, Milton Klein (1981) has evaluated Mahler's formulations and concepts in the light of recent research on infants and has found a number of them seriously wanting and reflecting the almost complete neglect of the available research evidence. For example, it is doubtful that the infant is ever in a state of "normal autism," as described by Mahler and her co-workers. The evidence suggests that the infant is never in a state of total non-differentiation between self and other and that psychological and biological birth are simultaneous (that is, there is no need to posit a later and separate psychological birth). Hence, characterizations of the young infant in terms of such concepts as primary narcissism, objectlessness, fused, and so on, are, according to Klein, simply inaccurate.

Stern (1980) also presents convincing evidence that even at birth there is no total lack of differentiation between self and other. On the contrary, from the very beginning the infant reveals capacities and abilities which would permit him to form rudimentary conceptions of self and of other and to differentiate between the two. For example, the infant shows cross-modal equivalence (the ability to recognize in one modality an object one has only experienced in another modality); can visually orient to the source of a sound; shows temporal cross-modal integration (the infant reacts to two events sharing the same temporal structure as if they belonged together); can match the intensity of a stimulus experienced in one modality with the intensity experienced in another modality; can maintain the identity of a three-dimensional object despite changes in perspective; shows evidence of remembering an event experienced days before with the use of minimal cues such as context; and can distinguish between a constant and variable reinforcement schedule.

What is remarkable about all these abilities is not only that they are present within the first few months of life, but they are the very abilities necessary for the establishment of an early and rudimentary sense of self and other and differentiation between self and other. For example, the concept of an object implies the very abilities (such as cross-modal equivalence and temporal cross-modal integration) the infant has. To take another example, actions of the self upon the self involve a constant reinforcement schedule, while actions of the self upon others as well as actions of others upon the self involve a variable reinforcement schedule. The ability of the young infant to distinguish between these different reinforcement schedules then represents at least one basis for discriminating between self and other.

Both Klein and Stern make important distinctions which are often blurred in Mahler's formulations. For example, there is a critical difference between relative lack of discrimination between self and other based on normal developmental stages of cognitive-affective growth on the one hand and fusion or merging on the other, which may be a pathological phenomenon and is based on complex and high-level cognitions beyond the capacity of the infant. Stern urges that concepts such as "self-objects," "symbiotic objects," and "part-objects," which may be appropriate to the description of certain adult pathological phenomena, "not be borrowed to be retrospectively installed as normal parts of the infants' affective-cognitive experience" (p. 28) (a tendency Klein describes as the "pathomorphic" myth). And conversely, he decries the tendency to conceptualize adult pathology as reactivations of normal developmental phases.

Many of Klein's and Stern's criticisms were stated earlier by Peterfreund (1978), who noted certain disturbing tendencies in psychoanalytic conceptions of infancy. He also observes and decries the tendency to characterize normal stages of infancy in terms of adult pathology (a combination of "adultomophism" and "pathomorphism"). For example, the infant is described as "disoriented" or "delusional" rather than recognized as oriented and realistic to the extent of his functioning abilities. Along with Klein and Stern, Peterfreund also questions the accuracy of descriptions of the infant as totally "undifferentiated" or "fused" or "narcissistic."

It is obvious that many of the above criticisms can be (and indeed, are) directed to certain aspects of Mahler's characterization of the infant and his development. However, if I may be permitted this figure of speech, there is a danger of throwing out the baby with the bathwater. That is, even if Mahler's characterization of the infant as totally undifferentiated and in a state of complete fusion with mother, for example, is incorrect, what remains as an important contribution is her emphasis on separation-individuation as the major dimension of psychological development. Thus, even if, as Klein, Stern, Peterfreund, and others have argued, individuation and differentiation begin at birth, there is no question that they are present only at a rudimentary level, continue to develop as part of the child's psychological growth, and constitute an essential dimension of that growth.

In developing the concept of separation-individuation, Mahler has identified a truly universal dimension applicable to all members of the species and, in appropriate form, to members of other species. Further, in describing the unfolding of this dimension, Mahler has suggested certain relationships (for example, between "safe anchorage" and exploratory behavior) which, as we shall see, have received wide and systematic support. Finally, it is important to note that concepts such as symbiotic gratification and particularly separation-individuation are most meaningfully understood, not in terms of (sexual or aggressive) drive gratification, but in terms of attachment behavior. As I will try to show, although Mahler often employs the language of libido and drive, one can essentially ignore this language in understanding her more basic formulations.

In common with all other animals who show attachment behavior, the child must negotiate the often difficult path of individuation and independence expected and demanded of an adult member of the species. In infra-human species, failure to negotiate these demands successfully would undoubtedly imperil survival. In the much more complex and culture-bound human, such failures are manifested in uneven development, psychological disturbance, deviance, interpersonal deficiencies, etc. In other words, psychopathology and deviance are more likely to derive from the attachment related issues of symbiosis-individuation than from issues of sexual and aggressive drives. While sex and aggression undoubtedly play a part in personality development, separation-individuation is a truly universal and inevitable challenge, a challenge upon which personality most often founders. This is undoubtedly something of what Fairbairn (1952) had in mind when he claimed that all psychopathology was in one way or another related to the persistence and vicissitudes of infantile dependency. Indeed, it is likely that the capacity to gratify sexual needs adequately and the frequency and quality of certain pathological aggressive behavior is strongly influenced by early attachment experiences. Thus, Harlow's infant monkeys taken from their natural mothers and raised by artificial wire and terrycloth surrogate mothers manifested in adulthood severe incapacities in sexual functioning and the presence of deviant aggressive behavior (Harlow, 1974).

It appears, then, that a clear implication of Mahler's concepts of symbiosis and separation-individuation is the primary role of the attachment system and the secondary role of sexual and aggressive drives in personality development and serious psychopathology. And yet, symbiosis and separation-individuation are linked by Mahler, not to the ideas of an autonomous attachment system, but to the Freudian instinctual drives. This is, I believe, partly so because, as noted earlier, in the history of the psychoanalytic movement adherence to instinct theory has been viewed as the acid test of true Freudianism and rejection or radical alterations of the primary role of the dual instincts has traditionally been equivalent to neo-Freudian apostasy.

The attempt, however, to squeeze object relations and self into instinct theory often results in patent theoretical awkwardness and at times, one must say, nearly incoherent jargon. For example, Mahler *et al.* (1975) observe that identity "includes, in part, ... a cathexis of the body with libidinal energy" (p. 8). It is not at all clear that a phrase such as this has any empirical meaning at all. Or to take a more extreme example: "The primordial energy reservoir that is vested in the undifferentiated 'ego-id' still contains an undifferentiated mixture of libido and aggression. As several have pointed out, the libidinal cathexis invested in symbiosis, by reinforcing the inborn instinctual stimulus barrier, protects the rudimentary ego from premature phase-unspecific strain from stress traumata" (Mahler, 1969, p. 9). What is one to make of such passages?

It is important to note again that Mahler's formulation and discussion of separation-individuation can be understood quite apart from the above type of jargon and indeed, quite apart from instinct theory and energy concepts and, as such, represent a real contribution to a psychoanalytic theory of psychopathology and personality development.

What is important and rather distinctive about Mahler's work is the strong empirical support which certain of her central formulations and observations receive from a wide body of research outside the psychoanalytic context. Consider the concepts of "emotional refueling" and "safe anchorage" proposed by Mahler and her co-workers. As noted earlier, the basic idea suggested by these concepts is that the child will more freely engage in independent and exploratory behavior if he can periodically return to mother for "refueling." What is also specifically implied here is that the mother's presence will be positively related to exploration. And, indeed, in confirmation of Mahler's hypotheses, one finds that the general relationship between availability of what has been referred to as the "safe base" and exploratory behavior has received strong empirical support among a wide range of species, including birds (e.g., Hogan and Abel, 1971; Wilson and Rajecki, 1974); monkeys (e.g., Harlow and Harlow, 1965, 1972; Kaufman, 1974) and humans (Ainsworth *et al.*, 1971; Ainsworth, 1974). Further, there is evidence that stimuli other than mother can serve as safe base. Thus, Candland and Mason (1968) found a lower heart rate for young monkeys in an unfamiliar room when a towel is present as compared with no towel present. And Hill and McCormack (cited in Mason, 1970) reported a lower cortisol level for young monkeys in a strange environment when they have access to a surrogate. In children, it is established that exploratory behavior increases or diminishes as the mother is present or absent (Cox and Campbell, 1968; Ainsworth and Wittig, 1969; Feldman and Ingham, 1975; Rheingold and Eckerman, 1970). But exploratory behavior also varies with *pictures* of mother (Passman and Erck, 1977) and with security blanket for "blanket-attached" toddlers, although for "non-blanket-attached" toddlers, the blanket does not have this effect (Passman and Weisberg, 1975).

What is also implied in Mahler's (as well as Winnicott's [1958; 1965]) formulations is that the more secure the attachment between mother and child, the greater the likelihood of independent and exploratory behavior. Whether or not mother is physically present, the child who experiences secure attachment (in Winncott's [1965] terms, who has introjected the "ego supportive environment") will be more capable of exploratory behavior. To the extent that secure attachment implies an internalized "safe base," this hypothesis is an extension of the previous one. Again, the empirical evidence outside the psychoanalytic context provides strong support for this hypothesized relationship. Those whose relationship to mother can be characterized as indicating anxious attachment are more likely to show disturbances in play, in exploratory behavior, and in autonomous activity. And conversely, secure attachment is associated with greater freedom in these areas (Ainsworth and Wittig, 1969; Ainsworth, Bell, and Stayton, 1971; Ainsworth, in press).

Mahler has also articulated an additional later critical factor influencing separation-individuation. She has suggested that optimally the mother should achieve a balance between being physically and emotionally available during the child's independent forays (what Mahler desribes as the "hatching" process) and permitting and encouraging these moves toward separation and autonomy.[12] Although there has been little systematic research with humans in this area, the posited relationship between the balance described above and independent behavior is supported by animal observations. One can observe in infrahuman species the mother's complex role in both weaning of early attachment through discouraging excessive proximity and alert availability when the infant is in a situation of potential danger or may otherwise need her (see, e.g., Hinde, 1975; Marvin, 1977). What has also been observed in both humans (Devore and Konner, 1974) and monkeys (Kaufman, 1974) is the role of peers and older juveniles in the moves toward separation and autonomy. In other words, separation-individuation not only involves a move *away* from mother, but a move *toward* a new social context of peers and juveniles. (It is worth noting, as an aside, that the role of peers in development has been relatively underemphasized).

Mahler's success in identifying certain basic developmental dimensions is, in large part, attributable to the fact that she and her co-workers have observed children's behavior and mother-child interactions outside the consulting room. Her experiences in this area and her willingness to use data not derived from the analytic situation is rare among analysts. Indeed, as the previous material demonstrates, those of Mahler's formulations which are closer to actual observations are most useful and most fully supported by other data, while the formulations that are nearly wholly derived from traditional theory are more likely to be unsupported and/or suffused with virtually undecipherable jargon.

4

TWO-FACTOR THEORY:
Modell's Attempted Integration of Object
Relations and Freudian Instinct Theory

A recent straightforward attempt to integrate challenges from object relations theory with traditional Freudian theory has been made by Modell (1975). Borrowing from Kuhn's (1962) analysis, Modell notes that psychoanalysis is now at a point of crisis, created by the discrepancy between the traditional theory on the one hand, which comfortably held sway during the period of "normal science," and emerging new facts which come mainly from the "psychopathology of object relations" on the other. Modell asserts that "It is this new dimension of object relations that has yet to be integrated within Freud's model of *The Ego and the Id*" (p. 58), an attempt to which Modell devotes his work.

Modell's attempted integration of object relations phenomena with the traditional Freudian model takes the following form: first he suggests that one must now accept two classes of instincts: the sexual and aggressive instincts of the id, and the newly recognized object relational instincts which are ego instincts associated with object relations.[13] The latter instincts differ from the Freudian id instincts in that they are "quieter," cannot easily be attributed to a physiological source, are best characterized by process and interaction rather than discharge, and are gratified by stimuli which do not arise from within the organism, but arise from the environment in which "a fitting in of specific responses from other persons" constitutes the gratification. The specific responses required add up to the need for, in Winnicott's (1965) terms, "good enough" object relations which "are essential for

29

the formation of a special structure of the ego itself—the sense of self or the sense of identity" (p. 64). As for the relationship between the two classes of instincts, "object relations provide the setting for the normal unfolding of the instincts of the id" (p. 63) and also serve to tame and control id instincts. The ego is able to gain control over id instincts mainly by means of identification with a "good object." As far as I can understand Modell (and I don't think he is entirely clear on this issue), he is proposing that identification helps tame id instincts in two ways: by contributing to the development of a firm sense of self and, as Freud (1923, p. 29) suggested, as "the sole condition under which the id can give up its objects."

As noted earlier, Modell acknowledges that "if object relation theory cannot be integrated within *The Ego and the Id*, this latter itself will not survive as the central paradigm of psychoanalysis" (p. 58). He also acknowledges that "if the need for an object reflects the workings of an instinct, it will have to be acknowledged that the concept of instinct here is quite different from Freud's use of the term" (p. 61). And finally, it is to be noted that Modell departs from traditional Freudian theory by acknowledging the autonomy and even the primacy of objects relations and the development of self.[14] Specifically, he observes that "object relations provide the setting for the normal unfolding of the instincts of the id" (p. 63), a direction of contingency quite the contrary of the traditional view in which, as noted, the vicissitudes of id instincts are believed to be the setting for the unfolding of object relations.

Despite Modell's noteworthy efforts, the attempt to graft onto existing Freudian theory the newer object relational ego instincts involves him in inevitable difficulties and inconsistencies. First and most generally, talk about instincts belonging to the id and those belonging to the ego is difficult to understand clearly. Instinctual systems pertain to the organism or individual, not to an id or ego. Furthermore, if there are instincts not associated with the id, what happens to the concept of id as the psychical representation and reservoir of biological instincts? The central logic of the id-ego model rests on the contrast between biological instincts on the one hand and reality-testing and controlling structures on the other. (Surely, so-called object relational instincts are no less biological than the traditional id instincts). How can one claim to retain the basic id-ego model when one talks about instincts associated with the ego? It would have been more consistent with the current id-ego model had Modell enlarged and reconceptualized the concept of id so that it would include instinctual propensities linked to object relations (e.g., Bowlby's attachment as an instinctual system).

The distinction between the two sets of instincts drawn by Modell simply does not hold up for additional reasons. Consider Modell's characterization of object relational instincts as difficult to trace to a physiological source and as showing the property that "the stimulus for the gratification of (these) instincts does not arise from within the organism, but arises from the environment; the gratification of the instinct requires a fitting in of specific responses from other persons" (p. 62). With regard to the difficulty of tracing object relations instincts to a physiological source, surely this is at least partly a matter of the state of our knowledge (and the more recent "discovery" and interest in attachment behavior) rather than an essential substantive difference between so-called id and ego instincts. The evidence that tactile and kinesthetic stimulation are necessary for normal psychological and physical development suggests something about the physiological substrate mediating so-called object relations instincts. As for the second part of his characterization, "the stimulus for the gratification" of sexual instincts also "does not arise from within the organism" and the gratification of sexual instincts also "requires a fitting in of specific responses from other persons." It is difficult to understand the nature of the distinction Modell is making here. Modell may have in mind the fact that sexual gratification can occur through, for example, oral and anal stimulation, masturbatory activity, perversions, and both displacement and sublimation activities—none of which appear necessarily to entail "the fitting in of specific responses from other persons." Whatever he has in mind, however, one can say here: one, that normally sexual gratification *does* involve specific responses from other persons; and two, that for "object relational instincts" too, one may find evidence of parallel perversions, displacement, and substitution. Indeed, it can be claimed that certain deviant sexual behavior can be a response to unmet object relational needs (see Kohut, 1977).[15]

Modell seems to have been led to these untenable distinctions by looking at and trying to fit object relations phenomena into the framework of Freud's *The Ego and the Id*. He accepts a basic antithesis in which "the ego alone is in contact with the external world and the id corresponds to that which is the interior of the organism cut off from the external world" (p. 66). However, whatever is known about sexual and aggressive behavior suggests that this is an untenable distinction. Such behavior in both man and other animals is strongly influenced by and interacts with external stimuli.

There are two other difficulties with Modell's attempted integration of object relations and instinct theory. Modell writes that "the study of borderline and narcissistic character disorders . . . has confirmed

Freud's central thesis that an identification serves to mitigate the intensity of instinctual demands" (p. 60). And further on, Modell observes that for the borderline patient who shows failures in the process of identification and therefore, in the sense of self, "affects associated with anger and love are experienced with such intensity as to induce a sense of annihilation . . ." (p. 61). In short, according to Modell one of the main salutary consequences of a firm sense of identity is the taming of id instincts, while one of the primary pathogenic consequences of failure to develop a cohesive self is the experience of instincts at such a level of intensity that a sense of annihilation is induced. A number of comments are in order.

With regard to Freud's view on the relationship between identification and instincts, in the passage cited by Modell, Freud (1923, p. 29) wrote, "It may be that this identification is the sole condition under which the id can give up its objects." The context of this passage makes clear that what Freud had in mind here is that the boy's identification with the father permits him to give up his aggressive wishes toward the father and his incestuous wishes toward the mother. Nothing is said about identification specifically taming instincts.

More important, however, just how identification presumably tames instincts is not made explicit by Modell. If Modell has in mind that a cohesive self permits a greater sense of control of id instincts and, therefore, less of a sense of threat from such instincts, then he is inaccurate and misleading in talking about identification serving "to mitigate the intensity of instinctual demands" or serving to "tame instincts." It is not a question of increased or decreased intensity of instinctual demands, but of a cohesive self feeling less threatened by demands coming either from within or from the environment. This is tantamount to saying that someone with a strong ego will feel less threatened by inner processes and demands.[16] More important, however, the idea that the sense of annihilation experienced by the borderline patient and other patients suffering from severe disorders of the self is derived from the intensity of id instincts (in Modell's words, "anger and love . . . experienced with [great] intensity") reflects a confusing intermixing of a psychology of the self and a psychology of id instincts.

It seems to me that this confusion and this intermixing of two frames of reference is generated by and is an example of the kind of "piecemeal patching" of Freudian theory referred to by Gedo (1979). Is there really solid clinical evidence that the sense of annihilation or, in Kohut's terms, "disintegration anxiety," is derived from the intensity of instincts or affects? Or is such a formulation dictated by the theoretical view positing a "primary antagonism" between ego and id (A. Freud, 1966)? Someone holding such a view would assume, on non-empirical grounds, that the experience of "disintegration anxiety" or sense of annihilation necessarily comes from the ego being overwhelmed by instincts and their derivative affects. In fact, however, one clinically observes, particularly among schizoid personalities, narcissistic personality disorders, and some borderline patients (all of whom are presumably suffering from disorders of the self), reports of emptiness and flatness and inability to experience intense affect of any kind. The explanation more faithful to clinical evidence and to the phenomenology of such experiences is more likely to be close to the one proposed by Kohut (1977) and by Fairbairn (1952)—namely, that the sense of annihilation experienced by individuals with a lack of cohesive self is engendered, not by instinctual intensity, but by any intensely anxiety-provoking experiences which bring to the fore the sense of a non-intact self. Primary among the situations which engender such anxiety and a consequent sense of annihilation in these individuals is finding themselves separated from or without the support of an important supportive object or finding themselves at the mercy of a persecutory internalized object.

Consider, for example, the syndrome of agoraphobia, particularly when it takes the familiar form of persistent, multiple fears in which some degree of anxiety is experienced in practically all situations and in which intensity of anxiety can be seen to be a function of distance from the safety of home and of the presence or absence of a supportive figure. Under the impact of increasing knowledge and clinical experience, early psychoanalytic formulations, focusing primarily on sexual impulses (e.g., street-walking fantasies, Freud [1887–1902]) and aggressive impulses (e.g., hostility toward the necessary companion, Deutsch [1932]) have given way to the awareness that the chronic multiple agoraphobic is primarily exhibiting severe problems in separation-individuation and experiences an inability to survive without the presence of supportive self-objects.[17] The "disintegration anxiety" or sense of annihilation experienced by the severe agoraphobic is not a function of intense sexual and aggressive impulses which presumably assail him when he is away from the safety of home, but rather is explained by the fact that someone who has not achieved adequate individuation and an adequate capacity to separate feels that he cannot survive without the presence of animate and inanimate, actual and symbolic, supportive self-objects. The agoraphobic must also deal with danger from the other side of the conflict—namely, the regressive and symbiotic merging wishes which also threaten the integrity of the self. Hence, he often remains in a chronic state of anxiety even when not confronted by the agoraphobic situation (see Eagle, 1979 for a further discussion of this issue).

Modell's attempt to integrate the Freudian model of *The Ego and the Id* with the newer object relations findings does not work primarily because he is really interpreting the latter from the traditional perspective of the former. That is, although he recognizes that object relational experiences, autonomous of id instinct gratification, are critical in the formation of the aspect of the ego comprising the sense or self (Modell, in contrast to Kohut, views sense of self as an aspect of the ego), the main functions he appears to give to this sense of self are the controlling, taming, and modulating of id instincts. It follows from this view that the psychopathology associated with disturbed object relations and an impaired sense of self is to be understood mainly in terms of the failure of the ego to control, tame, and modulate id instincts. Hence, a specific symptom of this kind of psychopathology, such as a sense of annihilation, is believed to be induced by overly intense instinctual demand and overly intense "affects associated with anger and love."

In short, however much recognition he gives to the new object relational phenomena and the challenges they represent, Modell is interpreting the psychopathology of object relations and of self within the framework of the traditional model in which the primary psychological danger to the individual comes from intensity of id instincts. This is not integration but incorporation. And only incorporation rather than integration (and rather than modifications in theory which accurately reflect more recent findings and knowledge) is possible as long as one clings to the theoretical position that the primary threat to the individual is represented by id instincts. From this theoretical perspective, the most dire psychological threat that can confront an individual—the sense of disintegration and annihilation of self—is believed to represent a yet more arcane and basic danger, namely, intense id impulses.

Although he does not succeed in integrating traditional theory with more recent formulations, Modell's real contribution is to face squarely the fact that the id-ego central paradigm is severely challenged by object relations and self phenomena. We turn next to the most prominent recent challenge to the traditional psychoanalytic id-ego model.

5

TWO-FACTOR THEORY:
Kohut's Rejection of the Id-Ego Model

Kohut's work can be seen both as a two-factor theory in which a self psychology is meant to complement traditional theory and as an all-embracing self psychology intended to replace the id-ego model of psychoanalysis. His earlier work is characterized by the former and both his later work and that of his followers are characterized by the latter. Kohut's work with narcissistic personality disorders has led him to clinical and theoretical formulations in which the traditional primacy of the sexual instinctual drives is replaced by a major emphasis on a psychology of self and of object relations.

Broadly speaking, Kohut's main theoretical departure from traditional theory is to posit a separate narcissistic line of development independent of and prior to psychosexual and ego development.[18] Kohut's main emphasis has been on the developmental achievement of a cohesive self. He has argued that this aspect or dimension of psychological growth, which he refers to as a narcissistic line of development, is a central one and should be considered quite apart from the traditional emphasis on psychosexual sequences or even ego development. Indeed, with regard to the latter, for Kohut, experience of a unitary self is an important precondition for an adequately functioning ego.

Before undertaking a critical discussion of Kohut's work, it would be useful to summarize some of his main ideas concerning the development of a cohesive self. According to Kohut's formulation, which is not essentially different from other similar conceptions (e.g., Freud [1914];

35

Mahler [1968]), the earliest phase in the narcissistic line of development is that of autoerotism[19] in which only a "fragmented self" and "ego nuclei" exist. Then, the "mother's exultant response to the total child . . . supports, at the appropriate phase, the development from autoerotism to narcissism—from the stage of the fragmented self . . . to the stage of the cohesive self . . ." (1971, p. 118).

Somewhere along the line of development, the "absolute perfection" allegedly experienced by the infant (which, I assume, bears some relationship to the concepts of infantile omnipotence and symbiotic union) is upset by the unavoidable shortcomings of maternal care. However, the child's "narcissistic equilibrium" is now maintained by the development of a grandiose and exhibitionistic self and "by giving over the previous perfection to an admired, omnipotent (transitional) self-object: the *idealized parent image*" (1971, p. 25).

Both early mirroring and later idealization facilitate the smooth development of the normal and necessary narcissistic phase of grandiosity and exhibitionism and the construction of an "idealized parent image." The experience of grandiosity and the availability of an idealized image permit the child to feel powerful and full rather than powerless and empty in the face of the unavoidable shortcomings and frustrations of reality. And as long as union is maintained with these self-objects, the child feels powerful, full, and secure rather than powerless, empty, and insecure.

In normal development, mainly through empathic mirroring and opportunities for parental idealization, such archaic grandiosity and exhibitionism are tamed, modulated, and transformed into "healthy narcissism," as manifested in a cohesive self, adequate regulation of self-esteem, and the development of ambitions, values, and ideals. In pathological developments, which are mainly a consequence of failures in the provision of mirroring and opportunities for idealization, self-cohesiveness is not adequately established, archaic grandiosity and exhibitionism remain, and the "psyche continues to cling to a vaguely delimited image of absolute perfection . . ." (1971, p. 65).

One critical aspect of the narcissistic line of development is the changing nature of object relations. During early phases, the child relates to others, not as fully separate others, but as "self-objects." That is, the self-object is relied upon to carry out such vital psychological functions as tension regulation, maintenance of self cohesiveness, and regulation of self-esteem. In normal development, there is a gradual relinquishment of this use of self-objects and an increasing ability to carry out vital psychological functions for oneself. One shows an increasing capacity to experience others as separate others and as objects of instinctual gratification. In pathological development, one continues to respond to others as self-objects and to rely on them to carry out those psychological functions which one would normally carry out for oneself. Most importantly, one looks to others for the maintenance of self-cohesiveness and for the regulation of self-esteem. Further, without a feeling of union with the idealized self-object, the individual feels empty, powerless, and vulnerable to "disintegration anxiety." Such people are described by Kohut as suffering from narcissistic personality disorders and, in treatment, also relate to the therapist as a self-object in the context of developing mirroring and idealizing transferences (that is, relationships paralleling the early, traumatically involved mirroring and idealizing experiences with parents).

According to Kohut, the formation of a cohesive self and the general growth of psychic structures comes about through a process he calls "transmuting internalizations." Kohut is not very clear as to what he means by this term, but from what one can glean from his writings, the basic hypothesis is that internal structures are somehow formed through withdrawal of narcissistic cathexis (he does not specify what that is) from self-object images and through some subsequent process of internalization. A most important developmental consequence of this process of internalization and of the formation of internal psychic structures is that the child now performs functions which previously he relied on the object to perform—functions which include reality-testing, a sense of self-cohesiveness, and regulation of self-esteem.

While in his earlier work, Kohut (1971) presented his concept of self as a component of the ego, in his later work (1977), the self is presented as a superordinate structure, with drives and defenses as subordinate components. Thus, according to Kohut, neither drive fixations nor ego defects are primary. Rather, "it is the self of the child that . . . has not been securely established, and it is the enfeebled and fragmentation-prone self that . . . turns defensively toward pleasure aims through the stimulation of erogenic zones, and then, secondarily brings about the oral (and anal) drive orientation and the ego's enslavement to the drive aims correlated to the stimulated body zones" (1977, p. 74). (As will be shown, this view is identical to Fairbairn's [1952]). Elsewhere, Kohut notes that "from the beginning the drive experience is subordinated to the child's experience of the relation between the self and self-objects" (1977, p. 80). For example, for Kohut aggression is "not the manifestation of a primary drive . . . , but . . . a disintegration product which, while it is primitive is not psychologically primal" (1977, p. 114). Destructive rage ". . . is always motivated by an injury to the self" (1977, p. 116). (This is a central theme stated by Rochlin [1973], but no note is made of Rochlin's work by Kohut). In general, Kohut argues for a conceptual disjunction between drive gratification and other aspects of mothering when he notes that a mother can satisfy every drive demand of the child and nevertheless expose the child to traumatic experiences by failing to provide "confirming and admiring responses of approval" and "maternal empathy" (p. 79). Here we see Kohut clearly and explicitly stating a theoretical position in which drives are secondary to considerations of self and of object relations, a position which is the reverse of the traditional Freudian one.

Perhaps the clearest expression of Kohut's conception of psychological functioning is contained in his description of what would need to be the case before one terminated treatment with someone suffering from a narcissistic personality disorder. According to Kohut, such a condition would obtain "when (treatment) has been able to establish one sector within the realm of the self through which an uninterrupted flow of the narcissistic strivings can proceed toward creative expression. . . . Such a sector includes always a central pattern of exhibitionism and grandiose ambitions, a set of firmly internalized ideals of perfection, and a correlated system of talents and skills, which mediate between exhibitionism, and ambitions, and grandiosity, on the one hand and ideals of perfection, on the other" (1977, pp. 53–54). Other aspects of healthy functioning noted by Kohut include the continued development of the self structure—via "transmuting internalizations"—such that one's self-cohesiveness and self-esteem is not so intensely and totally linked to the overestimated and idealized self-object; the ability to relate to others as more fully separate others; and the capacity of a "firmly and more satisfactorily cathected self" to "calmly and relaxedly become the center and coordination of object-directed pursuits—freeing the latter from the burden of having to be undertaken in the service of defensively sought-after needs for the enhancement of self-esteem" (1977, p. 41).

According to Kohut, these above changes occur in treatment, not through interpretation and insight, but "in consequence of the gradual internalizations that are brought about by the fact that the old experiences are repeatedly relived by the more mature psyche" (1977, p. 30). More specifically, the therapist's main role is to serve as a self-object (in the context of the inevitably developing mirroring and idealizing transferences) and thereby permit the resumption of the traumatically interrupted development of the self structure. That is, the patient uses the therapist as a self-object to substitute for poorly developed psychological structures of his own. Gradually, according to Kohut, the patient attenuates his narcissistic cathexis of the therapist and internalizes the anxiety-assuaging, delay-tolerating, and other realistic aspects of the therapist's image.

What should be clear from the above description is the degree to which Kohut maintains that the narcissistic line of development is a separate one, with its own phase-specific characteristics, quite independent of and even primary to the vicissitudes of drives, of psychosexual development, and of ego development. For Kohut, traumas in this sphere—mainly, early failures of empathic mirroring and of opportunities for idealization—lead to specific disorders of the self. And implicit in Kohut's writings is the claim that psychological health cannot be adequately and fully described without taking account of behavior and functioning in the narcissistic sphere. It would seem that for Kohut, one cannot be truly in touch with the "deep sources" of one's grandiosity and exhibitionism without the development of strong values and ideals, including ideals of perfection. These are the qualities emphasized in Kohut's conception of optimal functioning, and relatively under-emphasized are such traditional psychoanalytic goals as the ability to experience satisfaction and pleasure from spontaneous drive gratification, the capacity for genital functioning, and the experience of mutuality and intimacy in object relations.

Range of Applicability of Kohut's Formulations

Since Kohut's description and formulations are presented primarily in relation to narcissistic personality disorders, a question that arises is their intended range of applicability. Are they relevant, for example, to an understanding of neurosis which, after all, provided the main data for Freud's theory and to which it was mainly meant to apply? Here Kohut's position is somewhat ambiguous and ambivalent. This ambiguity and ambivalence is expressed in a number of ways.

On the one hand, particularly in his earlier work, Kohut presents a developmentally based two-factor theory and partitioning scheme in which a self psychology is intended to apply to the earlier periods and to the narcissistic line of development and traditional drive-conflict theory to later oedipal periods. As far as pathology is concerned, in this scheme a self psychology is meant to be relevant to disorders of the self (such as narcissistic personality disorders), while drive psychology is applicable to "structural neuroses." The primacy of drive for neuroses and self psychology for disorders of the self is also seen in Kohut's contrast between a class of anxiety in which the basic fear is of disintegration of the self and neurotic anxiety in which, given the establishment of a more or less cohesive self, the predominant fear is of danger situations presumably involving drive expressions.

According to this scheme, during the earliest periods of development, the predominant developmental challenges have mainly to do with such issues as the establishment of a firm and cohesive self; the regulation of self-esteem (the maintenance of "narcissistic equilibrium"), including the taming and transformation of archaic grandiosity and exhibitionism; and the transformation of relationships to self-objects such that they are related to as separate others. Only after these early developmental challenges have been relatively successfully negotiated, will the individual confront issues having to do with drive gratification, instinctual involvements with objects of the oedipal period, and intrapsychic conflict among presumably intact structures. For those people who have failed to develop more or less intact self structures, pathology centers around issues of self-defects and the compensatory and defensive structures erected in response to this failure. For those who have developed a cohesive self, pathology takes the form of "structural neuroses" which involve mainly conflict among relatively intact structures and oedipal instinctual issues.

This means that while those with self defects are likely to be struggling mainly with such issues as self-esteem, fantasies of merging with omnipotent self-objects, self-disintegration anxiety, grandiosity and exhibitionism, failure to develop internalized values, feelings of isolation and emptiness, pseudo self-sufficiency, and destructive rages following experienced narcissistic injuries, neurotic patients are likely to be struggling with such issues as conflict over sexual and aggressive impulses, guilt, castration anxiety, excessive involvement with parental images which interferes with achievement of intimacy in current relationships, failure to achieve sexual gratification, and fear of assertion and success. That is, those people who have been fortunate enough to develop intact self structures can, so to speak, afford to become involved mainly with more developmentally advanced oedipal issues in which conflicts around drive impulse and drive gratification are primary; while for those who have not developed intact self-structures, the main struggles will center on self-cohesiveness, as expressed in merging fantasies, disintegration anxiety, and so on.

Whatever its problems, the above represents a clear-cut two-factor or partitioning scheme in which a self psychology is intended to apply to the earliest periods of development, while traditional psychoanalytic theory is relegated to later periods of development. (Kohut [1977] incorrectly refers to this scheme as "complementarity"). However, particularly in his later writings, Kohut indicates that he has more imperialistic, all-embracing ambitions for his self psychology— that is, it is intended to apply across the board, quite independent of nosological category.

For example, the statement that ". . . from the beginning the drive experience is subordinated to the child's experience of the relation between the self and the self-objects" (1977, p. 80) is obviously meant to describe a general fact about psychic development without reference to this or that diagnostic category. Or, as another example, Kohut's claim that destructiveness is not the manifestation of a primary drive, but is a "disintegration product" is a general statement. In both of these (and other) claims, Kohut seems to be saying that *generally speaking*, drives and drive gratification are not primary factors in development but are subordinated to considerations of self and object relations. And at another point, Kohut states clearly that "abnormalities of the drives and of the ego are the symptomatic consequences of a central defect in the self" (1977, p. 82). This statement is a sweepingly general one and does not appear to be at all limited to narcissistic personality disorders.

What Kohut is proposing in these comments is that for *all* patients early object relational experiences having little, if anything, to do with drive gratification play the determinative role in the development of personality and self structures. This formulation of Kohut's is a statement referring to *general development* independent of nosological category. Indeed, the particular pathology developed in adulthood, including the question of whether oedipal issues or defects in the self will be primary factors in the pathology, will be determined, to an important degree, by these early non-drive experiences. A clear implication, then, of Kohut's views is that in the earliest period of development, a period most critical for the fate of self structures, considerations of drive and drive gratification are not especially crucial. What is to be noted here is that even when Kohut proposes a two-factor theory, his conception of early development and of which factors play a determinative role in early development is diametrically opposed to the traditional Freudian view.

The general shift from a two-factor theory to more all-embracing claims for self psychology is also seen in the changing conception of self from Kohut's earlier to later writings. In his earlier work (1971), the self is conceptualized as a component of the ego structure, while in his later thinking (1977), the self is presented as a superordinate structure, with drives and defenses as, at most, constituent components.

What is more, as I have argued elsewhere (Eagle, 1982) the partitioning scheme in which neurosis is assigned to traditional theory (with its emphasis on sexual and aggressive drives, "structural conflict," and oedipal issues) and disorders of the self to self psychology is far from unambiguously presented. For one, as noted, in certain passages Kohut suggests that difficulties with sex and aggression are often, if not always, subordinated to issues of self and the relationship between self and self-objects. Two, Kohut views oedipal conflict as much a developmental achievement (marking an ability to become sexually interested in persons as separate others) as a source of pathology, and he wonders whether the oedipus complex described in the classical view is "already the manifestation of a pathological development" (1977, p. 246). Three, a wide range of behavior viewed in one way by traditional theory can be and is seen in Kohut and his followers as indicative of defects in the self.

Rangell (1980) has noted that most, if not all, of the clinical phenomena described by Kohut and his followers have been encountered by many analysts who viewed them as within the range of neurotic pathology rather than as warranting the establishment of a distinct category. The point is that it is possible to see a wide range of pathological behavior and experiences as reflecting self defects. If so, it becomes more and more likely that Kohut's self psychology is essentially intended as *a new way of looking at pathology* rather than as a means of elucidating a specific category of pathology, namely disorders of the self.[20] Furthermore, even if the latter is intended, we are told by Kohut that it is precisely disorders of the self which are now widespread because of presumed changes in family structure and in interaction between parents and children. The implication is that today's modal patient is likely to be suffering from self pathology and that one should not expect to find too many patients whose difficulties are understood and best dealt with by traditional theory. The two-factor theory and partitioning scheme, then, as I have argued elsewhere, is tantamount to offering "a partitioning scheme in which one compartment is given a near zero value" (Eagle, 1983).

Kohut's conflict between positing a two-factor theory, which constitutes what Mitchell (1979) refers to as a "psychoanalytic form of ecumenicism," and the more "imperialistic" ambition of the *overall* replacement of traditional theory with self psychology finds expression both in logical contradictions and in the failure to spell out logical implications of his own position. With regard to the former, Mitchell raises the following question: "If drives are disintegration products reflecting a breakdown of primary relational configurations, how can 'structural neuroses' contain at one and the same time no self pathology and conflicts concerning drives which, by definition, reflect severe self pathology" (p. 181)?

As for failure to spell out logical implications, if, as Kohut argues, forms of pathology are shifting more and more in the direction of narcissistic disorders; and if it is true that self psychology is uniquely appropriate to these phenomena; and if it is further true that the traditional theory of intrapsychic conflict is *inappropriate* to these phenomena, it follows that in relatively short order self psychology will *fully replace* traditional theory. It also follows—sort of retroactively—from the original premise that, as the earlier neo-Freudian "cultural" critics claimed, the validity and applicability of traditional psychoanalytic theory are culture- and era-bound and linked to particular character types rather than, as Freudians claim, timeless and universal. This implication Kohut and others have failed to make explicit.

Finally, the partitioning assumption that traditional theory is relevant to neurotic pathology, while the province of self psychology is the more severe and preoedipal pathologies of the self does not appear to be accepted by at least some of Kohut's followers. Thus, Goldberg (1973) argues that "one cannot correlate narcissistic disorders with early, primitive, or sicker" and goes on to state that "disorders of narcissism range from psychoses . . . to mild disturbances of everyday life . . ." (p. 28). This furthers one's suspicion that at least some of Kohut's followers always intended his psychology to represent a way of looking at a wide range of pathology, perhaps a dimension or aspect of all pathology, rather than a point of view limited to narcissistic personality and related disorders, and complementary to traditional theory. In a certain sense, Goldberg articulates the implications of Kohut's self psychology more fully than Kohut himself does. For if one wants to posit a narcissistic line of development as a basic dimension of personality, separate and apart from psychosexual and ego development, then one should expect the claim that developmental achievements as well as disorders will run the gamut from, so to speak, least to most. As Goldberg puts it, "if narcissism is a separate and distinct line of development from object love (and hate), then it has its own stages of development and its own evidences of disorder" (p. 28).

Since "success" in all areas of personality development and functioning is always relative, always a question of more or less, and always a function of life circumstances and situational demands, it is likely that issues having to do with intactness of self structures will also appear in the pathology and treatment of the "structural neuroses" (as we shall see later, a point made by Gedo, 1980). Kohut hedges on this point. On the one hand, he suggests that intactness of self structure will not be relevant to the treatment of neurosis. And on the other hand, he suggests that this issue will appear in all or, at least, many analyses when the "deepest levels" are reached. What is implied in this latter view is that for some more traumatized and disturbed individuals, self issues will be primary and immediately prominent. For others, whose developmental history was a more fortunate one, these concerns will not be apparent, but will be seen to underlie the more neurotic symptoms and defenses when the "deepest levels" of analysis are reached. As will be seen, this is precisely the position taken by Fairbairn (1952) and Guntrip (1968) who argue that the basic and ultimate issues in all pathology have to do with a lack of an intact sense of self rather than with sexual and aggressive drives. Although Kohut does not unambiguously and explicitly take this position, it is, as noted, implied by some of his comments.

Kohut's Conception of Anxiety

Kohut's ambiguity regarding the range of phenomena and pathology to which he wants his formulations to apply is also reflected in his discussion of anxiety. First, he clearly proposes two classes of anxiety: one, for people whose self is more or less intact, "the emphasis of the experience lies in essence in the specific danger (that is, the specific danger situations discussed by Freud [1926]) and not on the state of the "self" (1977, p. 102). The second class of anxiety "comprises the anxieties experienced by a person who is becoming aware that his self is beginning to disintegrate" (p. 102). Kohut then observes that Freud's (1923, p. 57) discussion of "libidinal danger" in terms of "fear of being overwhelmed or annihilated" and "excessive degree of excitation" (1926, p. 94) and Anna Freud's description of one kind of anxiety (fear of instincts) as a "dread of strength of the instincts" represent "attempts to deal with disintegration anxiety within the framework of the mental apparatus psychology" (p. 104). According to Kohut, the kind of overwhelming anxiety in which fear of annihilation is experienced is not the fear of the drive, i.e., is not a "libidinal danger, but is the anticipation of the break up of the self" (p. 104).

Kohut is, I believe, correct in questioning whether overwhelming anxiety is most meaningfully thought of as a "libidinal danger." He is also undoubtedly accurate in his clinical observations regarding different intensities of anxiety (I am translating his two classes of anxiety into different degrees of anxiety). The question is whether his analysis of the nature of anxiety goes sufficiently deep. The question he fails to pose is the sense in which *any* class or degree of anxiety is specifically a libidinal danger. There are at least two ways "libidinal danger" can be interpreted. On the one hand, what Freud seems to mean by "libidinal danger" is the external punishment with which instinctual wishes are associated and on the other, it can be interpreted as referring to the danger of excessive excitation carried by instinct.

According to the first model, the link between instinct and anxiety is one in which an instinctual wish triggers an anticipation of punishment (because of a past association between instinctual wish and actual or threatened punishment), in particular punishments which bring about the danger situations of loss of the object, loss of the object's love, castration anxiety, and superego disapproval. It is the anticipation of these danger situations which constitutes anxiety. Consider the example of castration anxiety. In what sense is castration anxiety a "libidinal danger"? Although castration anxiety is the consequence of libidinal (incestuous) and aggressive wishes, it is not itself, at least in any obvious sense, a "libidinal danger"—that is, a direct threat carried by the drive impulse itself. Rather, it is a fear of punishment in the form of mutilation carried out by an external agency (and later internalized). Similarly with loss of the object and loss of the object's love. While these dangers may attend or follow from libidinal and aggressive wishes, they are essentially external punishments initially to be carried out by an external source.

The implication in the above examples is that the anxiety surrounding libidinal and aggressive impulses is entirely a matter of externally (socially) imposed prohibition and were it not for such social prohibitions—were society and one's upbringing more permissive, for example—there would be little or no anxiety associated with libidinal and aggressive wishes. However plausible and frequent this interpretation of the Freudian theory of anxiety, it is, I believe, essentially incorrect or at least incomplete.

While it is true that the internalization of external prohibitions and punishments makes one susceptible to anxiety and guilt, according to the logic of Freudian instinct theory, the absence of external punishment would not necessarily render libidinal and aggressive wishes benign nor remove their anxiety-arousing potential. A. Freud (1966) makes this point explicit when she speaks of the "ego's primary antagonism to instinct" (p. 157). Insofar as instincts are said always to carry the possibility of ego-damaging excessive excitation, they are, according to the logic of instinct theory, the natural foe of the ego—all this quite independent of particular cultural and social prohibitions and punishments.

Because instinctual pressures cannot be resolved by fight or flight (one cannot physically battle or run away from one's own wishes), they are particularly likely to present the theoretically ultimate dangers of excessive excitation and consequent ego damage and hence to constitute the natural foe of the ego. I review all these elements in Freudian theory in order to make the point that what is overlooked by Kohut (and others) is that for Freud the invariant element of and ultimate threat represented by all forms of anxiety is excessive excitation. Thus, what castration, loss of the object, and loss of the object's love have in common is that because they leave the individual with no opportunity for instinctual discharge, they present the organism with the potential for an excessive degree of excitation and thereby constitute the ultimate danger of ego damage.[21] In other words, they represent the danger of a traumatic situation in which utter helplessness in the face of intense excitation is experienced and in which damage to the ego is the basic threat.

It is the excessive degree of excitation and its associated threat of ego damage that constitute the basic danger to the organism, not instinctual impulses and demands *per se*. Indeed, as Freud (1926) notes, external situations in which one cannot readily escape overwhelming stimulation carry the same danger that excessive degree of excitation may lead to ego damage.[22] Such a situation of excessive degree of excitation beyond the capacity of the organism to cope with or tolerate, Freud described as a "traumatic situation." And it is the primary function of signal anxiety to avoid "traumatic situations" by alerting the organism in "danger situations"—that is, those situations which could degenerate into "traumatic situations" if some coping mechanism (e.g., mainly defense, but also such behaviors as physical flight or avoidance as in the case of phobias) were not mobilized.

In the present context, the point to be noted in this discussion is that Kohut's sharp distinction between anxiety linked to "libidinal danger" and anxiety related to fear of disintegration of the self is not entirely tenable. It overlooks the fact that for Freud, too, the essence of anxiety is fear of ego damage, a concept which does not seem too distant from what Kohut refers to as "anticipation of breakup of the self" or fear of disintegration of self.[23]

Although Freud's mode of discourse deals with mental apparatuses and Kohut's perspective is presumably a subjective one from the point of view of the individual's phenomenal experience, it seems to me that implicit in Freud's conception of the relationship among instinct, excitation, anxiety, and the ego, as discussed above, is the idea that the ultimate threat of anxiety is to the very integrity of the self. The differences between Freud and Kohut (as well as between Freud and the object relations theorists) lie not in the conception of the nature of the ultimate threat in anxiety, but in the ideas regarding the sources of this threat. For Freud, as noted, it is excessive degree of excitation resulting from, to put it as simply as possible, accumulating undischarged instinctual drive tensions. For Kohut (and for the object relations theorists) the threat to the self results from sensed and actual defects and weakness in the structure of the self interacting with situations in which one experiences oneself either isolated from or merged with the need object (in Kohut's terms the self-object). In any case, there is no "libidinal danger" to be contrasted with danger to the self. There is only danger to the self and different conceptions regarding the source of this danger.

Self Psychology and Oedipal Conflict

The ambiguity of Kohut's two-factor approach to the relationship between traditional theory and self psychology is seen in his discussion of the oedipal conflict. One implication of the two-factor approach and of the idea that treatment permits resumption of traumatically interrupted psychological development is that after patients with narcissistic personality disorders and other patients with self defects have achieved an increased degree of self-cohesiveness in successful treatment, they should begin to confront oedipal issues and show conflicts, defenses, and symptomatology typically associated with neurosis.[24]

On occasion, Kohut describes such a sequence, but his description is colored by such comments as patients "joyfully entering" into the oedipal period. In conjunction with other comments (to the effect that the oedipal phase, as described by traditional theory, may already be the manifestation of an earlier pathological development rather than an inevitable and ubiquitous phenomenon), one has reason to believe that Kohut does not take entirely seriously the implication of his own two-factor formulation that typically neurotic problems and issues follow upon the establishment of a firm and cohesive self. If, as is stated by the two-factor theory, narcissistic patients who experience an increased degree of self-cohesiveness are now at a developmental point similar to the one occupied by neurotic patients (i.e., facing "structural conflicts," oedipal issues, etc.), why do they seem so much more joyful, creative, and self-accepting than many neurotic patients?

What seems to be implied, however, subtly, in these clinical case descriptions, is that while from a psychosexual point of view one can be functioning on a pre-oedipal level, one can nevertheless lead a creative, joyful, and rewarding life in which one is able to pursue realistic and meaningful ambitions and to develop deep and sustaining values and ideals. This may or may not, in fact, be true, but the point I am making here is that Kohut's clinical descriptions belie and contradict the implications of his two-factor theory of development. The former implies, in contradiction to the latter, that therapeutic growth in the dimension of narcissism alone (i.e., the move from pathological to "healthy narcissism") can make for a rich and meaningful life, in which, among other things, ambitions are pursued, self-esteem is adequately regulated, and ideals and values are developed, all quite independent of whether or not progress has occurred in the realm of psychosexual development or conflicts associated with that realm. This is, of course, another way of saying that as far as leading a rich, meaningful, and pleasurable life is concerned, issues of psychosexual development and conflicts around sexuality and aggression are really irrelevant and all that matters is the achievement of self-cohesiveness and the successful move from pathological to "healthy narcissism." More specifically and concretely, what Kohut seems to be saying by implication is that one can lead a full and satisfying life without having adequately resolved such issues as object love and hate and the capacity for intimacy—as long as one has achieved self-cohesiveness and "healthy narcissism."[25]

Kohut's interest in geniuses and the "great man" is another indirect expression of what appears to be his underlying belief that what really matters in life, what really makes life worth living, are the development of abiding values and ideals, the pursuit and accomplishment of ambitions informed and fueled by these values and ideals along with one's talents, and the achievement of self-esteem through these values, ideals, and ambitions. To be noted here is that these activities and accomplishments are mainly ones that one carries out on one's own. In Kohut's theory, others are necessary etiologically and developmentally—to provide the mirroring and opportunity for idealization necessary for the development of a cohesive self and for the smooth transformation of archaic grandiosity to "healthy narcissism." But once these others have played their role, healthy narcissism—which the genius and/or hero possesses par excellence—permits going off alone to accomplish one's life's tasks.

To what extent, one wonders, was the development of Kohut's self psychology necessitated by the clinical phenomena of disorders of the self and to what extent is it an expression of his own values, in particular his belief that the full life is the one that in its achievement of "healthy narcissism" most approaches the life of the genius and hero?

6

KOHUT'S PSYCHOLOGY OF NARCISSISM:
A Critical Overview

One central question that arises from the discussion in Chapter 5 is the relationship between Kohut's self psychology and his psychology of narcissism. Although it has been customary, in considering Kohut's work, to equate the two, I believe it is a mistake to do so. Indeed, although Kohut's psychology is called (by himself and others) a self psychology, I think it is more accurate to describe it as an extended treatise on narcissism.

In other work—Mahler's (1968), for example—dealing with the early establishment of a sense of self, the reasonable assumption is made that the formation of a concept of self involves and requires an adequate differentiation between self and other. Prior to this differentiation, the infant is said to be in a state of primary narcissism. This seemingly simple and core assumption has been the basis for linking the development of a sense of self with a psychology of narcissism and, for that matter, with such related conceptions as that of object constancy and object relations. Thus, one could say that a child who has not successfully negotiated this differentiation—who, for example, has remained too long in a symbiotic relationship—will inevitably show failures in the establishment of a firm and cohesive sense of self. And, although stated in different language, Kohut is describing similar vicissitudes when he links self defects and the need for others as self-objects. That is, someone who relates to others as self-objects rather than as fully separate others has obviously not successfully achieved adequate self-other differentiation. Thus far, there is no difficulty in linking narcissism and the development of self—insofar as unsuccessful self-other differentiation can be seen as a failure in the narcissistic line of development and as a critical aspect of self defects.

The difficulties with Kohut's self psychology and its embeddedness in a psychology of narcissism center on such assumptions and conceptualizations as the phase of a grandiose and exhibitionistic self: narcissistic, idealizing, grandiose libido, and "healthy narcissism." With regard to the first assumption, the basis for positing an inevitable and universal phase of a grandiose and exhibitionistic self is not at all clear and, indeed, seems somewhat arbitrary. There is little, if any, evidence to warrant the assumption that grandiosity is a normal stage in development. Certainly, Kohut presents no evidence from longitudinal studies of children which demonstrate that grandiosity regularly appears at a certain stage in development. Kohut's only "supporting evidence" for this etiological and developmental assertion is the material obtained from adult patients in treatment—or, more accurately, material as selected, reported, and interpreted by Kohut and his followers. Further, no degree of sensitive and accurate empathy with adult patients would permit legitimate inferences regarding the existence of an early grandiose and exhibitionistic self.

Rather than being based on solid empirical grounds, it is Kohut's theorizing that has called for and has generated the concept of a grandiose and exhibitionistic self. This concept is based on an elaborate model in which the "absolute perfection" presumably experienced by the infant during the stage of primary narcissism, disturbed by the impact of the unavoidable shortcomings of maternal care, is now replaced by the "narcissistic equilibrium"—maintaining a grandiose and exhibitionistic self. This grandiose and exhibitionistic self, after being duly tamed and modulated, becomes the basis for subsequent "healthy narcissism." One can see how central this idea of a grandiose and exhibitionistic self is to Kohut's theorizing. But its centrality should not blind one to the lack of empirical support. Furthermore, even from a purely theoretical point of view and quite apart from empirical data, the notion of a grandiose, exhibitionistic phase seems arbitrary. Why should, for example, shortcomings in maternal care and disturbances in "narcissistic equilibrium" (that is, in the experience of "absolute perfection") inevitably lead to a phase of grandiosity and exhibitionism? Why don't unavoidable shortcomings in maternal care function in the same manner as "optimal frustrations" do? or, to use Winnicot's (1965) phrase, as "gradual failures in adaptation" do, contributing slowly and cumulatively to a realistic rather than a grandiose sense of self and of object?[26] Or, when such shortcomings assume traumatic proportions, why don't they result in a sense of basic mistrust (Erikson, 1959) or a sense of insecurity regarding the reliability of the environment? Why is the consequence specifically grandiosity and exhibitionism?

Other questions about Kohut's elaborate model arise. For example, as Gedo (1980) asks, what is the evidence, in the first place, that children require the unconditional admiration of their caretakers and that failure to provide such unconditional admiration has significant developmental consequences of any kind?

Also, it is not at all clear that infants need to experience "absolute perfection" in order to maintain "narcissistic equilibrium" or even what it means for an infant to experience "absolute perfection." In Freud's (1914) original conception of narcissism, magical thinking and "omnipotence of thought" are posited and it is these attributes which are stressed in Freud's reference to the "grandiosity" and "megalomania" of the infant (as well as, he argued, of the schizophrenic and the so-called primitive man). Whether Freud was correct or incorrect, one can understand what he had in mind: the basic idea is that wishing will make it so ("hallucination of the breast" during hunger is the classic example). But what is the nature of the narcissistic grandiosity and "absolute perfection" posited by Kohut?

As Peterfreund (1978) points out, all these psychoanalytic characterizations of infancy—primary narcissism, omnipotence, and, I would add, absolute perfection—are "adultomorphic" in that they imply adult standards. If an adult behaved the way a normal infant does, he might be seen as narcissistic or believing in his omnipotence or absolute perfection. But the infant behaves the way he does because there is no other way available in the light of his functioning abilities. As for subjective experiences specifically, how can one assume that the infant is *experiencing* omnipotence or absolute perfection or a self-centered grandiosity? Such attributions seems so clearly to be arbitrary adult intrusions and projections.

Kohut's idiosyncratic conception of narcissism and its somewhat arbitrary link to self psychology is also noted by Gedo (1980). In examining the Goldberg (1978) casebook, Gedo notes that in many of the cases reported, difficulties in tension regulation and in organization of behavior are prominent. Why, Gedo questions, are such difficulties seen in the context of narcissism? In what sense are they specifically narcissistic disorders? In a self psychology not arbitrarily embedded in the context of narcissism, such difficulties would be seen as failures of integration on the part of a superordinate structure which can be conceptualized as self-organization (but which, in another theoretical framework, can be viewed in terms of the synthesizing function of the ego) (see G. S. Klein [1976] and Gedo [1979] for a self psychology outside the framework of narcissism).

Consider also the relationship between the non-cohesiveness of self on the one hand and grandiosity and exhibitionism on the other. What is the relationship between the two? Again, simply from a theoretical point of view, why should non-cohesiveness of self be expressed in and so closely linked to grandiosity and exhibitionism? Now, from an ordinary common sense point of view, it is often observed that people who are self-absorbed, boastful, and grandiose (that is, narcissistic in the ordinary sense of the term) are often defensively reacting to and compensating for an underlying inner sense of inadequacy and low esteem. If this were the essential nature of the link posited between self defects and exhibitionistic grandiosity, it would be a reasonable connection and, of course, not a very novel one. And, indeed, some of Kohut's formulations linking self defects and grandiosity seem to me to be stating, in a very obtuse way, just this common sense idea. Thus, we are told that a person with a defective self remains fixated at the level of archaic grandiosity and exhibitionistism and continues "to cling to a vaguely delimited image of absolute perfection . . ." (1971, p. 65)—presumably because the very sense of self defect and vulnerability (to "distintegration anxiety," for example) requires the compensation of grandiosity. But Kohut goes further and observes that the continuation of archaic grandiosity and exhibitionism somehow weakens the self. Now if what is meant here is that unrealistic grandiosity interferes with realistic appraisal and experience of who one really is (including one's talents, skills, limitations, etc.) and with realistic planning of life goals, this would be a reasonable though, again, not very original idea. But instead we are told that "the danger against which the ego defends itself by keeping the grandiose self dissociated and/or in repression is the dedifferentiating influx of unneutralized narcissistic libido . . ." (1971, p. 152). This is, of course, pure jargon and has only the vaguest, if any, coherent meaning. Further, it gives no indication of, nor does it even address, the question of mediating processes linking non-cohesiveness of self and grandiosity.[27]

Other questions concerning Kohut's formulations arise, such as whether the capacity to develop ambitions and interests and pursue values and ideals is so entirely a function of early mirroring and idealization, whether it is so inextricably linked to early grandiosity and exhibitionism, and whether narcissism (healthy or otherwise) is the most meaningful theoretical context in which to understand such behaviors. With regard to the first two points, suffice it to say here that to base the acquisition of ambitions, interests, and particularly, values and ideals so exclusively on presumed events in infancy is to ignore utterly both later experiences and events in the life of the individual and the broader social context influencing the development of these attributes. It is the last point however—the concept of "healthy narcissism"—that I want to pursue more fully here.

Healthy Narcissism

As noted earlier, Kohut has argued that a basic dimension of personality growth is the narcissistic line of development. Thus, according to Kohut, broadly speaking, not only do we show a regular sequence, known as the psychosexual stages, in the zones and modes by which we gain sexual gratification, but we also exhibit regular developmental sequences in the means employed for self-maintenance and self-enhancement. Just as we move from immature to mature means of sexual gratification in psychosexual development, so do we progress from more primitive to more mature modes of self-maintenance and self-enhancement in the line of narcissistic development. For example, one typically goes, according to Kohut, from archaic and untamed grandiosity and exhibitionism to a tamed and modulated grandiosity which is integrated into ego organization and expressed in realistic ambitions and pursuits.

It is clear, then, that Kohut is proposing a line of personality development and a set of motives parallel to and every bit as basic as psychosexal growth and sexual motivation. Indeed, what is strongly suggested in Kohut's writings is his belief that the narcissistic line of development is more primary and more basic. Kohut has made clear his belief that traditional psychoanalysis has overemphasized object interest and his intention to correct this imbalance with a recognition of the importance of self-love, self-esteem, and self-development.

Traditional psychoanalytic theory, Kohut tells us, has placed too exclusive an emphasis on libidinal investment in the object and has looked upon narcissistic investment in the self mainly in pejorative terms—e.g., as developmentally primitive or pathological. An aim of psychoanalytic self psychology is to correct this imbalance and to argue that an optimal level of narcissistic self-esteem, self-love, and even modulated grandiosity is necessary for a full and joyful life. It also notes that beyond object investment, a certain degree of narcissistic investment of the self is necessary to undertake various projects and actions.[28] The accomplishments of the "hero" and artistic genius—types in whom Kohut has long had an interest—are prototypic examples of narcissistically motivated and sustained activities. Thus, while traditional theory is exclusively concerned with object-instinctual gratification, self psychology points to the psychological importance of the more narcissistically oriented activities of pursuing ambitions and goals, exercising one's creative talents and skills, and behaving in accord with ideals and values. A clear implication of this view is that maintenance and enhancement of self are at least as important motives in behavior as object-linked instinctual gratification. Indeed, as I have tried to show, in his later writings Kohut's implicit position has seemed to be that successfully negotiating the narcissistic line of development—from archaic and primitive narcissism to mature and healthy narcissism—is *the* pivotal determinant of a successful and fulfilling life. In other words, more and more, Kohut replaces the traditional concept of psychosexual stages with the narcissistic line of development as the central dimension of personality formation.

It seems to me that Kohut has made a valid and important contribution in attempting to correct an imbalance of psychoanalytic theory and in pointing to the fact that some basic behaviors, ambitions and strivings, for example, cannot be accounted for exclusively in the context of psychosexual functioning and in oedipal terms of instinctual gratification (or sublimations thereof), but are motivated by self-maintenance and self enhancement.[29] Indeed, if one relinquishes an instinctual-tension-reduction model of human motivation, one can recognize that sexual gratification itself may relate to what G. S. Klein (1976) refers to as "self-values." There is evidence that the capacity for interests and goals and the possession of strong ideals and values can contribute to psychological intactness in dire circumstances (e.g., concentration camps or prisoner-of-war camps). And, in general, there is evidence supporting Kohut's claim of a link between a firm and cohesive self on the one hand and the capacity for values and ideals on the other (Eagle, 1982).

However, the matter is not as simple as suggested by Kohut. For one thing, the relationship between ambitions, etc., and cohesiveness of self is likely to be bi-directional rather than, as is suggested by Kohut, uni-directional. I have tried to show elsewhere (Eagle, 1982) that the possession of special talents and gifts and the organization of a major part of one's life around them can serve to sustain and shore up an otherwise shaky and non-cohesive self. Also, one cannot ignore the possibility that some individuals with a non-cohesive self are capable of developing strong, often fanatic, ideals and values and overriding ambitions, indeed partly motivated by the need to firm up an inadequate sense of self. Clearly, these issues require further investigation.

Having noted Kohut's contributions in this area, there are nevertheless remaining difficulties with his concept of "healthy narcissism." First, it will perhaps be useful to remind oneself what is meant by the term narcissism. An examination of the psychoanalytic literature suggests three related dimensions: one, lack of differentiation between self and other, as in primary narcissism; two, regulation of self-love and self-esteem; and three, self-absorption and self-preoccupation. With regard to the first two dimensions, there is little difficulty in conceptualizing a developmental move along the line of narcissism from relative lack of differentiation between self and other to increasing differentiation, to an increasing sense of self and of self-regard, and to an increasing capacity to regulate self-esteem.[30] As I will try to show, it is in regard to the third dimension that Kohut's difficulties arise. We recognize that in the course of psychological development, we move from relative egocentricity and self-absorption to an increasing capacity for concern for, interest in, and taking the role of the other (emphasizing different aspects of personality; this has been described and discussed by, for example, Piaget [1969] and Winnicott [1965]). What is not clear is whether Kohut's conception of "healthy narcissism" takes adequate account of this third aspect of narcissistic development.

The most obvious difficulty with Kohut's formulations is the relatively little room left for autonomous object-directed pursuits and interests which are not in the service of self-maintenance and self-enhancement, that is, which are not particularly implicated in narcissistic motives, pathological or healthy. Kohut, of course, recognizes that with increasing maturity and health, one becomes better able to engage in object-directed pursuits free "from the burden of having to be undertaken in the service of defensively sought-after needs for the enhancement of self-esteem" (1977, p. 41). But by referring to this increased capacity as *healthy narcissism* Kohut is suggesting that these object-directed pursuits are, in some fashion, in the service of self-enhancement. Otherwise, why are they deemed to be expressions specifically of narcissism? And to the extent that Kohut proposes that even object-directed pursuits (including and particularly those that comprise one's ambitions and goals) are, in part, motivated by tamed grandiosity and exhibitionism, he obviously does believe that such activities contain a necessary and ineradicable narcissistic component.

Kohut's formulations imply the ubiquitousness of narcissistic motives. In pathological narcissism, the self-absorption and the defensive
and desperate search for self-maintenance and self-enhancement are
blatant, while in "healthy narcissism" the self-absorption is tamed
and the motives of self-maintenance and self-enhancements are modulated and successfully integrated into one's pursuits and activities.
But what remains ubiquitous is the inevitable dominating presence of
narcissistic motives. The irony is that there is an exact parallel here to
Freudian instinct theory. Just as in the latter all behavior is, directly or
indirectly, overtly or covertly, in the service of drive gratification,
Kohut's writings (particularly his concept of "healthy narcissism") imply that all behavior is, in some manner, in the service of self-
maintenance and self-enhancement. The result is that, just as in Freudian instinct theory there is little or no room for autonomous ego
activities independent of drive gratification, so in Kohut's system
there is little or no room for autonomous object-directed pursuits relatively independent of self-maintaining and self-enhancing motives.[31]

The fact is that frequently people engage in object-directed pursuits
largely because of an autonomous interest in these activities with
little or no regard for the question of whether or not they are self-
enhancing. And in fact, the self-maintaining and self-enhancing
efficacy of such activities is often a *by-product* of the fact of their
being carried out rather than constituting the motive for the activities.
Hence, it is misleading to speak of such behavior as expressions of
narcissism, pathological or healthy. In ordinary discourse, we say of
people who are fully engaged in object-directed pursuits and accordingly more absorbed in an external object and less self-absorbed that
they are being *less narcissistic,* not more healthfully narcissistic. Here
is an instance where ordinary discourse is less confusing than special-
ized meanings. Rather than speak of healthy narcissism, I believe it is
less confusing to say that the development of a basic sense of intactness, of self-esteem, and of self-worth permits one to relinquish predominantly narcissistic motives as the organizing theme in one's behavior and in one's relationships.

My above argument rests on the assumption that there is a reciprocity between object-directed pursuits and self-absorption, an ordinary
discourse version of the reciprocity Freud (1914) posited between
narcissistic and object libidinal investments. Contrastingly, Kohut's
concept of "healthy narcissism" implies a rejection of this reciprocity
principle insofar as the former permits the concurrent operation of
both object involvement and narcissistic motives. Taking up this issue
in support of Kohut's position, Stolorow (1975) also rejects the reci-

procity principle and cites as evidence for this rejection the fact that narcissistic people can be intensely involved with objects. He points out that such people may even require the presence of objects in order to maintain a sense of self-cohesiveness.[32] He then goes on to suggest that one adopt a "functional definition of narcissism" such that behavior is narcissistic to the degree that it is *"in the service of"* maintaining and enhancing the self (I interpret "in the service of" to mean motivated by the need to maintain and enhance the self). In accord with the logic of Kohut's formulations, he then distinguishes pathological from healthy narcissism in terms of the *degree of success* in accomplishing the goal of maintaining and enhancing the self.

If "healthy narcissism" is simply a matter of degree of success in maintaining and enhancing the self, then the narcissistic personality disorder's relationship to self-objects and the exploitative use of others would have to be viewed as somewhat healthy insofar as it can succeed, for long periods of time, in maintaining and enhancing the self. And, by Stolorow's logic, one might have to view precipitous drops in self-esteem following realistic failures and violations of one's ideals and moral code as expressions of pathological narcissism. Most importantly, the kinds of activities described as "healthy narcissism" by Kohut and Stolorow—ambitions, ideals, object involvements, etc.—*are generally not primarily motivated by the need to maintain and enhance the self. Rather, as noted earlier the contribution to firmness of self and self-esteem are often by-products of these activities.* They tend to be engaged in for such reasons as the interest they arouse and the enjoyment and gratification they provide (to use Hunt's [1965] phrase, they are "intrinsically motivated." Or, as White (1959; 1965; 1966) observes, while certain activities, such as exploration and manipulation, have evident survival value, they are often "done for the fun of it" and "part of the fun can be described as a feeling of efficacy—or sense of mastery— . . ." (1966, pp. 247–248).

Consider for example Stolorow's suggestion that a set of firmly internalized ideals is an instance of healthy narcissism because it is likely to be successful in contributing to the maintenance and enhancement of self. Firstly, as noted above, a set of firmly internalized ideals does not necessarily guarantee self-esteem and, indeed, carries the potential of assaults to self-esteem insofar as one may not measure up to one's standards and ideals. More to the point however, one does not pursue and live by standards and ideals *in order to* maintain and enhance the self or "in the service of" maintaining and enhancing the self. The enhancement of self is often a by-product of conducting one's life in accord with certain ideals and values rather than a direct

motive of such behavior. Similarly with ambitions and goals and object-directed (rather than narcissistically directed) pursuits and involvements. In general, it seems to me that it makes both clinical and
theoretical sense to say that given a certain minimal degree of self-
cohesiveness and of self-esteem, behavior is free to become increasingly directed, not to narcissistic motives (healthy or otherwise), but
to object involvements and object directed pursuits. To repeat, to link
such object involvements and object directed pursuits to "narcissistic
fulfillment," to (tamed) grandiosity and exhibitionism, to an "organized flow of grandiose-exhibitionistic libido," to idealizing libido,
and to other similar conceptions and conditions is based, not on clinical data or the requirements of theoretical elegance, but on Kohut's
central assumption that the most appropriate context for an understanding of adult success and fulfillment in the areas of ambitions,
ideals, and object directed pursuits is to be found in the narcissistic
line of development, including the vicissitudes of an earlier phase of
grandiosity and exhibitionism.

With regard to the issue of reciprocity between object-pursuits and
narcissism, Stolorow (1975) states that "narcissistic objectives may be
characterized by a very intense overt attachment to external objects.
In other words, increased involvement with the self is not necessarily
accompanied by a decreased cathexis of objects. . . . Freud's [1914]
economic hypothesis of a mutually excluding reciprocity between
narcissistic libido and object libido does not appear to hold up clinically. . . . It is clear that an intensely cathected object relationship can
serve a primarily narcissistic function" (p. 182).

It is, of course, true, as Stolorow notes, that "narcissistic object ties
may be characterized by a very intense overt attachment to external
objects." But I believe Stolorow misses a critical point. The critical
point has to do not with the intensity but the *nature* of the attachment
to objects characteristic of narcissistic ties as compared with non-
narcissistic involvements (that is, object directed ties). Kohut himself
points out that narcissistic patients respond to others, not as separate
others, but as "self-objects," and, at times, as parts of themselves. In
other words, it is really not accurate, in the case of narcissistic ties, to
speak unqualifiedly of "attachment to external objects" insofar as,
psychologically speaking, in this type of tie the other is as much a part
of the self as a separate object. This is the whole point behind Kohut's
referring to them as "self-objects."

A central insight emerging from considering the role of self-other
differentiation in development (a basic dimension of narcissism) is
that not every interpersonal interaction is necessarily a full object
relation between a self and another. This insight suggests that from

one point of view, to say that "an intensely cathected object relationship can serve a primarily narcissistic function" is somewhat of a contradiction in terms. To the extent that the other serves "a primarily narcissistic function" and is not a fully separate other, one is not involved in an object relationship, but in a relationship to, in Kohut's term, a self-object. It is useful to recall that in the original myth, Narcissus is also intensely involved with an external object. The object, however, is, of course, the mirror image of himself. (In another context—e.g., see Fairbairn [1952] or Volkan [1976]—one would speak of internalized object relations). That narcissistic involvements, however intense, do not involve true object relations has long been recognized. For example, Fromm (1955) notes that "narcissism is the essence of all severe pathology. For the narcissistically involved person, there is only one reality, that of his own thought processes, feelings, and needs. The world outside is not experienced or perceived *objectively* [Fromm's emphasis], i.e., as existing in its own terms, conditions and needs" (pp. 35–36).

The above considerations suggest that Freud was essentially correct in positing a reciprocal relationship between narcissistic self-involvement and object cathexis. More specifically, I believe that the observation that narcissistic ties can involve "intense . . . attachment to external objects" does not contradict Freud's reciprocity claim if one fully understands the implications of Freud's formulations and if one keeps in mind the above clarification that the "external object" in narcissistic ties (which, of course, is not fully external) does not have the same status as external objects in non-narcissistic involvements. The essence of what is implied in Freud's concept of object-libido is a libidinal investment in an object in its capacity to provide instinctual gratification. By contrast, the central meaning of narcissistic libido is an erotic or libidinal involvement with oneself, even if an object is the vehicle for such involvement.

When Kohut describes the move from pathology to relative health as one in which the individual now could "become the center and coordinator of object-directed pursuits—freeing the latter from the burden of having to be undertaken in the service of defensively sought-after needs for the enhancement of self-esteem" (1977, p. 41) he is, it seems to me, accepting Freud's basic insight that self-preoccupation is incompatible with the free exercise of object directed pursuits. This insight is then lost with the introduction of the concept of "healthy narcissism." For the incompatibility between narcissism and object pursuits remains, whatever the reasons for and nature of the narcissism. That is, whether the self absorption is a function of lack of self-cohesiveness and archaic grandiosity or tamed grandiosity, it remains incompatible with true object investment. About the only meaning healthy narcissism could have and still remain compatible with object involvement is some optimal degree of self-love and self-esteem which, once developmentally established, becomes characterologically stable and need not be constantly replenished. But note that by this definition, "healthy narcissism" becomes equivalent to minimal narcissism.

In the simplest, commonsense terms, what Freud's reciprocity principle claims is that to the extent that one is self-absorbed, one will be less interested in and involved with external people and things, and conversely, to the extent that one is absorbed in genuine concern for others and genuine object directed pursuits and interests, one will be less self preoccupied. It seems to me that both on the level of commonsense wisdom and of clinical evidence, this principle is thoroughly supported. The observation that self-absorbed people can also show intense attachment to objects does not contradict the principle when one considers the nature of the attachment—it is but another expression of self-absorption. To bring this part of the discussion to a close, I offer the following illustrative joke: A Hollywood mogul is going on, seemingly endlessly, about himself to a young starlet. At one point, in a rare moment of apparent self-awareness, he says, "That's enough about me. Let's talk about you. What do you think of me?"

Some final comments regarding the roots of "healthy narcissism": for Kohut, the early foundation of "healthy narcissism" is the experience of "absolute perfection" which in the course of development becomes duly tamed and modulated. What characterizes the narcissistic personality disorder is a traumatic disturbance to this early sense of perfection and a set of defensive and compensatory reactions to this disturbance. In an important sense, in Kohut's scheme the narcissistic personality disorder is not overly narcissistic, but does not possess sufficient "healthy narcissism." That is, his early sense of perfection was traumatically disturbed and, in consequence, neither adequately retained nor transformed. His self-absorption, archaic grandiosity, etc., that is, his pathological narcissism, is a consequence of and reaction to a traumatic disturbance to his "healthy narcissism."

According to Kohut, were one less disturbed in the early sense of perfection, one would be less narcissistic in the sense of being grandiose, etc. This idea is, of course, not too different from the everyday observation that people who are self-absorbed, boastful, and grandiose are often defensively reacting to and compensating for an underlying inner sense of inferiority and inadequacy, while people who have a sense of adequacy and self-esteem do not need to be so self-preoccupied, grandiose, and exhibitionistic. But note that in this commonsense view the opposite of narcissistic self-preoccupation, etc., is simply an ordinary sense of adequacy and self-esteem. What is *not* assumed is that the foundation for this ordinary feeling of adequacy and self-esteem is an early sense of narcissistic perfection. I believe that this latter additional assumption made by Kohut confuses matters. It also seems arbitrary in its claim that somehow as a natural stage of development we are all guaranteed a sense of "absolute perfection"— which is then upset and disturbed by the failures of parental care, including not only the inevitable shortcomings, but the traumatic failures to mirror and to permit idealization. Not only is there no evidence for this claim, but it seems to betray a romanticization of what would seem to be the only reasonable meaning of early narcissism— namely, a relative lack of differentiation (not only between self and other, but between various aspects and components of one's own personality). Such a relatively global, undifferentiated state would hardly seem capable of yielding a sense of perfection (or imperfection, for that matter).

The alternative to this understanding of primary narcissism is to posit some early state of perfect integrative achievement, following an earlier autoerotic stage of "the fragmented self" or "self nuclei." That Kohut has something like this alternative meaning in mind is suggested by the following passage: ". . . the mother's exultant response to the total child . . . . supports, at the appropriate phase, the development from autoerotism to narcissism—from the stage of the fragmented self . . . to the stage of the cohesive self" (1971, p. 118). If one takes this passage literally, it would follow that the so-called narcissistic personality disorder is not someone who is overly narcissistic, but someone who has not fully yet achieved the stage of narcissism.[33]

Other Problems in Kohut's Formulations

In this section, I will consider some difficulties with Kohut's formulations which were not covered in the earlier discussion of his concepts of anxiety and of narcissism.

Consider first Kohut's invocation of the principle of complementarity "such that both a conflict–drive psychology and a self psychology, existing side by side, explain general personality development and psychopathology equally well." What Kohut overlooks is that the principle of complementarity refers to two different models of equal explanatory status *for the same set of phenomena*—not, as is suggested by Kohut in other passages, different explanations for what turns out to be different phenomena (e.g., pathology at different levels of development).

A basic difficulty with Kohut's partitioning scheme is the radical dichotomy it suggests between developmental self-defects on the one hand and intrapsychic conflict on the other. This issue is sufficiently important to merit full discussion and the next chapter is devoted to such a discussion. Suffice it to say here that there is good reason to doubt the accuracy of Kohut's claim that patients suffering primarily from self-defects (such as narcissistic personality disorders) do not experience oedipal conflicts because they have not yet reached that level of development. As I will argue in another chapter, I do not believe that this is an accurate picture of the nature of psychological development.

Kohut's implicit model of psychological development is not in accord with the clinical data or with the actual nature of development. Interestingly, quite apart from the specific content of his psychosexual stages, the *structure* implicit in Freud's concept of psychosexual sequences is a more useful and more accurate model of development. In this model, despite arrests at one stage (conceptualized as fixations), development proceeds to subsequent stages, although the manner and success with which one negotiates later stages continue to be influenced by the consequences of earlier arrests and fixations. In Freud's model there is no hard and fast distinction between defects and arrests on the one hand and wishes, fears, and conflicts on the other. They are simply different aspects of and different perspectives on the same phenomenon. Thus, a fixation at a given psychosexual stage can be viewed both as a developmental defect or arrest *and* in terms of the stage-specific wishes, conflicts, and defenses which continue to persist into subsequent stages. By contrast, Kohut (along with other current psychoanalytic writers) makes a sharp dichotomy between developmental defects and arrests on the one hand and "structural conflicts" on the other.

Paralleling the dichotomy between developmental defects and "structural conflicts" espoused by Kohut and his followers is the general sharp distinction between a self psychology and a conflict psychology. Thus, a follower of Kohut, Ornstein (1978) writes: "Is integration of conflict psychology within the new paradigm of self-psychology the logical next step in psychoanalysis? The answer to this question is a decisive No." Just why, however, a concern with the concept of self should be incompatible or unintegratable with a recognition of conflict is not made clear by Ornstein. Given the general thrust of Kohut's self psychology, one can surmise the reason. As

Wallerstein (1980) has pointed out and as I have noted earlier in discussing Kohut's implicit "deficiency-compensation" model of therapy, Kohut and his followers believe that formation of the self is a straightforward product of the degree to which certain ingredients (such as empathic mirroring) have been provided and does not entail intrapsychic conflict. It seems to me, however, that Kohut has overlooked two important considerations. One is, as I have tried to show earlier, that even gross failures to provide psychologically "nurturing" ingredients do not lead only to deficiency states, but often to *conflicts* surrounding the area of deprivation. For example, someone deprived of adequate love and empathy early in life may have to cope, not only with deprivation of these "ingredients," but with such conflict-laden issues as destructive rage, ambivalence, greed, etc.

The second critical consideration Kohut has overlooked in positing a sharp dichotomy between self psychology and conflict psychology is the simple recognition that, in G. S. Klein's (1976) words, the failure to carry out successfully the "resolution of incompatibilities" (i.e., conflicts) is threatening to one's self-organization. As we shall see in a later chapter, Klein's formulations demonstrate that an emphasis on the integrity and continuity of self as an overriding motive in behavior need not be incongruent with a "conflict psychology." What distinguishes Klein from Kohut is the former's recognition that in an organism as complex as a human being, incompatible aims and tendencies are inevitable. It follows that any superordinate, coordinating, and integrative structure—which is, after all, an essential aspect of the concept of self—will have as a primary task the integration of these complex and conflicting aims and tendencies. It also follows that the cohesiveness and integrity of this self-structure will bear an important relationship to the degree of success with which this primary task is accomplished. Thus, to separate radically a self psychology from a conflict psychology is not only unnecessary, but also misguided in that it keeps the former from dealing with some of its most significant phenomena and issues.

I want to make note of Kohut's tendency to employ, both in his clinical descriptions and in his theorizing, what Slap and Levine (1978) refer to as "hybrid concepts," and relate this tendency to Kohut's espousal of empathic introspection as the guiding and special means of acquiring knowledge in psychoanalysis. Certainly, Kohut is not alone in the use of "hybrid concepts," but it is noteworthy that Slap and Levine focus mainly on Kohut's formulations to illustrate this phenomenon. First, let me provide some examples taken from their paper. In the first example, Kohut (1971) states that "the patient comprehends that the [pathological] condition is due to the fact that his self had temporarily become deprived of its cohesive narcissistic cathexis which had been uncontrollably siphoned into his actions" (p. 128). Assuming that one understands the terms employed, is narcissistic cathexis the kind of thing one can experience or comprehend being deprived of? Consider another example offered by Slap and Levine. "The presence of an unconscious fellatio fantasy in which swallowing the magical semen stands for the unachieved internalization and structure formation might well be assumed . . . "[Kohut, 1971, p. 72 N]. How can a fantasy stand for a metapsychological construct such as internalization or structure formation?

In the above examples, the level of experience–near and observation–near description is intermixed with highly abstract, metapsychological constructs distant from experience and observation, as if both levels referred to people's actual experiences and behavior. It is ironic that Kohut, who so definitively espouses empathy and introspection as *the* distinctive hallmark of the psychoanalytic approach, can so easily confuse what someone is experiencing or could be experiencing with an abstract metapsychological account or an etiological account. The latter, given its level of discourse, could not possibly represent simply an empathic understanding of what another is feeling, nor should it be expected to represent that. Similarly, how can one empathically know the etiological-causative role of a patient's early experience (or even what that early experience was)? Or, to take another example, how can empathy permit one to make "blind" diagnoses of the patient's parents? Also, although one may empathically resonate with another's feelings and fears, how does one empathically know about a patient's *structural defects?* How does one distinguish, empathically, someone's feelings and fantasies of being defective from the fact of having a structural defect (I'm assuming that we really know what we mean by the latter)? Is the latter the kind of knowledge one can ever gain empathically? Indeed, as Levine (1979) points out, for a therapist to claim empathic knowledge regarding a patient's self-defects may work to confirm the latter's fantasies about being defective and may also foreclose analytic exploration of such fantasies. To paraphrase an old saw: With empathy like this, one doesn't need misunderstanding.

All psychoanalytic interpretations and formulations entail the risk that they will be inherently incongruent with what is really going on and with what the patient is experiencing.[34] It is easier to be alert to and recognize this possibility when one acknowledges that one's interpretation is, after all, an inference. However, the claim that one's interpretations and formulations are based exclusively upon empathy can block or delay the recognition of one's fallibility insofar as it permits one to believe that this route grants direct and privileged access to what another is experiencing. In any case, despite Kohut's elevation of empathy, a careful reading of his work—both clinical accounts and theory—demonstrates, I believe, that his descriptions and formulations are not, in any obvious way, more experience–near or even more experientially anchored than most psychoanalytic writing.

A striking feature of Kohut's writings is the degree to which he makes etiological assertions without any evidence other than adult patients' reports—or, more accurately, the analyst's interpretations of adult patients' reports—regarding what they are currently experiencing and/or remember experiencing in their childhood. Because they are said so frequently and with so much assurance by Kohut and his followers, one can lose sight of the stark and startling fact that formulations concerning, for example, the effects of early empathic mirroring (or the lack of it) and of early idealization (or the lack of it) rest on no reliable and systematic evidence and do not include even a single longitudinal or follow-up study on the effects of these factors upon later development. But in this regard perhaps Kohut is no more culpable than many other psychoanalytic writers, who make similar assertions with equal lack of evidence. This issue will be discussed further in a later section.

As Stolorow (1976) points out, there are clear similarities between Kohut's self psychology and Rogers's (e.g., 1952) client-centered theory (which, it should be noted, he also conceptualizes as a self psychology). I state this similarity as a "problem" because of Kohut's failure to acknowledge fully influences and predecessors. To set the scholarly record straight, it is important to at least mention some of the striking parallels Stolorow notes between Kohut's and Rogers's formulations: The injunction against interpretation that can be experienced as threats to the patient's (client's) grandiose wishful self; the parallel between Kohut's mirroring transference and Rogers's reflection and the need for the patient to feel "prized"; the common emphasis on empathy and the patient's (client's) phenomenal world; the internalization of the therapists' attitudes, of "unconditional positive regard" in the case of Rogers and empathic mirroring in the case of Kohut; and finally, the parallel between Kohut's goal of taming the archaic grandiose self and Rogers's goal of tempering the ideal self and reducing the discrepancy between it and the real self.

Finally, I come to Kohut's (and his followers') tendency to reify the concept of self and to appear to confuse contexts of discourse in discussing self psychology. As Hartmann (1950) pointed out some time ago, the simplest and least problematic definition of the self is "one's own person" (p. 127). Rubinstein (1981) has further clarified the definition by noting that the self refers to the subjective aspect of the person and "is the person a person is to himself" (p. 13). In other words, one can and often does appear to oneself in a way that is different from the way one appears to others. For example, when we say that someone has a "grandiose self," we mean that he sees himself in a certain unrealistically extravagant way and endows himself with certain extravagant qualities that is very different from the way others see him and very different from the qualities with which others endow him (I am not getting into the issue of what this grandiose self is purportedly a reaction to). Or, to take another example from Rubinstein, to say "He loves *his self*" or "He hates his *self*" can be replaced by the use of a reflexive pronoun, as in "He loves himself" or "He hates himself." In either case, the sentences mean respectively, "He loves the person he is" (or, I would add, "He loves certain aspects of the person he is") or "He hates the person he is" (or "He hates certain aspects of the person he is"). But, as Rubinstein points out, what some psychoanalytic theorists, including Kohut, seem to do is take the first set of sentences literally—that is, treat the concept of self as a separate substance or entity, divorced from the concept of person. Or they use the concept of self sometimes as referring to the subjective aspect of the person and sometimes as a structure in the world of organisms. Thus, at one point, clearly having in mind the world of persons, Kohut (1977) refers to the self "as the center of the psychological universe" (p. XV); while at another point (on the very same page), he refers to the self "as a content of mental apparatus" (p. XV).

One finds the same confusion and vacillation of contexts in Kohut's discussions of a *fragmented self*. At times, when he writes about "disintegrating anxiety," for example, he writes about it in subjective terms, from the point of view of the patient. Thus, in experiencing "disintegration anxiety" one may *feel* fragmented, as if one were splintering into pieces. And, indeed, one may feel generally fragmented, torn, unintegrated, etc. However, at other times, Kohut and his followers write about *lack of self-cohesiveness, fragmented self*, and *self defects* as if they were referring to actual "cracks" in a substantive structural entity, much like one would describe faults in a geological structure. The question that Rubinstein poses here is whether a term such as *fragmented self* is anything more than a metaphor or shorthand description of a "patient's widely scattered failings" and symptoms. There is nothing wrong with using metaphors and shorthand descriptions. The difficulty arises when one confuses these metaphors and descriptions with existent entities and when one believes that one has provided an explanation for these widely scattered failings and symptoms.

One reason, I believe, for the strong response on the part of many to talk about *fragmented self* and *lack of self cohesiveness* is the emotional conviction that such talk taps a deeper, gut level of experience. I have observed this response when I have given graduate seminars on psychoanalytic self psychology. People do not react that way to talk about id, ego, and superego or even talk about unconscious wishes. But some people do react strongly to talk about *lack of self cohesiveness* because it resonates with *the way they often feel about themselves.* In other words, the description of an observer regarding the kind of person a person is to oneself seems to resonate with the *subjective feelings* regarding the kind of person one is to oneself. This is certainly a critical aspect of what we normally mean by empathy. However, it is very important to note that a person's *subjective feelings* of being fragmented does not mean that he *possesses* a structure—a self—which is fragmented. The latter claim which, as I noted earlier, has nothing to do with empathy, trades on the convincingness of the metaphor *"fragmented self"* and its ability to resonate empathically with a person's subjective feelings. The explanatory vacuousness of Kohut's formulations becomes apparent when one realizes that he is purportedly explaining or somehow accounting for *feelings* of being fragmented or for seeing oneself as a fragmented person by referring to a *fragmented self.* What causes feelings of being fragmented? The answer: a fragmented self.

Earlier, I noted Levine's (1979) criticisms that Kohut fails to distinguish between a patient's fantasies about being defective and in fact, his being defective; and that he fails to analyze such fantasies. These criticisms were presented in the context of therapeutic import. My above comments make essentially the same point in the context of showing their explanatory emptiness.

Finally, I remind the reader of Slap and Levine's (1978) observation that Kohut makes abundant use of "hybrid concepts," that is, abstract, metapsychological concepts which are used as if they referred to a person's actual experience. It seems to me that self and a variety of other self concepts (such as *fragmented self*) are, as used by Kohut, essentially "hybrid concepts" which sometimes refer to the world of the subjective person and sometimes to the non-personal world of organisms—or worse yet, which are used as if they belonged to one world when, in fact, they belong to the other.

Implications for Treatment

I want to consider briefly the implications of some of Kohut's formulations for treatment. Consider first the implications of Kohut's model of development. As noted earlier, I do not believe that one can assume that, because the patient is a narcissistic personality disorder or borderline or schizoid, one can limit one's attention to self defects or other presumably preoedipal concerns and ignore oedipal issues on the grounds that the latter are developmentally later and therefore relevant only to neurotic patients. This assumption, which finds widespread expression in much current literature, is based, as I have tried to show, on an inaccurate theory of the nature of psychological development. I believe that, as far as treatment is concerned, it is more realistic to expect that for all patients, material from many different levels of development will emerge and need to be dealt with, although there will be variations among patients in specific content, in coping style, and in the degree to which a particular level predominates (see Gedo, 1979 for a further elaboration of this point of view).

The dichotomy between defects on the one hand and intrapsychic conflicts on the other is also expressed in Kohut's conception of "disintegration anxiety," which I have discussed earlier. In Kohut's scheme, this kind of anxiety is, as Levine (1977) has pointed out, a passive experience based on real defects rather than a dynamic event which involves wishes, conflict, and defense. As noted earlier, a potentially insidious therapeutic consequence of the general view that the patient's difficulties and anxieties are based on actual early defects is the degree to which it confirms the patient's fantasy that he is, after all, defective (Levine, 1979).

Another difficulty with the therapeutic approach espoused by Kohut and his followers—at least as far as viewing it as psychoanalytic treatment is concerned—is that it tends to lend itself to the substitution of gratification for interpretation. Levine (1979) has shown in his analysis of the case studies published by Goldberg (1973) that although followers of Kohut advocate the use of interpretation in treatment, in specific instances, interpretation is foresworn and gratifications are offered instead. (See Levine, 1979 for specific clinical examples).

I have always had difficulty with descriptions of therapy with adults which conceptualize therapeutic change wholly or primarily in terms of resumption of an interrupted developmental process. An adult patient is, after all, chronologically, physically, socially and, in many significant areas, psychologically an adult and cannot resume development in the same manner as a child normally goes through the developmental process. Thus, to take the specific example discussed earlier, I do not believe that after achieving greater self-cohesiveness, the chronologically adult patient simply "enters" the oedipal period in a manner similar to or even analogous to the young child. As Levine (1977) reminds us, an adult is in a totally different situation—different socially, physically, and psychologically—from that of the child. Also, as Loewald (1979) reminds us, "the analysis of adults, no matter how much given to regression or [how] immature they are in significant areas of their functioning, is a venture in which the analysand not only is, in fact chronologically a grown-up, but which makes sense only if his or her adult potential, as manifested in certain significant areas of life, is in evidence" (pp. 163–164).

In his descriptions of some patients, Kohut (along with other psychoanalytic writers) often does not seem sufficiently aware of these basic facts Loewald calls to our attention. For example, Kohut writes about certain patients as if they had not proceeded beyond the earliest stages of "ego fragmentation" and "ego nuclei," stages which presumably characterize early infancy. Now, it seems difficult to understand or even imagine how an adult patient can resume development from this presumed earliest period of growth. What kind of processes could one imagine being involved? Also, we must ask, how is it possible for someone fixated or arrested at such a primitive and early stage in a central area of personality (i.e., self or ego structure) to function as an adult in so many areas of life? How is it possible for these people to do such things as think, communicate, relate to others (even if in a deeply troubled way), learn, make a living, etc.? It seems to me that the clinical and metapsychological speculations of many current psychoanalytic writers—and I believe Kohut is one of them—become almost fanciful in the degree to which they tend to ignore some of these most basic realities about patients. There is a troubling tendency on the part of many current psychoanalytic writers to engage in what I have referred to elsewhere (Eagle, 1982b) as "metapsychological infantilizing" of patients. If one took with utter seriousness some of these descriptions of patients, one would not understand how they could function within any degree of intactness in any significant area of life.

One difficulty which Kohut also shares with other psychoanalytic writers is an unnecessary degree of vagueness, even obfuscation, in descriptions of the processes mediating change in therapy. This is not always the case, for at times Kohut is quite laudably specific regarding the factors he believes to be responsible for therapeutic change. For example, Kohut makes quite clear his belief that real transformations in therapy take place not as a consequence of intellectual insights, but "in consequence of the gradual internalizations that are brought about by the fact that the old experiences are repeatedly relived by the more mature psyche" (1977, p. 30). This kind of claim, whether correct or incorrect, has a reasonably clear empirical meaning, can be related to previous similar formulations, can be made more precise, and can, in principle, be more rigorously evaluated. Or, as other examples, Kohut's emphasis on the importance of such factors as permitting idealization of the therapist, identification with the therapist, and the relinquishment of fantasies for narcissistic union with the therapist all seem to me to have substantial empirical content and are therefore, however difficult and complex the implementation might be, in principle susceptible to rigorous and controlled testing. However, one of the key theoretical concepts Kohut appeals to account for therapeutic change—"transmuting internalizations"—is as vague as can be.

According to Kohut, the general growth of psychic structures comes about through transmuting internalizations both in and outside of therapy. Generally, the concept of internalization in the psychoanalytic literature is confused and confusing, and Kohut's concept is no exception (see Meissner [1980] and Schafer [1968] for recent attempts to create some order in this area). When one attempts to ascertain what Kohut means, specifically, by "transmuting internalizations," one reads, for example, that this involves the creation of internal psychic structures through the withdrawal of cathexes from object images. But what are psychic structures? And what does it mean to withdraw cathexes from object images? Unless one's responses to these questions are reasonably clear and with empirical content and reference, the explanations of "transmuting internalizations" remain as vague as the term itself. Unfortunately, I believe one has to conclude that at this point, this key concept, employed by Kohut to describe and explain therapeutic change, has at best only approximate or perhaps only apparent meaning.

Finally, a problem characteristic of Kohut and other psychoanalytic writers is that it is difficult to ascertain from their writings what actually and precisely goes on in treatment. It is all well and good to talk about mirroring empathy, idealization, transmuting internalizations, etc., but that leaves unclear precisely what therapists actually *do* in a given session and the precise nature of the patient-therapist interaction. Until such questions are clarified, one does not know, for example, how Kohut's mirroring empathy differs, for example, from Rogers's (1959; 1961) non-directive reflections.

Some General Contributions of Kohut's Work

The reader familiar with Kohut's work can judge for himself the degree to which it represents a contribution to psychoanalytic theory and practice. In my view, there are some relatively clear-cut contributions which should be noted. First, Kohut's writings contribute to the general body of recent psychoanalytic literature which, taken together, makes an exceedingly strong and cogent case that, as Wallerstein (1980) puts it, psychosexual theory is not a sufficient framework in which to view psychological development. Or, to state it more specifically and forcefully (as Loewald [1979] does), that self-object differentiation is a more universal phenomenon than psychosexual conflict. In this regard, Kohut's work takes its place alongside the contributions of, for example, Mahler (1968), Jacobson (1964), Klein (1976), and Fairbairn (1952).

If one views self-object differentiation as a central and universal dimension, it becomes apparent that issues related to this dimension will play a significant role in treatment, particularly with more disturbed patients. As Gedo (1980) observes, Kohut's recognition of the importance of and the need to deal with symbiotic wishes[35] in the treatment of certain patients represents a possible contribution to the effectiveness of such treatment and to what has come to be referred to as the broadening scope of psychoanalytically oriented treatment.

A general contribution made by Kohut (some would consider it retrogressive—I do not) is the extent to which he has facilitated the introduction or re-introduction of the concept of self into psychoanalytic theory. In this regard, Kohut's work takes its place alongside the formulations of Sullivan (1947; 1953), Erikson (1959; 1963), Jacobson (1964), G. S. Klein (1976), and Gedo (1979), all of whom, whatever their differences (and they are considerable), have considered it essential that a theory of human behavior have a central place for a concept of self and of self-organization. I said "re-introduction" of the concept of self above because some have argued (e.g., Brandt [1966]) that originally traditional psychoanalysis did have a concept of self, Freud's "Das Ich," and that had that term been more accurately translated into "the I" or "the self," that fact would have remained apparent.

Finally, I think it is also worth singling out as a contribution Kohut's emphasis on the importance of goals and guiding values and ideals as both a reflection of and a maintainer of psychic health. These factors have not played any prominent role in traditional psychoanalytic formulations (Jacobson's [1964] work has represented an outstanding exception to this generalization) and have been extensively dealt with mainly by Erikson (1959; 1963) in the context of writing about ego identity. Whether or not one agrees with Kohut's conceptualization of the development of goals, values, and ideals, it is to his credit that he has recognized their psychological importance.

Summary

One finds in Kohut's writings three contradictory points of view toward traditional instinct theory. One, the idea that such theory is relevant to a circumscribed area, namely, the "structural neuroses"; two, the "principle of complementarity" in which both drive theory and a psychology of self constitute different perspectives on essentially the same set of phenomena; and three, the most radical position, in which drive theory is replaced by a psychology of self across the entire range of developmental and pathological phenomena. Kohut suggests but is reluctant to adopt explicitly this last position. It is this last position, however, which Kohut and his followers have come more and more to adopt, both implicitly and explicitly.

This last position amounts to a thoroughgoing rejection of Freudian instinct theory and to saying boldly and simply that when all is said and done the basic issues in development and in pathology do not have to do primarily with conflict among instinctual wishes, ego and superego, but with the development of an intact and cohesive self characterized by a clear sense of identity, by the capacity to express one's talents, ambitions, and aspirations, by the development of interests, values, ideals, and goals, and by the capacity to relate to others in the world.

What seems to be implied in Kohut's writings is that other problems that occur in the course of living, such as sexual guilt or guilt in relation to competitive strivings, are likely to be susceptible to relatively economical means of intervention (e.g., brief psychotherapy) when they are present in the context of a firm and cohesive self and are likely to resist such intervention when present in an individual without a cohesive self. In either case, the typical neurotic problems *per se* do not constitute the major therapeutic challenge of our time. As Erikson (1963) noted some time ago, ". . . the patient of today suffers most under the problem of what he should believe in and who he should—or, indeed, might—be or become, while the patient of early psychoanalysis suffered most under inhibitions which prevented him from being what and who he thought he knew he was" (p. 279).

As a rule, today's patients do not simply present classically neurotic problems of an oedipal nature. Rather, they present the kinds of problems which have come to be labeled schizoid, borderline, and narcissistic. For whatever reasons, problems of self and of object relations— experienced as feelings of meaninglessness, feelings of emptiness, pervasive depression, lack of sustaining interests, goals, ideals and values, and feelings of unrelatedness—are the overwhelmingly predominant symptoms in today's modal patient.[36] Furthermore, since as early as 1954, Winnicott (1958) warned young analysts that they would be unlikely to be seeing many classically neurotic patients in their practices, it is clear that we are witnessing a phenomenon of some duration.

I want to comment in passing on this question of the changing nature of pathology if, indeed, such changes have occurred. As Morgenthau and Person (1978) point out, psychoanalytic theorists, even when they do acknowledge the influence of broader social factors on personality and pathology, tend to reduce these factors to early experiences and child rearing. That is, if social factors influence personality development, they do so mainly through the vehicle of child-rearing processes. This is seen, for example, in Kohut's (1977) speculation that the self pathology of our time is a consequence of parental under-stimulation (which, in turn, is a function of working parents, time consumed in traveling to and from work, etc.) in contrast to the over-stimulation purportedly characteristic of neurotic patients.

It is, however, possible that given an "average expectable environment" of early caretaking experiences (with regard to empathic mirroring, "holding," symbiotic gratification, etc.) a greater frequency of self disorders may nevertheless occur because of certain social factors which are not mediated through mothering and child-rearing experiences. For example, the lack of stable ideologies and values or a particular set of values or an atmosphere of disillusionment and cynicism in the surrounding society may be potent factors contributing to experiences of emptiness and meaninglessness, and may be most operative, not in infancy and childhood, but in the period from preadolescence to young adulthood. In any case, this whole area requires further investigation and further careful thought.

To return to the summary of Kohut's views: when one spells out what I have called the radical position in Kohut's writings, it becomes apparent that it is similar, in important respects, to the position taken by the so-called object relations theorists. Fairbairn and Guntrip have essentially argued that *the* core problem in all psychopathology centers on the lack of intact self structures. Problems which are classified as neurotic in classical theory (Kohut's "structural neuroses") are seen by Fairbairn and Guntrip as defenses against the core problem of the experience of a lack of an intact sense of self.

According to this view, there is only more severe and less severe pathology of the self rather than qualitatively different nosological categories of the neuroses on the one hand, in which drive and structural conflict are primary, and disorders of the self on the other. In contrast to Kohut, this is directly and unambiguously stated by Fairbairn and Guntrip, who do not have to attempt to make room somehow for classical drive theory since their object relations theory, from the start, is based on an explicit and outright rejection of Freudian instinct theory. In the next section, I will present the formulations of Fairbairn, as representative of the British object relations theorists. Although others, such as Guntrip, Winnicott, and Balint have made important contributions in this area, Fairbairn's writings have been the most systematic and comprehensive.

7

REPLACEMENT OF INSTINCT THEORY BY OBJECT RELATIONS THEORY:
The Work of Fairbairn

As noted in Chapter 6, the work of Fairbairn is characterized by an outright rejection of Freudian instinct theory and its substitution by a thoroughgoing object relational theory. Fairbairn's approach to human behavior is most concisely expressed in the following summary offered by Ernest Jones (presented in the preface of Fairbairn's book, *Psychoanalytic Studies of the Personality*):

> "If it were possible to condense Dr. Fairbairn's new ideas into one sentence, it might run somewhat as follows. Instead of starting, as Freud did, from stimulation of the nervous system proceeding from excitation of various erotogenous zones and internal tension arising from gonadic activity, Dr. Fairbairn starts at the centre of the personality, the ego, and depicts its strivings and difficulties in its endeavor to reach an object where it may find support" (p. v).

An even more concise description of Fairbairn's basic differences with Freudian theory is his own statement that "the ultimate principle from which the whole of my special views are derived may be formulated in the general proposition that libido is not primarily pleasure-seeking, but object-seeking" (1952, p. 137). Elsewhere, Fairbairn notes that "from the point of view which I have now come to adopt, psychology may be said to resolve itself into a study of the relationships of the individual to his objects, whilst, in similar terms, psychopathology may be said to resolve itself more specifically into a study of the relationships of the ego to its internalized objects" (1952, p. 60). Although Guntrip (1968) has described object relations theory as the British parallel to Sullivanian interpersonal theory, it is the Kleinian concept of internalized objects, Guntrip's claim notwithstanding, which more than anything else clearly distinguishes the two approaches—and I shall have more to say about the concept of internalized objects later.

From the perspective of the central idea that the ego is object-seeking, Fairbairn reinterprets many traditional Freudian formulations. For example, what are repressed are not id impulses, but split-off ego structures and internalized objects which appear intolerably bad. Psychosexual stages are techniques employed by the ego for regulating relationships with objects. Tension reduction is not the basic direction of the individual, but a deteriorative principle which operates when there is a failure of object-relationships. "It is . . . not a means of achieving libidinal aims (which are, of course, object relational), but a means of mitigating the failure of these aims" (1952, p. 140). (Note the similarity between Fairbairn's and Kohut's views here). Aggression is not an inborn instinct, but a reaction to deprivation and frustration. The personality is not divided into structureless energy (id) and energyless structure (ego). Rather, the ego is a structure with its own dynamic aims. Hence, intrapsychic conflict is not conceptualized in terms of an id-ego model, but rather in terms of splits in the ego.

It would be useful to present Fairbairn's views more fully and in their own right, instead of through specific comparisons with Freudian theory. In a certain sense, Fairbairn's formulations constitute as much an ego psychology as what has come to be known as psychoanalytic ego psychology (i.e., the work of Hartmann, Rapaport, and others). That is, personality development, psychopathology, and behavior in general are viewed from the point of view of the ego, and, in particular, from the point of view of the ego's relationship with external and internalized objects. Of course, what distinguishes Fairbairn's from Hartmann's ego psychology is not only the former's emphasis on object relations, but also its rejection of the id-ego paradigm. In Fairbairn's theory, there is no id from which the ego is primarily or secondarily autonomous. There are only ego structures with their own dynamic aims and impulses. The ego's autonomy is not conditional but thoroughgoing. In Fairbairn's system, ego development and personality development in general is viewed, not in terms of vicissitudes of instinct or in terms of ego apparatuses, but in terms of an individual's movement from an early state of infantile dependence, based on primary identification with the object, to a state of mature dependence based on differentiation of the self from the object. (Note the similarity of this view to Mahler's conception of psychological development in terms of separation-individuation and to other general conceptions—Kohut's, for example—in which a central perspective from which development is viewed is differentiation of self from object).

Three stages to be noted in ego development are: 1) infantile dependence, 2) a transitional stage, and 3) adult or mature dependence. According to Fairbairn, underlying all pathology are developmental failures (due to traumas and deprivations) to move successfully from the early state of infantile dependence and one's defensive reactions to these failures. The basic conflicts underlying all pathology are either the schizoid one of "to love or not to love" and the accompanying dilemma of how to love without destroyng the needed object with one's devouring love, or the depressive one "of to love or to hate" and the accompanying dilemma of destroying the needed object with one's hate.

It is at the earliest stage of infantile dependence that ego splitting, a universal phenomenon underlying all pathology, occurs. The concept ego splitting plays a central role in Fairbairn's theorizing. According to Fairbairn, it is the essence of the schizoid position and is found, in different degrees, in overt schizophrenia and in neurosis. What is ego splitting? How does Fairbairn conceptualize it? I believe that Fairbairn's description of ego splitting reveals a murky, convoluted metapsychology which is difficult to understand and whose empirical referents are, to state it mildly, not at all clear. As best I can understand it, it goes somewhat as follows:

Initially, the infant splits the figure of the mother into good and bad objects in order to ameliorate the experienced ambivalence of the object. He then internalizes the bad object in order "to remove it from outer reality, where it eludes his control, to the sphere of inner reality," where it can be better controlled. The ambivalent qualities of the bad object form the basis for the split of the internalized object into an "exciting object" and "rejecting object." Both these internalized objects are then repressed by the (central) ego. Because parts of the ego remain attached to the repressed objects, the repression of the objects means that parts of the ego itself become split off and repressed. Those parts of the ego split off from the central ego are referred to by Fairbairn as the "libidinal ego" (the ego structure attached to the exciting object) and the "anti-libidinal ego" or "internal saboteur" (the ego structure attached to the rejecting object).

There are many questions that can be directed to Fairbairn's formulations, both from an internal and external perspective. For example, staying entirely within his system, one question that arises is whether only bad objects are internalized. Although at times Fairbairn writes about the internalization of good objects, the thrust of most of his remarks and the logic of his theorizing suggests that early internalization is intended to apply only to bad objects. Thus, in contrast to Melanie Klein, for Fairbairn, internalization occurs under the impact of deprivation and frustration and is motivated by the need to deal with the badness of the object, even by assuming and taking the badness into oneself. Indeed, the first defense of the infant against negative experiences, Fairbairn tells us, is mental internalization of the object associated with the negative experiences. Although Fairbairn does not explicitly make this link, it would also appear that the early "primary identification" between infant and caretaker would also predispose the infant to internalization of the object.

Guntrip (1969) has attempted to clarify this issue of internalization of only bad objects versus internalization of both good and bad objects by distinguishing between two kinds of internalization. Good experiences, he argues, are internalized as memories and serve as psychic aliment, as it were, for the building of psychic structures. One can further elucidate the differences between internalization of good versus bad objects by using the analogy of eating and digesting (borrowed from Piaget [1976], who uses the analogy in another context). Edible foods which are eaten and digested are metabolized as basic substances which are assimilated by the organism and serve as aliment for the building and energizing of bodily structure and processes. In a word, the ingested food becomes a natural part of and assimilated to the body. By contrast, indigestible substances which are ingested cannot be digested and metabolized, cannot be assimilated, and cannot serve as aliment to energize and build. They remain as foreign bodies and retain their identity as foreign substances. A similar contrast holds, Guntrip tells us, between the internalizations of good and bad experiences. The former are internalized as memories which serve as aliment for the build-up of cognitive and affective psychic structures and of identity. In bad experiences, the bad object is internalized as object, undigested and unassimilated, and hence remains as a foreign body within the psychic structure of the individual.[37]

From an external perspective—that is, from the point of view of a critic who stands outside Fairbairn's system—many criticisms and questions can be directed to Fairbairn's formulations. In my view, the most serious of these criticisms and questions have to do with the vagueness and murkiness of certain basic concepts. For example, what precisely is meant by such concepts as internalization and internalized objects? Which, if any, common psychological processes, about which we have some substantive knowledge, are involved in the internalization of objects? What does it mean to say that parts of one's ego become attached to internalized objects? And what does it mean to talk about the repression of internalized objects and ego structures? These are only some of the basic questions that need to be asked.

Consider first the concept of internalized object. The psychoanalytic literature on internalization processes—which include incorporation, introjection, and identification—has been vast and, for the most part, confusing and confused. Fairbairn's concept of internalized object seems to belong to this tradition. However, some minimal attempt at clarification can be made. It might be useful to begin by noting that what Fairbairn describes as an internalized object seems closest to what others in the literature have referred to as an *introject*, and what Fairbairn describes as internalization (of the object) others have considered *introjection*. Having translated "internalized object" into "introject," we need to take a closer look at the latter. Most psychoanalytic descriptions of introjection include the essential idea of taking in and making part of oneself some set of experienced representations (including traits, evaluations, prohibitions, and functions) of the other. Now this process of taking in and making part of oneself is common to all internalization processes, including incorporation and identification. What distinguishes introjection from other internalization processes? It seems to me that what Fairbairn wants to convey by internalized object and what others want to convey by the concept of introjection is the idea that *what is taken in is not fully integrated into one's self-organization.* The result is that introjects or internalized objects are, as Schafer (1968) points out, often experienced as "felt" presences by which one feels assailed (or gratified) and in relation to which one feels passive.[38] For example, some patients may report the experience of some evil or destructive force which prompts a particular maladaptive behavior. By contrast, the hallmark of identification, a process in which what is taken in is more fully assimilated and integrated, is a characteristic "feel" of intentionality, will, and activity.[39]

Because the internalized object or introject is not fully integrated into one's self-organization, one relates to it as object—that is, it has an object-relational quality save that what was once a relationship to an external object is now replaced by a relationship to an internal one. Consider as a classic example of introjection Freud's description of the development of the superego (to which, Fairbairn tells us, the concept of internalized object can be traced). Punishments, prohibitions, evaluations, rules, etc., which were once experienced in relation to an external object are now internalized and made part of oneself. But frequently, they are not fully integrated into one's self-organization, as expressed in the common tendency to experience and describe these prohibitions, etc., as a homunculus standing outside oneself and observing what one does and thinks, and as expressed in such common locutions as "my conscience tells me . . ." What we are observing—at least, according to the definitions adopted here—is the presence of superego as introject rather than as the product of fully successful identifications.[40] The latter would be experienced as a relatively well assimilated set of moral values and standards that are intrinsic and integral to one's identity (see Meissner [1981] for a fuller description of this and related issues).

The link between internalized object and the Freudian superego suggests that what Fairbairn means by the former is a set of originally external valuations of oneself which become internalized and thereby part of one's self-evaluations (not unlike Sullivan's [1974] "reflected appraisals"). While the analogy with the concept of superego may be helpful, it leaves many other questions unanswered. For example, while one can perhaps understand what it means to internalize the "rejecting object" (the object's rejecting attitudes and values *toward me* are internalized so that I now reject certain aspects of myself), it is more difficult to understand what it means to internalize the "exciting object" in view of the fact that exciting object refers from the beginning, not to attitudes of the object toward me, but *reactions of mine toward the object.* In short, "rejecting object" and "exciting object" do not seem to be of comparable conceptual status as far as susceptibility to internalization is concerned.[41]

A perusal of Fairbairn indicates that internalization can be understood in two basic ways: one, the "natural" tendency of the oral dependent child to incorporate the object with which he is identified. This is expressed by Fairbairn as follows: ". . . infantile dependence is characterized not only by identification, but also by an oral attitude of incorporation. In virtue of this fact the object with which the individual is identified becomes equivalent to an incorporated object . . ." (1952, p. 42). The second context in which internalization can be understood is as the first defense of the child. As noted, Fairbairn tells us that the child internalizes the (bad) objects in order to make the environment more controllable and more benign. By "taking upon himself the burden of badness which appears to reside in his objects" and thus purging the objects of their badness, the child "is rewarded by that sense of security which an environment of good objects so characteristically confers" (1952, p. 65).

What Fairbairn seems to be suggesting here is that the child takes on as his own the "bad," that is, depriving and frustrating qualities of the object both because of his "natural" age-specific propensity to employ identification (this tendency would presumably not be limited to "bad" qualities) and his defensive need to make the environment more benign and tolerable. This raises a host of difficulties and questions, only a few of which can be sampled here. For example, a variant of the question often directed to Melanie Klein's work: Is the infant really capable of such terribly complex, purposive maneuvers such as taking on the object's badness in order to render the environment less bad?

There is still another difficulty with this notion of the child's taking on the "badness" of the object. Since the "bad" qualities of the object referred to are rejecting and depriving behavior, the taking on the "badness" of the object would mean that the child would also become and feel rejecting and depriving. Although presumably this outcome does occur (as in the case of a primitive and harsh superego or what Fairbairn refers to as the "internal saboteur"), often the "badness" of the child is *reciprocal* with the mother's rejection rather than a direct identification with it. That is to say, the child's "badness" takes the form not of feeling rejecting and depriving, but of feeling and being *worthy* of rejection and *deserving* of deprivation. In some of Fairbairn's own clinical descriptions, meant to provide concrete illustrations of internalization of objects, the child behaves, not in a rejecting and depriving manner, but as someone who is the *object of* and deserves little but rejection and deprivation. His self-picture reveals more, to use Sullivan's (1947) terms, the "reflected appraisals" of the object, rather than identification with the object. It is more a question of one's image of oneself being the product of *complying* with the appraisals of significant others. This process is different from internalizing directly the parents' rejecting attitude so that one rejects aspects of oneself and *then* feels unworthy. The former is a direct reflection of significant others' attitudes and appraisals, while the latter clearly implies intrapsychic conflict (in traditional terms, typically an id-superego conflict). Fairbairn does not make entirely clear the kind of internalization he has in mind.

Another aspect of the difficulties attending the concept of internalized object is the following one: The conception of internalized object as a foreign body that needs to be expelled implies a core of aspects of oneself that truly are oneself. That is, if a foreign body is to be expelled, it is expelled from a milieu to which it is foreign. But what is the nature of this core that is truly oneself and of the milieu in relation to which the internalized object is foreign or alien? Insofar as Fairbairn defines psychic structure (what he calls the "basic endopsychic situation") *almost entirely* in terms of internalized objects and the ego sub-structures which are attached to them, two further questions arise: 1) What else is there in personality structure (other than the central ego, which is the conscious, environment-oriented aspect of personality)? and 2) What is left when internalized objects are expelled? Fairbairn's only implicit answers to these questions seems to reside in the notion that prior to the internalization of objects and consequent "splits in the ego," the infant is endowed with an "original pristine unitary ego" which, in the present context, I take to represent Fairbairn's idea of the real core of the personality. (I shall have more to say about this notion below).

To illustrate in a more concrete, behavioral way: to interpret, let us say, feelings of low self-esteem in terms of an internalized object suggests a therapeutic model of exorcism and expulsion in which what remains after expulsion are feelings of worthiness emanating from the "original pristine unitary ego." It also suggests a concept of a pure pre-social and pre-interpersonal self which is revealed after exorcism of the foreign body. The question that must be posed is whether it makes theoretical or clinical sense to posit such a "pristine" pre-social self.

A theory that identifies various normal processes in personality development *can* meaningfully speak (even if only metaphorically) of the expulsion of introjects insofar as there are other aspects of personality (and more specifically, of self and of ego) remaining which have developed through processes *other than* internalization of objects. But, as noted above, Fairbairn describes personality development mainly in terms of internalization of objects and its consequences and has little, if anything, to say about other contributing processes. This silence about these contributing processes makes it difficult for him to answer the question regarding what remains of the personality when internalized objects are expelled, and forces him to fall back on the vague and unrealistic notion of an original pre-social ego or self whose "pristine unitariness" was destroyed by early defensive internalization.

This position also implies a model of therapy in which the main task and goal is to exorcize the internalized object and, following that, to re-discover what remains of the "original pristine unitary ego"—rather than a model in which therapy consists in a process of relearning and of slow growth. The former prompts talk about "re-birth" and other similar hyperbolic locutions (see Guntrip [1968], for example) while the latter suggests a more realistically slow and arduous process of new learning, trying out new attitudes and behaviors (working through), and experiencing new identifications.

By positing a concept such as the "pristine unitary ego," Fairbairn suggests that we are born whole and that only rejection, deprivation, and frustration (and our defensive reactions to them) tear us asunder. But here Fairbairn does not seem to distinguish between the "wholeness" inherent in lack of differentiation (in this sense, a blob is "whole") and wholeness emerging from differentiation and integration of various differentiated aspects of a structure. It may be that most of us are born with a potential for wholeness. But actual wholeness is a life-long integrative achievement. Too often, Fairbairn writes (and Guntrip does too, in explicating Fairbairn) as if, following exorcism of internalized objects, we can somehow return to a pristine, pre-split state of unity and wholeness. This is a harmful illusion which is too much connoted by concepts like "pristine unitary ego."[42]

One can go on with further theoretical examination of the central concept of internalized objects, but I believe that Fairbairn's clinical and behavioral descriptions rather than his metapsychological formulations will be more likely to tell us what he means. When Fairbairn writes in ordinary, clinically descriptive language his formulations concerning internalized objects suggest the following: When the child feels genuinely loved, he can separate psychologically from the object because he can safely depend upon his real objects. In the absence of such security, the child experiences difficulty in renouncing and overcoming infantile dependence "for such renunciation would be equivalent in his eyes to forfeiting all hope of ever obtaining the satisfaction of his unsatisfied emotional needs" (Fairbairn, 1952, p. 39). Manifestations of this state of infantile dependence include failure to differentiate from the object ("primary identification," in Fairbairn's terms) and a preoccupation with the object in which the individual keeps hoping for change in the object. Because for Fairbairn internalization of the object and failure to differentiate from the object are essentially equivalent (as expression of infantile dependence), "the task of differentiating (from) the object tends to resolve itself into a problem of expelling an incorporated object . . ." (1952, p. 42).

When Fairbairn discusses specific clinical symptoms, his formulations are stated more straightforwardly and predominantly in the above terms of differentiation and separation from the object. For example, in discussing phobias, he writes that "it may accordingly be inferred that it is to the conflict between the progressive urge toward separation from the object and the regressive lure of identification with the object that we must look for the explanation of the phobic state" (1952, p. 43). And in discussing the difficulties of schizoid and depressive soldiers, Fairbairn notes that "the abandonment of infantile dependence involves an abandonment of relationships based upon primary identification in favor of relationships with differentiated objects" (1952, p. 42). Looking at development and at pathology in these terms is, it will be recognized, remarkably close to more current conceptions in which the central dimension of psychological development is, in Mahler's (1968) terms, the move toward separation-individuation and, in more general terms, the differentiation of self from other.

It seems to me that much of Fairbairn's convoluted metapsychology of internalized objects and associated split-off ego structures can be more simply and more meaningfully re-stated in terms of self-valuations and cognitive-affective responses, derived from experiences with the object, which have not been successfully integrated within the personality. For example, one set of aims (represented by the term "libidinal ego")—let us say, to be taken care of and to merge with the object—may conflict with the set of aims stemming from the desire to differentiate from the object and may also arouse one's own contempt and hatred represented by the term "anti-libidinal ego." Restating matters in this form not only simplifies them, but keeps intact Fairbairn's insistence that intrapsychic conflict be conceptualized, not in terms of ego structure versus instinctual aims, but in terms of different structures, each with its own aims. Or, to state it even more simply, intrapsychic conflict is a question of different *aim systems* (see G. S. Klein, 1976).

Before leaving Fairbairn's work, there is one point of contrast with Freud that is worth pursuing. It will be recalled that for Fairbairn mental internalization is the basic defense, the infant's first defense. It is, in fact, the starting point for Fairbairn's whole elaborate metapsychology of internalized objects, splits in the object, and splits in the ego. In direct contrast, for Freud the basic defense is the making external of what is internal. Thus, for Fairbairn, the starting point for defense is internalizing what was external, while for Freud, defense consists in making external what was internal.[43] In this contrast lies an insight into some basic differences in viewpoint between Fairbairn and Freud. For Freud, it is a prohibited inner wish or *impulse* that constitutes a threat and requires defense. Hence, the need to disavow and expel, to deny that the wish is one's own. By contrast, for Fairbairn it is the negative rejecting and depriving *experiences* at the hands of *an external object* (that is, a "bad" environment) which constitute the basic threat and require defense. Hence, the need to internalize the environment in order to deny and control its badness.

While for Freud, the *inherent* nature of instinctual wish is such that, even under ideal circumstances, it will be irreducibly opposed to civilization, implicit in Fairbairn is the utopian idea that in an ideally "good" environment defense would not be necessary.[44] Another way of stating the difference is to say that for Freud one's basic problems arise out of incompatible and conflicting aims and the defensive means of dealing with these incompatibilities. For example, as G. S. Klein (1976) points out, repression and other forms of disavowal of one set of aims tend to *fractionate* the personality (note the links to pre-psychoanalytic concepts of dissociation). For Fairbairn, however, one's basic problems arise out of negative experience in a "bad" environment and the defensive internalization that follows such negative experiences. It is no wonder, then, that Fairbairn's conception of psychotherapy emphasizes the exorcism of internalized bad objects and the provision of a "good" object situation, while in the Freudian conception of treatment there is an unrelenting emphasis on insight and understanding.

It will be recognized that these contrasting views already anticipate much current debate regarding the nature of pathology and the proper therapeutic approach to its treatment. For example, Fairbairn shares with Kohut the view that pathology, particularly of the self, is the result of a "bad" environment (with lack of mirroring and empathic mothering as the particular aspects of "badness" stressed by Kohut). Hence, for Fairbairn, as for Kohut, psychotherapy must prominently include the provision of a "good object" situation. I must repeat the comment made earlier in relation to Kohut's work, however. One can speak of treatment as constituting "good object" situations (necessary to "dissolve" the internalized bad object), "holding environments," and other similar descriptions. However, these characterizations have limited value without detailed descriptions of the patient-therapist interactions and of ongoing therapeutic processes illustrating these ideas.

In an attempt to evaluate, in an overall fashion, the significance of Fairbairn's work, what is important, it seems to me, are not the specific, complex metapsychological formulations regarding internalized objects and split-off ego structures, but the broad emphasis on the importance of early object relations, the conception of psychological development in terms of differentiation between self and object, and progress from infantile dependence to mature dependence. And paralleling these positive emphases is Fairbairn's rejection of Freudian instinct theory and the concomitant implicit and explicit claim that object-seeking propensities are as primary and as biological as the sexual and aggressive drives of instinct theory. In all these respects, Fairbairn's work anticipated and was instrumental in generating the current ferment in psychoanalytic theory and practice.

It is also important to note again that Fairbairn's clinically based intuitions regarding our inborn object-seeking propensities and the autonomy of object relational needs receive strong empirical support from the research evidence that has become available since Fairbairn's formulations (see pp. 10–16).

8

A REFORMULATION OF PSYCHOANALYTIC THEORY:
The Work of G. S. Klein

In this section, I will present the work of G. S. Klein which, in certain respects, is quite similar to Fairbairn's. The similarity is particularly interesting because Klein attempted to stay within the bounds of traditional Freudian theory rather than reject significant aspects of it. His attempt was to revamp and rationalize psychoanalytic theory rather than formulate a new theory. Unfortunately and tragically, an early death cut short the continuation of his clearly important and original contributions.

Without expressly stating it, Klein (1976) essentially reformulated psychoanalytic theory as a psychology of self. In this sense, his work is part of that general movement within psychoanalysis which has placed increasing emphasis on the central motivational role of the maintenance of self-integrity. The elaboration of the notion of aims and their relationship to a concept of self form a major part of his book, *Psychoanalytic Theory.* According to Klein, from the psychoanalytic point of view, human development and behavior are most meaningfully viewed as attempts at "constant resolution of incompatible aims and tendencies." The idea of incompatibilities and their resolution is certainly not new to psychoanalytic theory. But what is distinctive in Klein's view is his claim that the resolution of these incompatibilities is conditioned by the need for a coherent and integrated self. Klein posits the need for a unified self as a pervasive, all-embracing, and underlying motive for behavior. The links between these ideas and both recent formulations such as Kohut's (1971, 1977) and earlier for-

87

mulations of object relation theorists such as Fairbairn (1952) and Guntrip (1968) should be evident.

Taking a self psychology as his basic starting point, Klein reinterprets in a fresh and challenging way many hallowed, traditional, psychoanalytic concepts. For example, he redefines repression as "a meaning scheme that is dissociated from the person's self-conception" (p. 241). He expresses what to many analysts will seem the shocking view that the essence of repression is not to be found in the concept of the unconscious or of unconscious content and activity, but in the fact that "'lived' meanings are . . . segregated from understanding, i.e., *dissociated from the self* (Klein's italics)" (p. 251). Conflict is viewed, not as a phenomenon occurring between forces, but always in relation to self-conception. Klein defines anxiety not in quantitative terms of excessive stimulation, but as "always [involving] issues of identity and selfhood." Ego and id are defined, respectively, as experiences and actions owned and related to the self and those occurring without self as center (definitions, which as noted earlier, some would claim are closer than the current uses to Freud's original use of "Das Ich" and "Das Es"—for example, see Brandt [1966]).

Fundamental to all these above reinterpretations is the image of a person trying to preserve and maintain, as well as he can and with whatever means are available, a coherent and unified self. In his discussion of the two main means—"fractionation and identification"—by which the person tries to guarantee unity and continuity of selfhood, Klein is at his most stimulating. In fractionation, of which repression is the prime example, an attempt is made to preserve unity by splitting off a meaning schema from the self-structure. In identification, of which reversal of voice from passive to active (a concept Klein attributes to Loevinger, 1966) is the prime example, one attempts to preserve unity by changing the self-schema. In repression, the experience is dissociated from the self but continues to influence behavior. In reversal of voice, one attempts to recreate in an active mode, for the purpose of mastery, what was passively experienced and endured.

While Klein has no hesitation in rejecting Freudian metapsychology, his attitude toward the primary role given to instinctual impulses in Freudian theory is more complex and, I believe, more ambiguous. Klein has little to say about aggression and focuses his entire attention on the sexual drive. Klein's basic explicit attitude here is that one can get rid of the drive discharge model and of libido theory without undermining the Freudian insight into the central importance of sexuality. More specifically, Klein argues that one can reject Freudian libido theory without rejecting psychosexual theory. He assures us, in effect, that his reformulations of Freudian theory do not shortchange sexuality. Indeed, he warns against the danger of "re-repression of hard-won insights into the importance of sexuality" (p. 7). Here Klein shows a sensitivity to a tradition in the history of psychoanalysis in which one's attitude toward Freudian drive theory constituted the major criterion for whether or not one's views would be seen as apostasy (see also Holt, 1976).

The fact is, however, that despite Klein's assurances, when he discusses specifically the role of sexuality in behavior he departs radically from Freudian conceptions. Consider the passage in which Klein interprets preemptive and nagging sexual craving in terms of "some more encompassing need in which self-conception and self-status are at issue." In that same passage, he continues as follows: "In such instances what hurts and disturbs is not the tension of unreleased sexual energy but the failure to actualize the self-value which has come to be symbolized through sexual accomplishment" (p. 97). This is not a Freudian concept of sexuality. Quite contrary to the Freudian view, in the above formulations, what is central is not sexual discharge or gratification, or even sensual pleasure, but the overriding need for unity and cohesiveness of self.

In short, despite Klein's insistence on the centrality of sexuality, it is not central in the sense in which Freud intended. To say that sex is important in behavior is hardly itself distinctively Freudian and should not obscure Klein's departure from the Freudian view. What is distinctively Freudian is a conception in which all behavior, including patently non-drive behavior, is seen to be, directly or indirectly, in the service of drive gratification. Klein reverses this position by arguing that sexual gratification is primarily in the service of maintaining unity of self. Thus, his formulations entail a rejection not only of the libido or drive-discharge components of the Freudian theory of sexuality, but of the fundamental Freudian proposition that sexuality has a special, central, and ubiquitous motivating role in behavior. The former Klein explicitly states; the latter, although unacknowledged by Klein, is implicit in his examples and in his "superordinate" self psychology. Klein believed he could separate libido theory from the general Freudian position regarding the centrality of sexuality in behavior, but, in fact, they are too intimately linked for that to be easily accomplished. That is, what permits one to view manifestly non-sexual behavior as sexually motivated, as entailing indirect sexual gratification, and as a displacement of sexual aims (as in sublimation)—in short, what permits one to see sexuality as a central motivation in a wide range of behaviors—are precisely the assumptions contained in instinct theory and libido theory. Without such assumptions, sexuality takes its place as only one among many motives.

My observation that Klein rejects the essentials of the Freudian drive theory of sexuality is not intended as a criticism of Klein, for I believe he is correct in his position. But the ambiguity and ambivalence of the rejection is worth noting. Klein's ambivalence in this area helps account for certain inconsistencies in his treatment of the Freudian theory of sexuality and for his failure to draw the full implications of a psychology in which maintenance and unity of self are taken to be the superordinate goals guiding the individual's behavior.

As an example of this inconsistency, Klein notes approvingly that in his concept of sexuality, "Freud was able to relate such diverse phenomena as perversions and strong [non-sexual] interests" (p. 25). But is this an achievement or a deficiency in the theory? Klein notes that a major developmental and ongoing psychological problem facing the individual is maintaining the integrity of self in the face of incompatible aims and tendencies. He notes further that aims incompatible with the self-structure are the major source of anxiety and threat to the self and that maladaptive, "fractionating" attempts to deal with such threats are a major condition for psychopathology. Now, the point here is that, according to Klein's formulation, *any* set of aims incompatible with the self-structure constitutes the primary conditions of anxiety and threat. There is no necessary special status for psychosexual aims. In short, it is difficult to reconcile Klein's conceptions of anxiety, defense, conflict, development, and the conditions of pathology in terms of incompatibility with self-structure, with his claim that he is accepting Freud's ideas regarding the centrality of sexuality.

It is interesting to note that in important respects, Klein's self psychology is similar to early Freudian formulations of hysteria in which the major pathogens were psychic trends dissociated from what would now be called self-structure. Freud (1893–1895) writes that "it turns out to be a *sine qua non* for the acquisition of hysteria that an incompatibility should develop between the ego and some idea" (p. 122). He does not specify that the idea need be sexual in content. Such formulations show obvious links to the non-psychoanalytic continental psychiatry of Janet and Binet (a link acknowledged by Freud), the American psychiatry of Morton Prince (1929a,b) and Sullivan's self psychology (1953, 1955). (I cannot resist noting, in passing, the remarkable absence of any reference to Sullivan in recent emphases on object relations and self).

The centrality in Klein's thinking of the idea of aims incompatible with the self-structure is also seen in his treatment of the concept of repression which, in turn, has important implications for recent emphases on splitting as defense. Klein defines repression (and other defenses) not so much in the traditional terms of keeping certain ideas and impulses out of awareness, but rather in terms of a "split-off cognitive-affective structure which exerts a selective influence on behavior" (p. 198). Or, as Klein notes at another point, in repression, "self-continuity and integrity are resolved through dissociation from self" (pp. 293–294). The idea of split-off cognitive-affective structures (read as motivational aim systems) is, as noted earlier, reminiscent of early Freud (1893–1895). It is also, however, reminiscent of the last of his writings in which he is concerned with the relationship between repression and ego splitting (1940a, 1940b), as if some of his earlier ideas returned for reconsideration.

This idea of splitting as a defense is also exceedingly prominent in recent descriptions of borderline conditions (e.g., Kernberg, 1975, 1976; Masterson, 1976). Indeed, in these discussions, the pervasive presence of splitting, in contrast to the presumably more developmentally mature repression, is frequently cited as a differentiating hallmark of such conditions. Now, the question implicitly posed by Klein's (and Freud's) description of repression is: If repression, by definition, involves split-off cognitive-affective structures, how is it to be differentiated from the more pathological splitting observable in borderline conditions? I think that some answers to this question are implicit in Klein's work and need to be spelled out. The characterization of repression in terms of split-off cognitive-affective structures, dissociation from the self-structure, lack of comprehension, and failure to make connections (rather than simply failure of awareness) helps make clear the relationship between repression and splitting. What is implied in repression is that there is present a predominant, relatively stable self-structure from which cognitive-affective structures *can* be split off. It is the "option" open to someone with a relatively cohesive self. By contrast, in the clinical phenomena described by splitting, there is less of a predominant, cohesive self-structure from which cognitions and affects are split off. Rather there are, so to speak, alternations of different self-structures with no one structure being a decisive and stable determinant of identity. It is the "option" open to someone who has not yet achieved a stable self-structure. Thus, the person employing splitting is all-loving and idealizing on one occasion and all-hating and denigrating on another. The clinical descriptions would be similar to multiple personalities or fugue states were it not for the fact that while the person is in state 1 (the all-loving state), he *remembers* many of the cognitions and affects of state 2 (the all-hating state).

It really is a matter of range of integrations. Whereas those employing repression have achieved integration within the set of aims defined by a cohesive self (but have not been able to integrate what is split off from the self), the range of integration achieved by those employing splitting is limited to "intra-self" valuative and affective (good vs. bad, love vs. hate) "islands" within a relatively diffuse and unstable self-structure.

The former can rely on a relatively stable and reliable executive coordinator and integrator which has succeeded in coordinating and integrating the major components (or sub-routines) of the personality, even if some components remain unintegrated. In the latter case, semi-autonomous components or structures of the personality operate in alternating or parallel fashion, unintegrated by an executive coordinator. Of course, it can be seen that these are merely quasi computer-language translations of, what in another context, would be described as a cohesive versus a non-cohesive self. Other clarifications contributed by Klein include a formulation of repression which is more consistent with the importance of object relations and a conception of the ego not simply as "pure" structure controlling and channeling id aims, but as a structure with its own aims (see Apfelbaum, 1966, for further discussion of this issue).

Klein's work takes its place alongside the contributions of others discussed here who have forged this new direction. Klein's work is further evidence that we are witnessing in our time a major shift in, to borrow from Kuhn (1962), the basic "paradigm" of psychoanalytic theory. This shift is characterized by a central concern with the development and vicissitudes of object relations and of an individuated and cohesive self—precisely those domains emphasized by Klein.

I want to make one final point regarding Klein's contributions. By positing the "constant resolution of incompatible aims and tendencies" as the central psychic challenge facing the individual, by linking degree of such resolution to degree of self-integrity, and by insisting that basic aims are always pursued in the context of object relations, Klein has implicitly demonstrated that, contrary to Kohut's partitioning scheme and current radical distinctions, it is possible to integrate a self psychology and a psychology of object relations with a psychology of intrapsychic conflict.

Gedo's Epigenetic-Hierarchical Model

Gedo (1979; 1980) is another contemporary psychoanalytic theorist who, similar to Klein, conceives of self-relevant goals as superordinate overriding ones. His avowed purpose is to replace traditional drive theory with his epigenetic-hierarchical model. More specifically, Gedo replaces Freud's sexual and aggressive aims with personal autonomy and self-definition as superordinate goals, expressed through a multiplicity of strivings and ambitions. Self-organization is defined as "the cohesive hierarchy" of these aims and strivings and it is the threat to self-organization (rather than instinctual impulses) that is the main stimulus for the eliciting of anxiety.

Gedo presents a hierarchical model in which psychological development is conceptualized along two interrelated dimensions: one, which he calls "phases," moves from differentiation of body boundaries to consolidation of self-organization to formation of the superego to formation of the repression barrier; along the other dimension, which Gedo refers to as "modes," development is viewed in terms of different governing principles and typical problem situations. Thus, at the earliest point in development (corresponding to the phases of differentiation of body boundaries and consolidation of self-organization), the governing principle is avoidance of unpleasure and the typical problem situation faced by the individual is the danger of overstimulation. At the next stage of development, the pleasure principle is the governing one and persistence of illusions is the typical problem. The reality principle comes into play as the governing rule at the next stage of development and the associated typical problem is intrapsychic conflict. Finally, at the last stage creativity emerges as the ruling principle and frustration is the typical problem faced by the individual.

In contrast to Kohut's assertion that traditional psychoanalytic theory is adequate for dealing with neurotic "structural conflicts," while self psychology is necessary to explain self defects, Gedo is explicitly interested in presenting a unified psychoanalytic theory which will be applicable to all psychopathology. In support of his belief in the need for a unified theory, Gedo insists that one must deal with all phases of development in psychotherapy, particularly in view of the fact that how one reacts to later developmental issues is strongly influenced by earlier disturbances and successes.

The specific content of Gedo's "phases" and "modes" has a certain vagueness and arbitrariness and raises a number of questions. For example, why does the pleasure principle developmentally follow the principle of self-definition as a regulating principle? Or, as another example, while avoidance of unpleasure, the pleasure principle, and even self-definition can be construed as motivational aims and principles, in what way is the "principle of creativity" primarily motivational in nature? Is creativity a motivational principle of behavior or rather an outcome of a particular set of interests (e.g., in a particular phenomenon or problem) and gifts? Finally, self-definition and self-organization are presented by Gedo both as superordinate overriding themes and motives and as a specific phase and mode characteristic of a particular level of development. These are only some of the questions that can be directed to Gedo's scheme. But what is noteworthy about Gedo's model is that it represents an attempt to provide a systematic and comprehensive revision of psychoanalytic theory from the point of view of a self psychology.

9

A REFORMULATION OF
THE PSYCHOANALYTIC THEORY OF THERAPY:
The Work of Weiss, Sampson,
and their Colleagues

The final psychoanalytic development I will cover briefly is the work of Weiss, Sampson, and their colleagues at Mt. Zion Hospital in San Francisco. The work of this group comes closest to the development of what I refer to later as an autonomous theory of therapy. It also represents one of the very few instances of well-designed and rigorous research involving psychoanalytic psychotherapy. Although the formulations of the Mt. Zion group are made primarily in the context of therapy, they are also of general theoretical interest.

Weiss (1971; 1982) contrasts the early Freudian theory of therapy and of mental functioning with his own point of view which, he maintains, is derived from later Freud. According to Weiss, the early psychoanalytic theory of therapy is as follows: Under the impetus of regression and the psychoanalytic situation, infantile unconscious wishes and the surrounding conflicts and defenses are mobilized and are most directly expressed in the transference. The frustration of these wishes by the analyst's neutrality facilitates the emergence of unconscious contents into free association. Working against the emergence of these unconscious contents into consciousness is the ubiquitous resistance, which incldes the transference itself, specific defenses against the experience of anxiety-provoking unconscious wishes, and a reluctance both to give up the unconscious partial gratification which one's symptoms and neurosis provide and to relinquish one's fantasy of greater fulfillment of infantile wishes.

As for the general early Freudian theory of mental functioning, unconscious contents are mainly "impulses and defenses. The impulses seek their infantile gratifications, and the defenses—or, more precisely, the forces of repression—keep the impulses unconscious. Moreover, the impulses are additive. They are all, therefore, on the same level of the mental hierarchy. They interact dynamically with each other, and with the defenses, and by their dynamic interactions they determine behavior.

"Repression, according to the early theory, is maintained primarily to protect the infantile gratifications which the impulses unconsciously are obtaining. If a person were to become aware of such gratifications, he would have to relinquish them" (Weiss, 1982, pp. 1–2).

While the core psychoanalytic idea that certain unconscious contents are warded off is retained by the Mt. Zion group (as it is by most, if not all, critics of traditional psychoanalytic theory), what is modified is the conception of what is warded off and how such contents emerge in awareness. While in the early theory, it is mainly instinctual impulses seeking gratification that are warded off, the Mt. Zion group emphasizes warded off motives "stemming from the unconscious parts of the ego" and from the superego, such as, for example, the wish to comply with parents, or the wish to restore an object, or the wish to atone for an imagined crime against an object. Also warded off are "grim unconscious beliefs which arise in the traumas of childhood, such as the unconscious belief in castration as punishment" and the fears, anxieties, and guilt feelings connected to these beliefs.

As to how such contents emerge into conscious awareness: according to traditional theory, unconscious instinctual impulses are constantly striving for gratification and constantly pushing upward for conscious expression. Working against such expression are defenses and resistance. In this scheme, the pleasure principle *automatically* regulates emergence versus non-emergence of material into awareness. As noted earlier, in the analytic situation, the regressive components and the transference, among other things, tend to mobilize and strengthen unconscious impulses so that they are more likely to "spill over" into conscious awareness. According to the Mt. Zion group, however, what regulates the emergence of warded off contents into conscious awareness is the patient's unconscious assessment of danger and safety.

Rather than assume that the patient's basic motivational thrust is the wish to gratify unconscious infantile wishes, the radically different assumption made by the Mt. Zion group is that patients come to therapy with the conscious and unconscious desire to *master* early conflicts, traumas, and anxieties and with unconscious *plans* as to how this mastery can be achieved. In the service of mastery, the patient attempts to find and/or establish *conditions of safety* under which he can implement his unconscious plan. Under conditions of safety, one is able to take up again the struggle to attain the personal goals which, under the impact of trauma, conflict, and anxiety, were set aside during an earlier period in one's life. Accordingly, patients institute, largely unconsciously, *tests* which the therapist may either pass or fail. Test failures are more likely to be followed by increased anxiety, mobilization of defenses, and a decrease in the emergence of warded-off unconscious contents. By contrast, passing tests will be associated with reduction of anxiety, a greater depth of feeling, and an increased likelihood of emergence of warded-off contents.

As Weiss (1982) notes, according to traditional theory, therapy must induce the patient "to do what he does not want to do—that is, to relinquish his infantile gratifications." By contrast, according to the model put forth by the Mt. Zion group, "the therapist may help the patient by enabling him to do what he unconsciously wants to do— that is, to change his pathogenic beliefs and overcome the feelings of fear, anxiety, and guilt which stem from them" (p. 14). As to how the therapist enables the patient to do what he unconsciously wants to do, it is as noted, mainly by passing tests and helping establish conditions of safety.

This concept of conditions of safety is a deceptively simple one and should be elaborated and filled in by concrete clinical examples. The prototypic illustration for the concept is an experience from everyday life which Weiss (1952) refers to as "crying at the happy ending." Why, Weiss asks, does a person experience sadness and weep just at the moment when the happy ending should result in his being happy? It cannot be explained, in accord with early theory, as a consequence of an intensification and eruption of sadness into consciousness. For at the saddest moments, crying did not occur. Also, intensification of emotion would be accompanied by tension and anxiety, but, in fact, the crying person is not more tense nor more anxious and does not experience the sadness and crying as ego-alien. The answer that Weiss offers is that the happy ending provides the safety necessary to experience fully the sadness.

Consider the following clinical examples taken from treatment in which certain unconscious contents are warded off until it is safe to bring them into consciousness. Prior to a vacation break in the treatment, the patient denies that he will miss the therapist and, in fact, does not experience missing him during the break. However, upon return to treatment, the patient *then* feels that he missed the therapist and felt sad at not seeing him. This directly parallels the "crying at the happy ending" phenomenon. The next example involves the presentation of a test which the therapist can either pass or fail. The therapist's response to a male patient's gift is to tactfully refuse the gift and to remind the patient of the analytic contract. During the next session the patient begins to talk about homosexual fears and fantasies. The interpretation of this sequence of events is that the patient *tests* the analyst by offering him a gift, is reassured by the analyst's refusal, which is unconsciously tantamount to a communication that he will not be seduced and therefore constitutes test-passing, and then feels that it is safe to bring forth the warded-off homosexual contents. It should be evident from these examples that what constitutes conditions of safety will be strongly influenced by the nature of the patient's specific fears, anxieties, and conflicts.

The tests presented to therapists often center on the very themes that have been traumatic and anxiety-laden, not because of an instinctually driven repetition compulsion, but for the purpose of mastery. Thus, a patient who unconsciously believes that by competing with his father he had, in his childhood, hurt him, may compete with the analyst, not because he wants to hurt him, but "to assure himself that he *does not,* by competing with him, hurt him. A patient, by such testing, hopes to overcome the constricting idea that, by competing with authorities, he necessarily damages them" (Weiss and Sampson, 1982, p. 13).

Independent of the therapeutic context, Weiss and Sampson offer a conception of symptomatology different from the traditional one. Rather than understanding symptoms as disguised expressions of unconscious impulses seeking gratification they view them as "a person's attempts to remove himself from a situation of danger, or they may express the anxiety he feels when he faces the danger" (Weiss, 1982, p. 4). The following are concrete examples offered by Weiss and Sampson:

> The patient, who in childhood had assumed that she was much more attractive than her petulant mother, had competed with her mother for her father's love and, as she experienced it, defeated her. However, she became guilty about her victory. Indeed, she believed that by having so much fun with her father, she was devastating her mother. She was plagued with worry about her mother until she found a way of restoring her—namely, by having temper tantrums. She assumed, whether or not correctly, that she was, by her temper tantrums, enabling her mother both to feel morally superior to her

and to defeat her in her competition for her father. Her mother, who was usually somewhat depressed, would become lively and indignant when the patient had a temper tantrum and would, moreover, induce the patient's father to punish her. The mother, as the patient experienced it, would feel restored, as she demonstrated to the patient that her claims on the patient's father took precedence over those of the patient (1982, p. 8).

For example, a patient was traumatized during his fifth year when his father became crippled in an automobile accident. Since he was, at that time, succeeding in his struggle to become more independent and happy, he assumed that by becoming these things, he had caused the accident. He developed the unconscious pathogenic belief that were he again to become independent and happy, he would bring about another catastrophe, and that by suffering and by being dependent, he would stave off disaster.

As a young man, the patient had a great deal of trouble leaving home. He went to a college about 50 miles away, and though he was a friendly, outgoing person, he did not let himself enjoy the college social life. Indeed, he came home almost every weekend to be with his family.

In his analysis, his unconscious belief that if he were independent and happy he would bring on a trauma was a major theme. He became anxious when things were going well and would often, after a good day, become worried that something terrible would happen.

This patient's seeming dependency on his parents was not the expression of a primary wish to be dependent, stemming from a primary impulse seeking gratification, automatically, beyond the patient's control.

It was, instead, based on the patient's belief, which he had acquired in experience, that by being strong he would damage his parents. The patient was guided by this belief, not automatically, but by use, unconsciously, of his higher mental functions (1982, p. 10).

As noted earlier, the work of Weiss, Sampson, and their colleagues is rather unusual in the psychoanalytic community in that it includes rigorous and well-designed tests of formulations. In one study (Horowitz *et al.*, 1975), it was shown from information obtained from the first ten hours of process notes that there was high reliability among judges as to which later appearing themes had been warded off. Furthermore, the likelihood of a warded-off theme's emerging was greater when, following the patient's presentation of a test (e.g., disagreements with the therapist, anger at the therapist, making a demand of the therapist), the analyst was judged to be neutral rather than non-neutral. Finally, a drop in patient discomfort was associated with analyst neutrality and emergence of warded-off themes. Gassner

(1980) added to these results the additional important finding that warded-off contents tend to emerge *without* the analyst's interpretations.

In another study, Caston (1980) found high reliability for "blind" judgments of the degree to which therapist's interventions were compatible with the patient's unconscious plan, as independently formulated by another group of judges (the plan was that before she could master closeness and intimacy she first had to find it safe to be oppositional and then master that tendency). Most importantly, ratings for plan-compatibility of the interventions were correlated significantly with an independent measure of the boldness and insightfulness of the patient's responses immediately following the intervention (whereas plan-compatibility ratings were *not* correlated significantly with a control segment of the patient's responses).

Other research findings have been reported by the Mt. Zion group, but the above examples will suffice to provide the reader with some idea of this group's approach to therapy. The general picture of the therapeutic process (and, by extension, of mental functioning in general) that emerges is that of a patient who comes to therapy, not to gratify unconscious instinctual impulses, but to *master* certain conflicts, wishes, irrational beliefs, and anxieties originating from childhood traumas and experiences. With mastery as his basic goal, the patient presents *tests* to the therapists. The passing of tests constitutes *conditions of safety* which then make it safe for the patient to lift repression and *bring forth warded-off contents*. As Weiss (1979a) puts it, "the patient, in his analysis, takes up again his struggle to attain the goals which, in his childhood, he had set aside and, in his working to attain them unconsciously tests the analyst in order to assure himself that the analyst will not traumatize him as his parents had" (p. 5). The general therapeutic process is conceptualized here as "the dejeopardization (sic) of what the ego has erroneously regarded as dangerous. In essence, beneficial change in a previously unmastered area follows a series of re-appraisals by the ego that relevant safety obtains and conversely, either no therapeutic change, or a pathological regressive change follows appraisals of continuing or increased relevant danger" (Caston, 1980, p. 31).

A Critical Evaluation of Mt. Zion Work

As is the case with all the other recent developments in and modifications of psychoanalytic theory I have considered, the Mt.

Zion group both implicitly and explicitly rejects Freudian instinct and drive theory. The basic image of the person that emerges is not one who is primarily engaged in the direct and indirect pursuit of instinctual gratifications, but one who is seeking mastery of the conflicts, anxieties, and destructive beliefs that cause him suffering and limit his satisfaction, productiveness, and awareness. This emphasis on mastery links the work of the Mt. Zion group to the concepts of Hendrick (1943) and White (1960; 1963). Indeed, the formulations of the Mt. Zion group can be seen as an elaboration and application of Hendrick's and White's concepts to the therapeutic situation. One can also find links between the Mt. Zion formulations and both Fairbairn's emphasis on ego aims and certain of Rogers's (1959; 1961) concepts. However, Weiss and Sampson ignore all these links. Instead they try to show how their formulations are derived almost entirely from Freud's late writings, an attempt which appears more political than scholarly.

The concept of unconscious plans, assessments of conditions of safety, and decisions regarding whether or not to bring forth warded-off material might have seemed untenable some years ago to some skeptical critics. However, under the impact of developments and research in so-called cognitive science and cognitive theory, the idea of complex and purposive unconscious cognitive operations seems commonplace and entirely feasible. And yet, major emphasis continues to be placed by the Mt. Zion group on *awareness* and insight. In so much of their research, the bringing forth of unconscious, warded-off contents into conscious awareness is the dependent variable studied, undoubtedly based on the assumption that only the emergence of unconscious contents into consciousness can be therapeutic. It is, however, possible that therapeutic test-passing and the unconscious assessment that conditions of safety hold can produce therapeutic change *without* the emergence of warded-off contents into awareness. I offer such an example below.

I treated a patient whose presenting symptom, severe dyspareunia, dramatically disappeared following what I would refer to as an "enactment" with me of a pattern which she had characteristically carried out with men and with both her parents. The pattern was one in which defiance was followed by submission and physical and/or psychological pain. When she was age 3–4, she was a victim of child abuse (which was serious enough to reach the courts) at the hands of her mother, by the mother's account, for "defying" her. As an adolescent and adult, she believed, based on her father's expressed attitudes, that her father's acceptance of and love for her was contingent on his belief that she was a virgin. And on every occasion prior to sexual inter-course, she would have the obsessive, defiant thought, "if they could see me now," with the "they" clearly referring to her parents. This would be inevitably followed by severe pain during intercourse which she would silently endure. She expressed the thought that her partner would undoubtedly leave her were she to tell him about her pain.

On one occasion, the patient became enraged with me following my bringing up the possibility of her using the couch (she had been sit-ting up until that point). My suggestion was clearly experienced, at some level, as a seduction and as a demand that she submit. She did not, however, submit. Instead she rejected the idea with, as I've indi-cated, rage and verbal attack upon me. It was toward the end of the session (and also the end of the week) and I remained silent, offering no interpretation. The next session the patient said she felt she had "overreacted," but nevertheless felt uncomfortable and somewhat frightened at the idea of using the couch, "not ready for it," as she put it. I accepted her comments, again without interpretation, and we continued with therapy.

The very next session the patient came in elated and announced that the night before she had experienced sexual intercourse without pain for the first time in her life. She expressed both elation and fear that it "was all too good to be true" and "wouldn't last." She also informed me that she and her boyfriend were due to go away that weekend and she saw that as a kind of test of the lastingness of her new freedom from her symptom. The patient returned from the weekend, again elated, and reported that the symptom had not re-turned and that sexual intercourse was even enjoyable. As of this writing, a more than three-year follow-up indicates continued absence of the symptom and a continuation of other positive changes.

It is my belief that at a critical juncture, the patient's "enactment" in the therapy of the basic dynamic issue—submission and/or defiance, this time *not* followed by pain and/or rejection—helped ameliorate the conflict. It should be noted again that the "enactment" of this basic theme and the disappearance of the symptom occurred without interpretation on my part or articulated verbalized insight on the pa-tient's part regarding the dynamic meaning of the "enactment." Nor was there any obvious emergence of unconscious warded-off material into conscious awareness (a point to be taken up later).

Stated in terms of the model presented by the Mt. Zion group, the test that was "enacted" and passed was whether I could endure the patient's defiance and rage and continue treatment. This more dramatic test was preceded by earlier, more subtle tests of how I would react to her hositility and defiance. Her practically reflexive rejection of all transference interpretations can be seen in this light and is similiar to examples provided by Weiss and Sampson in which tests involving more modest risks are followed by tests with higher stakes. In the present case, the patient's outburst of defiance and rage was preceded by smaller doses of defiance and hostility which had no particular consequences—therapeutic work simply continued—and hence helped establish "conditions of safety." My suggestion that the patient use the couch provided the opportunity for a critical "enactment" and, once the test was passed (constituted by my silence and simple continuation of treatment), the presenting symptom disappeared.[45]

The above case, as well as the formulations of the Mt. Zion group, suggest a model of transference quite different from the traditional one. According to the traditional view, transference reactions are primarily an "automatic" outcome of the ever-present pressure for discharge of infantile instinctual urges, the particular mobilization of such urges by the regressive features of the therapeutic situation, and the ubiquitous presence and strength of resistance characterized by the patient's push to gratify rather than remember the conflictful urges. In this view, transference reactions are mainly pathological expressions which constitute "the most powerful resistance to the treatment" (Freud, 1912)—indeed, they constitute a full-blown neurosis—and it is only the *interpretive analysis* of transference that permits insights and therapeutic progress. Hence, an "enactment" rather than a remembering of material central to early conflicts and traumas would constitute resistance and would, if not interpreted, interfere with therapeutic progress.

What I am suggesting in the concept of "enactment" and what is suggested in the work of Weiss and Sampson is that rather than viewing transference reactions as necessarily constituting peremptory drive expressions, resistances, and the obligation "to repeat . . . instead of remembering . . ." (Freud, 1920), one can understand them as unconscious attempts to deal with, in the relative safety of the therapeutic situation, material related to early conflict and trauma, for the purpose of mastering such material.

Also suggested by the above case is that test-passing and the establishment of conditions of safety can lead to amelioration of symptoms (and other changes) without the intervening step of the emergence of warded-off contents into awareness and without articulated insight.[46] This seems to me to represent the essential modification of the concept of transference presented by Alexander and French (1946), particularly in their concept of "corrective emotional experience." According to this view, "in the transference neurosis, the patient learns to deal with small quantities of the same emotional tensions which he could not master in the past . . . ." (p. 17). Despite the disrepute into which Alexander and French's work has fallen within the psychoanalytic community, their concept of transference and of the therapeutic relationship is not essentially different from a number of current conceptions—for example, Kohut's (1977) belief that "essential structural transformations produced by working through . . . . are brought about by the fact that the old experiences are repeatedly relived by the more mature psyche" (p. 30); and Volkan's (1976) emphasis on the patient's learning to distinguish between archaic introjects and new objects (an idea already emphasized by Strachey, 1934).[47]

One implication of the Mt. Zion conception is that the failure of unconscious material to emerge and general failures to make progress in therapy are not so much a consequence of the patient's resistances, as defined in the traditional sense (which includes, for example, the idea of resistance to relinquishing the gratification of infantile wishes), but a function of the patient's unconscious judgment that conditions of safety do not obtain. A further implication is that therapist's failures of tests put forth by patients—perhaps frequently because of the therapists' own counter-transference reactions and difficulties—may be the most frequent reason for therapeutic failures.

As far as therapeutic *outcome* is concerned, one can only talk about implications of the Mt. Zion theory rather than empirical data because all the empirical work of this group has been concerned with therapeutic *process* rather than outcome. This is a definite limitation of their work. For while it is of interest to know the conditions under which new themes and warded-off contents emerge in psychoanalytically oriented therapy, it is of even greater interest and significance to determine whether such emergence is lawfully related to therapeutic *outcome*. The Mt. Zion group may make the tacit assumption that such a lawful relationship exists or must exist (given the hallowed roles of insight and awareness in psychoanalytic therapy), but that has yet to be demonstrated. And if it should turn out that no such relationship exists, one would have to acknowledge that the findings on emergence of warded-off contents would diminish in importance.

Another limitation of the Mt. Zion work is that their research is (necessarily?) restricted to very small numbers of subjects. This raises the usual question regarding generalizability of results. However, more specifically, it also raises the question of the type and range of patients to which their formulations apply. As I argued earlier, it is possible that certain aspects of their formulations, the importance of the emergence of warded-off contents in particular, may not apply equally to different kinds of patients. As for other factors, such as test-passing and the establishment of conditions of safety, it seems reasonable and even likely that they would apply to a wide range of patients (and, for that matter, to a wide range of therapeutic techniques). But however reasonable it may seem, it, too, has yet to be demonstrated.

A few final comments before leaving the work of the Mt. Zion group. One, I want to note the convergence between certain ideas of this group and G. S. Klein's (1976) emphasis on "reversal of voice" from passive to active (a term used by Loevinger, 1966) as a basic factor in the therapeutic process. The patient's active role in presenting tests, in determining whether or not conditions of safety exist, and in deciding whether or not to bring forth traumatic material all can be seen as instances of attempts to reverse passively endured traumatic experiences into active attempts at mastery.[48]

The second comment I want to make has to do with the frequently encountered distinction between the interpretive, insight-facilitating function of the therapist and the relationship factors such as the provision of empathic mirroring and a "holding environment." It seems to me that the concepts and findings discussed here argue against radical distinctions along these dimensions. The work at Mt. Zion teaches us that passing tests and establishing conditions of safety (which seems to be most effectively implemented by a non-impinging, benevolent neutrality) *both* facilitate insight and awareness (i.e., the emergence of warded-off contents) *and* constitute direct relationship factors which may be anxiety-reducing and thereby ameliorate symptoms. Also, the establishment of conditions of safety can itself be seen as an implicit interpretation to the effect that the patient is not in the original traumatic situation and that the therapist is different, in important respects, from traumatic figures of the past.

And finally, a few additional words regarding the concept of conditions of safety. It is a deceptively simple and subtle idea. Thus, it refers not only to external conditions, but may include the unconscious judgment that one has sufficient ego strength to attempt mastery of a situation which, at an earlier period, may have been too threatening or anxiety-provoking to confront (deciding to enter treatment may reflect such a judgment). Also, one can, I believe, be reasonably certain that interpreting the concept in terms of across-the-board prescriptions, such as warmth, love, and "unconditional positive regard" will not be very useful because, among other things, they are not sufficiently tuned to individual needs. The difficult clinical challenge is to be sensitive to what constitutes "conditions of safety" for a particular patient in the light of his or her particular constellation of early conflicts, fears, and traumas.

II

SELECTED ISSUES
IN PSYCHOANALYTIC THEORY

Having presented and summarized various individual contributions to the current ferment in psychoanalytic theory, in the succeeding sections I will examine and discuss broad themes and issues raised by these contributions from the point of view of their implications for psychoanalytic theory. I will begin with a discussion of the concept of anxiety, which is a central one in psychoanalytic theory.

10

THE PSYCHOANALYTIC
CONCEPTION OF ANXIETY

As we have seen, one issue frequently raised by contemporary psychoanalytic theorists concerns the primary source of anxiety and the nature of experienced threats to the ego and self. I would like to review and expand here the earlier discussion of anxiety. In traditional psychoanalytic theory, instinctual wishes are always and necessarily implicated in generating anxiety. A basic question one is entitled to ask is why sexual and aggressive impulses should be so threatening. This may seem to be a naïve question to anyone even generally familiar with psychoanalytic theory. Surely, one knows about castration anxiety, fear of loss of the object, of the object's love, and guilt and superego anxiety. But, as noted earlier, an examination of all these dangers eliciting anxiety indicates that they are based on one of two models. In the first, essentially a crime-punishment model, prohibited (sexual and aggressive) wishes constitute the crime and various forms of punishment, once placed in the outside world and now internalized, are expected as ones fitting the crime.

In the second, more all-embracing second model, sexual and aggressive wishes are naturally and *inherently inimical* to the self and thereby constitute threats to the very survival of the self. Freud (1926) writes that "the fundamental determinant of automatic anxiety [i.e., direct and automatic reaction to a trauma] is the occurrence of a traumatic situation; and the essence of this is an experience of helplessness on the part of the ego in the face of an accumulation of excitation, whether of external or internal origin, which cannot be dealt with" (p. 81). At a later point, he states, "The situation, then, which [the infant] regards as a 'danger' and against which it wants to be safeguarded is that of non-satisfaction of a *growing tension due to need* (Freud's italics), against which it is helpless. . . . The situation of non-satisfaction, in which the amounts of stimulation rise to an unpleasurable height without it being possible for them to be mastered psychically or discharged must for the infant be analagous to the experience of being born . . . what both situations have in common is the economic disturbance caused by an accumulation of amounts of stimulation which require to be disposed of. It is this factor, then, which is the essence of the 'danger.' In both cases the reaction of anxiety sets in" (p. 137).

Even the punishments of the first model derive their traumatic potential from the fact that were those punishments carried out, the organism would be left helpless in the face of overwhelming excitation emanating from non-gratification of instinctual drives. Freud (1926) writes: "When an infant has found out by experience that an external, perceptible object can put an end to the dangerous situation which is reminiscent of birth [by dangerous situation, Freud refers to the danger of being overwhelmed by excessive excitation], the content of the danger it fears is displaced from the economic situation to the condition which determined that situation, viz., the loss of the object" (pp. 137–138). In other words, the real danger represented by the loss of the object is the "economic situation" of excessive excitation.

In other writings, Freud makes clear that this applies to the other dangers of loss of the object's love, castration anxiety, and superego anxiety. For example, Freud (1926) notes with regard to castration anxiety, that "being deprived of it [his genitals] amounts to a new separation from her [the mother], and this in its turn means being helplessly exposed to an unpleasurable tension due to instinctual need, as was the case at birth" (p. 139). That this inherent threat does not depend on the traditional "crime–punishment" model of anxiety is recognized by A. Freud (1966) when she discusses the separate anxiety category of "fear of strength of instincts" (also see Waelder, 1960). And she obviously bases her thinking on Freud's (1940a) notion that "an excessive strength of instinct can damage the ego. . ." (p. 111). So we must ask why strength of instincts *per se* (independent of their association with punishment and disapproval) is believed to be so naturally and inherently inimical to the welfare of the self. Apart from civilization and its prohibitions, what is posited is a "primary antagonism" between id and ego. According to this view, it appears to be a misfortune of our biological heritage that we should be endowed both with instincts and an ego to which instincts are inherently inimical—somehow as if we are all born with a kind of auto-allergenic process.[49]

Why, then, should instincts *per se* be naturally inimical to the ego? Is there compelling clinical evidence that the experience of "disintegration anxiety" is necessarily brought on or accompanied by intense sexual and aggressive impulses and feelings? Is it really the case that "affects associated with anger and love are experienced with such intensity as to induce a sense of annihilation . . ." (Modell, 1975, p. 61)? The supposition that the intensity of instincts is threatening to the ego seems to be derived, not from clinical evidence, but from the central Freudian ideas that excessive excitation constitutes *the* prototypic danger situation for the ego and that the primary source of such excessive excitation is tension from undischarged instinctual demands. The idea that excessive excitation is a danger and that the central nervous system seeks to rid itself of excitation was not inductively based on the accumulation of clinical evidence, but was already present in Freud's (1887–1902) *"Project"* and remained thereafter as a central theme in his thinking. The idea that undischarged instinctual tensions lead to excessive excitation and thereby to anxiety can be seen to be both a hold-over from Freud's (1895) early, presumably discarded, theory of anxiety as accumulated and transformed libido and as an expression of the basic, never discarded, tension-reduction model in which all excitation is, to some degree, noxious and in which the primary motivating force in behavior is to discharge excitation. Instinctual tension is the prime candidate for contributing noxious excitation because its source is internal (endosomatic) and hence, in contrast to some kinds of external stimuli, one from which one cannot flee. In short, the idea that instinctual impulses, particularly those of great intensity, are *inherently* dangerous to the ego derives from an *a priori* tension-reduction model of human behavior and a conception of the nervous system as naturally and ideally quiescent, and disturbed, in varying degrees, by excitation. It is a specific example of what Cofer and Appley (1963; 1972) refers to as a "homeostatic drive" model of behavior.

While it is undoubtedly true that excessive excitation (arousal) can be damaging to the organism, it is unlikely that tension deriving from sexual and aggressive impulses is the primary source of excessive excitation. There is obviously an inherent relationship between excessive excitation and anxiety insofar as the latter is characterized by a high level of physiological arousal. Indeed, anxiety may in part be defined in terms of an excessively high level of arousal. But there is no evidence that instinctual impulses are a major source of excessive excitation.

What, then, is the critical feature which elicits anxiety in individuals? It seems to me that the general answer is *anything* that is experienced as threatening the integrity and intactness of the individual. Thus, if instinctual impulses are associated with such threats (e.g., loss of the object, which may be experienced as life-threatening), they will elicit anxiety. But, it should be noted, not because they are inherently antagonistic to the welfare of the ego.

A proneness to a high level of physiological arousal may itself predispose one to anxiety. As noted earlier, there is evidence that individuals who suffer chronic and intense anxiety are predisposed to a generally high level of arousal and, because they habituate to incoming stimuli very slowly, also respond to specific stimulation with excessive arousal (Lader and Wing, 1966). For those people, already at a high level of physiological arousal, *anything* which adds to the existing level of arousal—external stimulation, intense feelings, anxiety-provoking situations—may trigger intense anxiety. Consistent with Fenichel's (1945) description of anxiety-prone people, one can say that the signal function of anxiety fails in such people. Modest amounts of anxiety, which in others would trigger defensive reactions of one kind or another, when added to the already pre-existing excessively high level of arousal characteristic of anxiety-prone individuals, trigger the "traumatic situation" of an anxiety attack.

The chronic anxiety seen in some patients is probably largely attributable, not to instinctual impulses threatening to erupt, but to "structural" factors which, on one level of discourse, can be described as a proneness to an overly high level of arousal and, on another level, in terms of ego weakness and a non-intact sense of self. Someone without an intact sense of self will be more likely to exhibit the chronic vigilance associated with high arousal and is likely to experience a wide variety of situations as threatening. Hence, sooner or later such an individual will confront a situation that triggers intense anxiety. An easily elicited sense of danger to the self contributes to a vicious circle in which a sense of non-intactness renders one more likely to react to a variety of situations with intense anxiety which, in turn, intensifies the sense of "damage to the ego."

To the extent that instinctual wishes are involved in intense anxiety, they are likely to be not the traditional id instincts but, if one accepts Modell's distinction between two classes of instincts, the presumably "quieter" instincts associated with object relations. The urges and wishes that are most likely to threaten a sense of intact self are, as Fairbairn (1952) maintains, those having to do with the conflict between "the regressive lure of identification and the progressive urge to separate." That is, both symbiotic wishes and strivings in the direction of separation-individuation are likely to be centrally implicated in intense anxiety. As both Meissner (1981) and Sandler and Sandler (1978) point out, a wish for a particular kind of object relation is as much a wish against which one can defend as a sexual or aggressive wish.

Regressive longings and wishes to merge with self-objects are likely to evoke intense anxiety precisely *because such wishes and longings represent threats to the integrity of the self*. Here too a vicious circle is created: A shaky sense of self elicits regressive longings and wishes to merge with the supportive self-object which, in turn, threatens whatever intactness of the self is experienced. To take once again the example of agoraphobia, characteristic of the severe agoraphobic is not only the fear of leaving the relative safety of home, but also fear of his own regressive and merging wishes which threaten his shaky sense of self and contribute to the chronic anxiety present even when he is not in the phobic danger situation. In other words, for the agoraphobic and others in a similar conflict situation, threat to the self comes both from the more obvious direction of moves toward independence, away from the supportive self-object, and the wishes and longings associated with the self object. Thus, both the experience of finding oneself without support and the regressive wishes elicited by that experience contribute to the often chronic anxiety of the agoraphobic patient.

Separation-individuation strivings and regressive wishes, although instrumental in intense anxiety, are not easily construed as presenting excessive excitation to the organism. As Modell (1975) notes, the "quieter" instincts associated with object relations cannot easily be characterized in the same manner as the Freudian id instincts. That is, they cannot be easily fitted into a drive-reduction model in which instinctual endogenous sources are exerting constant peremptory demands on the organism.

As soon as one drops a drive-reduction model, it is difficult to see why the sheer intensity of sexual and aggressive impulses should endanger the ego. Patients do not generally report such experiences and were it not for the influence of instinct theory, it is doubtful that such inferences would be made on the basis of what patients do report. Freud's drive-reduction model, rooted in instinct theory, was a conjecture and paradigm *prior* to empirical clinical evidence and

strongly influenced how such evidence was interpreted and the nature of the inferences and formulations made. Clearly, one's theoretical ideas and preconceptions generally influence how one interprets
data, including clinical data, and this is inevitable. I am not suggesting
that this theoretical "bias" could be entirely eliminated. In the present case, what I am suggesting is that Freudian instinct theory does
not deal adequately with, among other things, the phenomenon of
anxiety and should be replaced with a more accurate and useful
theory.

11

INSTINCTS, THE ID-EGO MODEL,
AND SELF-ORGANIZATION

The terms id and ego have a double meaning in Freudian theory. The dominant meaning, reflecting an impulse-control model, defines id as instinctual impulses and ego in terms of controlling and mediating functions. The second meaning becomes clear if one keeps in mind the German "Das Es" and "Das Ich" which, in more direct English translation rather than the latinized version of id and ego, become "the it" and "the I." In this latter meaning, "the it" conveys that which in the personality is *impersonal* or disavowed, in contrast to "the I" which refers to that which is personal, owned, and experienced as part of oneself (see Brandt [1966] and Bettelheim [1982] for further discussion of the inadequacy of the English translations of Freud's works). By conflating both meanings, one arrives at a conceptualization in which the instinctual is necessarily and inherently impersonal and partaking of an "it" quality (in Hartmann's [1958] words, the id is cut off from reality and experience), while the ego mediates personal experience. As Bettelheim (1982) suggests in a recent article, the German terms "Ich" and "Es" convey the idea that the rational and controlling part of one's personality is the part one identifies as oneself, while the instinctual is made up of dark, underground forces which are experienced as impersonal happenings by which one can be overwhelmed. As we shall see, these continue to be the dominant images underlying the id-ego model.

I want to discuss three basic questions regarding the id-ego model as described above. The first is the adequacy of a model which dichotomizes between instinctual aims and energies on the one hand and controlling and mediating structures on the other. The second question I want to discuss is whether instinct is accurately conceptualized in Freudian theory. And the third and related question is the conflation of the two meanings of id—as instinctual wish and as impersonal "it." The basic issue here is why the instinctual is necessarily and inherently impersonal and of "it" status.

Modell's discussion of object relational instincts associated with the ego highlights an issue raised by Fairbairn (1952) and more recently by Apfelbaum (1966), Fingarette (1969), and Klein (1976), each in somewhat different contexts. As we have seen, Modell is correct in noting that so-called object relational instincts constitute challenges to the model presented in *The Ego and the Id*, but he minimizes the extent of these challenges. In the ego-id model and, as Apfelbaum notes, in the model presented in Hartmann's (1958) and Rapaport's (1950; 1951; 1958) formulations of psychoanalytic ego psychology, there are instinctual aims arising from the id and controlling and mediating structures and functions associated with the ego. According to this view, the blind, "seething cauldron" of the id, estranged from experience and external reality (see Hartmann, 1958), makes necessary the development of an organ of adaptiveness: the ego, which will control these blind forces and mediate between them and external reality (as well as between id and the structure of internalized prohibitions and rules known as the superego). The relationship between id instincts and ego pictured in this scheme is clearly expressed in A. Freud's (1966) claim, noted earlier, that there is a "primary antagonism" and "innate hostility" between id and ego and in Gill and Brenman's (1959, p. 182) explanation of the "consistency, reliability, and relative lack of intensity" of everyday behavior "as an achievement of autonomous ego structures in holding back an instinctual willfulness and abandon."

In this scheme, the motivational force of behavior is provided only by instinctual drives, while the ego is conceived of solely as a structure with a particular set of functions. That is, while instinctual drives provide energy and basic (discharge) aims, the ego provides adaptive channeling and control. This is as much the case in the later developments constituting psychoanalytic ego psychology as in the traditional model presented in *The Ego and the Id*. As Klein (1976) puts it, the psychoanalytic conception of drives as "'blind forces' that need to be controlled has trapped the ego concept; the ego is pictured predominantly as a controlling agency, and in the service of the 'reality principle'" (p. 175). Or, in Apfelbaum's (1966) description, Hartmann renders "the ego as an *organ* with a *function* rather than as a representation of a *drive* with an *aim*" (Apfelbaum's italics) (p. 457).

The insistence of psychoanalytic ego psychologists that the id remain the exclusive motivational domain is also seen in Rapaport's (1960) argument that clearly purposive exploratory, curious, and novelty-seeking behaviors be viewed as caused rather than as motivated. So committed is Rapaport to the conception of id as motivation and ego as controlling structure that any behavior that does not show the characteristics of id drives—which Rapaport identifies as peremptoriness, cyclicity, selectivity, and displaceability—is not to be viewed as motivated. This restriction forces Rapaport into the peculiar position of deeming a wide range of goal-directed and planned means-ends choice behavior as nonmotivational. This artificial and awkward categorization of behavior is testimony to the persistence of the idea that only drives provide behavior with aims and motives, while the ego provides structures and functions to control, modulate, and carry out these aims.

Insofar as Hartmann (1964) does occasionally refer to ego aims and to Freud's early concept of "ego interests," he seems to leave room for the possibility, indeed the ubiquitousness, of nonlibidinal motives and aims. However, mindful of Freud's use of the term, Hartmann continues to use "ego interests" essentially as an extension of self-preservative trends and notes that they "are . . . rooted in id tendencies" (p. 137) or "in narcissistic, exhibitionistic, aggressive, etc., drive tendencies" (p. 176). The result is, as Klein (1976) notes, that ego psychology offers neither a dynamic principle nor an explicit theory of nonlibidinal motivation and remains a structural psychology grafted on to a preexisting drive discharge theory of motivation.

To conceptualize the ego as anything but a structure with a particular set of functions would, indeed, introduce basic departures from the model of personality contained in *The Ego and the Id* and this Hartmann seems unwilling to do (p. 457). But, as Apfelbaum notes, in view of the talk of ego aims, urges toward mastery, etc.: "how far can the conception of apparatuses causing such behavior be carried before the organ metaphor breaks down and these apparatuses again take on the character of drives?" (p. 457). And Apfelbaum's question remains cogent even if one were to dispense entirely with the notion of drives. For he is essentially inquiring regarding the motivational status of ego aims in a theory which gives primary, perhaps exclusive, motivational force to instinctual drives. It is clear then, that in both traditional theory and ego psychology, the basic definitions treat id as motivational and ego as structural.

As discussed earlier, Modell makes a valiant effort to include ego aims in a psychoanalytic psychology. But for Modell to talk about object relational instincts associated with the ego is, his intentions notwithstanding, not to integrate "this new dimension of object relations . . . within Freud's model of *The Ego and the Id*," but to transform the latter so that it no longer stands "as the central paradigm of psychoanalysis." The theory as transformed bears closer resemblance to Freud's (1911, pp. 73–74; 1916–1917, pp. 414–415) earlier formulations positing both libidinal and ego instincts than it does to a theory in which instinct and ego are sharply distinct. And, despite Modell's criticism of Fairbairn, the transformations Modell suggested are in the direction suggested by Fairbairn's rejection of the id-ego dichotomy and his proposal of an ego structure with its own dynamic aims.

Another difficulty with the id-ego model is that the Freudian notion of instinct is empirically inaccurate. Thus, Modell is correct in noting that the instincts that underlie object relations appear to be quite different from the description of id instincts found in Freudian theory, in the former's interactional nature, their links to external objects, and their unsusceptibility to simple explanation in terms of somatic sources and tension-reduction. But what Modell overlooks is that the presumed properties of id instincts which are supposed to distinguish them from object relational instincts may be as little characteristic of the former as of the latter; or, to state it in the reverse way, the properties presumably distinctive of object relational instincts are, in fact, also characteristic of so-called id instincts. For example, sex and aggression in humans are as interactional, as linked to external objects, and as difficult to explain simply in terms of accumulation and discharge of tension as the so-called object relational instincts. As Klein (1976) notes, "aims are lived out in object relations." With regard to sexual behavior, consider the following passage from Beach (1956) (cited by Holt, 1976): "To a much greater extent than is true of hunger or thirst, the sexual tendencies depend for their arousal upon external stimuli." In speaking about the stag as an example, Beach states "it is most unlikely that in the absence of erotic stimuli he exists in a constant state of undischarged sexual tensions. This would be equally true for the human male, were it not for the potent effects of symbolic stimuli which he tends to carry with him wherever he goes" (p. 5). Fletcher (1966) too makes the point that instinctive "forces" are not constant, but are aroused by external stimuli.

As Holt (1976) notes, the Freudian concept of instinctual drive in terms of an inexorable accumulation of somatic stimulation and an ever-present need for discharge simply does not fit the facts about human and animal motivation, including sexual and aggressive behavior. It certainly does not fit the facts about motives having to do with self-esteem, curiosity, exploration, and a great range of other motivated behavior. Kaufman (1960), an analyst knowledgeable about ethological findings, writes that "evidence has accumulated which throw great doubt on the validity of the reservoir concept of behavior, according to which discharge of energy in an act brings the behavior to an end. It has become abundantly clear that most behavior is brought to an end not by the performance of an act but by the presence of a certain stimulus situation" (p. 321). Later, Kaufman goes on to state that "we need no longer postulate that the full panorama of sexuality . . . is derived from an inborn biological urge or force pressing inexorably for discharge" (p. 384). Rather, he argues, one should view the manifestations of sexuality in terms of inborn sensory-motor patterns which, in the course of maturational development and learning, become organized into a structure we call the sexual drive. Similarly, on the basis of the available facts, Holt concludes that Freud's concept of *Trieb*—of instinctual drive—is not tenable and proposes that one substitute Freud's earlier concept of wish.

I turn now to the third issue posed earlier, namely, the conception of the instinctual as necessarily impersonal. Let me say first that Freud himself was somewhat confused and inconsistent in his definitions of id and instinct. At times, he distinguishes between id and instinct in terms of mental versus biological. Thus, at one point he writes that "the forces which we assume to exist behind the tension caused by the needs of the id are called *instincts*" (Freud, 1940, p. 19). As the editor notes in *Instincts and Their Vicissitudes*, at times Freud (1915) spoke of instincts as "the psychical representative of organic forces" and at other times, he drew a sharp distinction between an instinct and its psychical representative. And, at still other times, Freud spoke of "the concept of instinct [as] . . . one of those lying on the frontier between the mental and the physical" (Freud, 1915, p. 168). And finally, Freud (1940a) writes about the instincts that "originate in the somatic organization and . . . find their first mental expression in the id in forms unknown to us" (p. 14).

Why are these forms unknown to us? Freud (1915) tells us that "an instinct can never become an object of consciousness—only the idea (Vorstellung) that represents the instinct can" (p. 177). But here Freud is obviously referring to the biological, the organic source; and, of course, it can never become an object of consciousness, just as one would say that the neuronal firing can never become an object of consciousness—only the percept that represents the neuronal pattern can. To say that only an idea representing the instinct can become an object of consciousness is no different than saying that only the percept or thought representing the neuronal firing can become objects of consciousness. It is also no different from saying that while hormonal secretions are not objects of consciousness, sexual desires and fantasies are. And finally, one can say that while the *processes* underlying ego functions, such as memory and thinking, are not objects of consciousness, particular memories and thoughts are. In short, something like this is generally true of the relationship between the biological and the psychological.

What Freud seems mainly to be doing by distinguishing between the instinct and the idea representing it is simply to demarcate different levels of phenomena, the biological and the psychological. In a certain sense, all experiences are "derivatives" of physiological processes which are themselves not represented. How something like a hormonal secretion or hypothalamatic stimulation finds its way, so to speak, into our behavior is a profoundly difficult question and ultimately is at the core of Freud's conception of psychoanalysis as biologically grounded. But then, how brain processes relate to the percepts we experience or the thoughts we think is a variant of the same basic question. Freud believed that because of our genetic-biological structure, certain classes of wishes will universally emerge. And whether or not he was correct as to the specific content of such wishes, I believe that he was correct regarding the general claim that our biological structure determines the kinds of wishes, aims, and desires we are likely to have.[50]

However, that our biological structure determines the nature of the wishes and desires we have does not require that one set aside as a separate component of personality a structure representing biological instincts. In short, biology "enters" our psychological world by being represented in what we think, perceive, feel, and want. But, it will be noted, what this amounts to saying is that as far as the psychological level is concerned, there are only the ego factors of cognitions, feelings, and desires. An instinctual wish is no less an ego factor than any other wish. The adjective "instinctual" merely describes the content of the wish. If it is instinctual in any other sense, it becomes biology, and hence one has reverted to mixing levels of discourse rather than referring to conceptually equivalent components of personality. While it makes sense to understand how these biological factors influence our wishes, desires, etc., it does not make sense to view these factors as a component of personality on the same level as personal plans and intentions.

In this sense, Fairbairn's (1952) intuitions were essentially correct in eliminating the concept of id and in constructing a "pure" ego psychology in which the focus is on various ego aims conflicting and interacting with each other. This step is also inherent in G. S. Klein's (1976) reformulation of psychoanalytic theory. And finally, I believe it is also implicit in both Freud's earlier work and in his late (1940) discussions of splitting of the ego in defense and in fetishism. In other words, as far as the psychological molar level is concerned, there are only the "ego" factors of cognitions, wishes, feelings, aims, etc. It is important to stress that this does not mean the elimination of biological factors in understanding human personality. On the contrary, a consideration of biological factors (of human nature, so to speak) is necessary to understand fully the kinds of wishes, feelings, etc., we are likely to have, what we need, and who we are. But, to repeat, these biological factors cannot be viewed as a component of personality on the same level as the wishes and feelings they influence and generate (just as a brain process cannot be viewed on the same level as the percept or thoughts it gives rise to). Just as it would not make sense to conceptualize brain processes that determine perception and thought as a component of personality. Wishes, desires, percepts, and thoughts are all "derivatives" of underlying biological processes. To conceptualize the id or reservoir of biological instincts as a psychological component of personality is to confuse levels of discourse and levels of phenomena. And to say that only id derivatives can be experienced and/or represented psychologically is to make a statement that applies logically to all psychological representations in relation to underlying biological processes.

In a general sense, there is no mystery regarding how something like hormonal secretion or hypothalamic stimulation (I employ these as crude examples of biological-instinctual factors) would "enter into" our behavior (although there is obviously an enormous mystery regarding the specific processes involved). It would do so by influencing or being reflected in what we think and perceive, what we feel, what we want to do, particularly if certain actions were experienced in an instrumental relation to the feelings and cognitions accompanying the hormonal secretion or hypothalamic stimulation. That is, as Delgado (1969) points out, if one wants to direct an animal's behavior via brain stimulation, one does so not by directly manipulating the organism's motor behavior (as occurs in the image of the robot), but by eliciting emotional experiences which the organism wants to repeat or avoid.

We return to the original question. If ideas corresponding to instincts and if id derivatives generally can be represented psychologically, why are the forms in which instincts find their mental expression necessarily unknown to us?

Why is it instincts, in particular, that are held to find their expression in forms unknown to us? Why is it not equally the case that the biological processes underlying ego functions find their expression in forms unknown to us?

It should be clear that these questions are variants of the original question as to why the instinctual and the impersonal are equated.

Could one not say that the forms in which instincts find their expression are wishing, desiring, fantasizing, feeling, urges, and so on? One can even claim that the content of such wishing and desiring will be primarily sexual and aggressive. Is it not the case that one can consciously and with full "ownership" experience sexual and aggressive feelings, wishes, and desires? In what sense, then, do such instinctual impulses belong to an impersonal "it" and in what sense do these impulses express themselves in forms unknown to us? It seems to me that what permeates Freud's treatment of the concept of id is his assumption that because the id is more closely linked to the mysterious organic source of instinct, it is both inherently biological, inherently unknowable, and inherently impersonal. However, as I have tried to show, to make this assumption is to confuse levels of discourse.

What remains is the proposal that id derivatives are rendered impersonal through the process of repression. Further, they are inherently susceptible to repression, according to Freud, because they are inimical to the requirements of civilization and, as discussed earlier, to the integrity of the ego. And this latter conception, in turn, rests on further notions of instincts in terms of excessive excitation and a general drive discharge model. However, as we have seen, this conception of instincts does not accord with the facts. Furthermore, on the general grounds of the logic of evolution, one wonders why organisms with instincts that are inherently opposed, not only to our social environment, but to another component of the personality, would have been selected out and survived. What adaptive advantage would be served by this kind of development?

Finally, there is a circular argument lurking here. For we turned to the consideration of repression only after finding that the idea of instinctual derivates' being inherently impersonal and alien to the personality was largely based on a confusion of levels of discourse. But then we learn that the special susceptibility of instinctual wishes to the fate of repression is based on the assumption that the ego is "alien territory to the instincts" (A. Freud, 1966, p. 59), that there is a natural "disposition to repudiate certain instincts" (p. 157) and that there is an "innate hostility between the ego and the instincts, which is indiscriminate, primary, and primitive" (pp. 157–158). In other words, it is not simply that instinctual derivatives are *rendered* impersonal and alien through repression (or some other defense), but that they are subject to repression because they are *inherently* alien and impersonal. Which, of course, returns us to the original issue of the adequacy of the grounds for viewing them as inherently impersonal.

On the basis of the above discussion, it seems clear that the id-ego model, with id as instinctual "seething cauldron" and ego as controlling structure is neither accurate nor useful. What does seem useful in the id-ego distinction is the idea of disowned versus owned aspects of the personality, particularly when the conception of the disowned is not conflated with the conception of the instinctual.

The dichotomous division of personality into a structure with motivational aims (provided, directly or indirectly, by instinctual drives) and a structure the function of which is to channel, mediate, and implement these aims gives way to the conception of persons as attempting to carry out a variety of aims—some in conflict with each other and others harmoniously, some infantile and others more mature, and all with varying degrees of conscious awareness and of acknowledgment as one's own aims, ranging from full conscious awareness and acknowledgment to total lack of awareness and disavowal. This picture is explicit in Holt's (1976) paper, referred to earlier, in Klein's (1976) work, in Fingarette's (1966) rendering of psychoanalytic concepts, in Schafer's (1976) recent work, and is implicit in the formulations of Fairbairn (1952) and Apfelbaum (1966).[51]

The development of selfhood enables one to acknowledge one's thoughts, memories, experiences, feelings, wishes, to use Fingarette's (1966) phrase, one's "engagement in the world," *as one's own*. It also permits one to fail to acknowledge as one's own, to *disavow* those "engagements" which are inimical to the maintenance of selfhood and self-esteem. (Among such "engagements" are sexual and aggressive thoughts and wishes). As Fingarette (1966) and Schafer (1976) note, such disavowal is the essence of the psychoanalytic concept of defense. That is, one part of the self is pursuing wishes and aims while another part of the self is disavowing these wishes and aims. This seems a more meaningful way of describing conflict than talk about instinctual impulses pressing for discharge and ego structures repressing and controlling them.

In a psychology so conceived, the concept of id, if retained at all, would be understood, not as a reservoir of instinctual impulses, but as an expression of the basic defense against acknowledging certain wishes and aims in conflict with one's dominant aims and values by experiencing them as "not-me" (Sullivan, 1953). That is, Freud's basic insight in distinguishing between an "it" and an "I" is retained and even enlarged by emphasizing degrees of disavowal and of disowning versus owning rather than impulses versus control. While sexual and aggressive impulses may be particularly subject to disavowal, what is critical about experiencing a wish or an aim as an "it" is not its presumed instinctual content, but its ego-alien "not-me" status.[52] It is not experienced as part of one's selfhood, is not subject to being reflected upon, and is thereby immunized from the corrective influence of experience, judgment, and criticism. As Apfelbaum (1966) notes, it is not only that an aim is necessarily repressed because it is infantile and anti-social, but also that what is repressed and thereby shielded from experience *remains* infantile and anti-social. If this is so, psychological growth or positive change in therapy is not only a question of increased structural control and renunciation of timelessly infantile impulses, but also consists in maturation and change in the aims themselves. (I will return to this issue in another section.)

This conception of personality in terms of different aims and different cognitive-affective systems, interestingly enough, is quite close to both Freud's earliest and latest formulations. In one of his earliest case histories, Freud (1893–1895) is concerned with "an incompatibility . . . between the ego and some idea presented to it" and notes that he hopes "to be able to show elsewhere how different neurotic disturbances arise from the different methods adopted by the 'ego' in order to escape from this incompatibility." A bit further, Freud writes that "the actual traumatic moment, then, is the one at which the incompatibility forces itself upon the ego and at which the latter decides on the repudiation of the incompatible idea. That idea is not annihilated by a repudiation of this kind, but merely repressed into the unconscious. When this process occurs for the first time there comes into being a nucleus and centre of crystallization for the formation of a psychical group divorced from the ego—a group around which everything which would imply an acceptance of the incompatible idea subsequently collects. This splitting of consciousness in these cases of acquired hysteria is accordingly a deliberate and intentional one" (p. 123). For the first fifteen years of his writings, as Holt (1976) points out, Freud was quite successful in conceiving of conflict and symptomatology in terms of different wishes and aims rather than drives and structures.

In his last work, Freud (1940b) returns to his earliest formulations and to "splitting" (of the ego) in particular. Thus, in discussing the co-existence in fetishism of both the disavowal and recognition of the perceptual fact that girls do not have a penis, Freud writes that "the two attitudes persist side by side throughout their lives without influencing each other" (p. 203). Here is what may rightly be called a "splitting of the ego." Freud's comment somewhat later on that "in the case of neuroses, . . . one of these attitudes belongs to the ego and the contrary one, which is repressed, belongs to the id" (p. 204), seems clearly an attempt to squeeze these notions of co-existence of disavowal and acknowledgment and "splitting of the ego" into the id-ego model. For even within the framework of Freud's own conceptions, it makes no sense to speak of the id as disavowing or acknowledging perceptual facts or as having this or that attitude (particularly, if the id is presumably cut off from the external environment).

Freud's concept of "splitting of the ego" is consistent with Fairbairn's (1952) formulations in which the core of psychopathology consists in ego splits, with Fingarette's notions of ego and counter-ego, with Federn's (1952) "ego-states," with Sullivan's (1956) concern with experiences dissociated from the self system, and with G. S. Klein's (1976) emphasis on incompatibilities of aims and their attempted resolution.[53] What all these related ideas have in common is an implicit emphasis on *integration* of cognitive-affective complexes into a superordinate structure as the core of psychic health and *lack of integration* of the complexes as the core of psychopathology. In all pathology there is failure, in varying degrees, to integrate conflicting sets of aims, cognitions, feelings, etc. Furthermore, as I noted in discussing G. S. Klein's work, self-cohesiveness is defined in terms of range and adequacy of integration of these cognitive-affective complexes.

A focus on the wishes and aims actually pursued by people means that one's description of behavior will be more likely to be based on empirical considerations rather than on the *a priori* theoretical biases that have too much characterized psychoanalysis and other approaches to human behavior. On a strictly empirical basis, one can no more claim that the wishes and aims pursued by people are all variants of sexual and aggressive motives then one can say that they are uniformly and preponderantly self-realizing in nature (Maslow, 1954; 1968; Rogers, 1959; 1961). Both attributions are based largely on theoretical speculations and preconceptions regarding human nature rather than on empirical findings.

Unfortunately, when one does posit such universal and all-embracing tendencies, such as those linked to the Freudian sexual and aggressive instincts, one manages to view all behavior, even behavior patently unrelated to these aims, as direct or indirect derivatives (including defenses against and sublimations of) these posited aims. Further, since according to Freudian theory all behavior, by definition, is in part and in some fashion an instinctual derivative (Waelder, 1960) and since there are few, if any, clear empirical criteria for determining when behavior is or is not a derivative of a sexual or aggressive instinct, the theoretical position becomes self-confirming and not subject to refutation by contrary evidence.[54] This is as true of Maslow's and Rogers's claim regarding basic self-realizing and ac- tualizing tendencies as it is of Freudian drive theory. With regard to the former, one can render all behavior as self-realizing or as reactions against the frustration of this all-embracing pursuit. I also believe that there are similar problems with viewing self-cohesiveness or self- integrity as a superordinate tendency or motive and will discuss this issue more fully in a subsequent section.[55]

An individual has a multiplicity of different and often conflicting aims, wishes, cognitions, feelings, values, etc., which he can integrate with varying degrees of success. To the extent that instincts play a part in behavior, they do so not as autonomous impulses which are pitted against other structures of personality, nor are they full blown, some- how embodied, aims which seek discharge. Rather, they are im- plicated in and are part of a complex of aims, behavior, feelings, and cognitions. As Holt (1976) points out, aims and wishes are cognitive- affective rather than drive concepts. For example, the attachment in- stinctual system is best conceptualized, not in terms of affiliative im- pulses seeking discharge, but in terms of a range of behavioral repertories, capacities, and aims which appear to be species-wide and, to use a term employed by ethologists, "environmentally stable." Whatever effect the attachment instinct has on behavior is integrated into the ongoing flow of individual plans and aims and means of relat- ing to others. There are no attachment instincts, as such, which exist as a separate structure of personality in a state of negotiated opposi- tion to other structures of personality.

Or to take sexual instincts as another example, there are no sexual impulses, as such, pressing for discharge (how would an impulse press for discharge?). Rather, sexual impulses and desires are reflected in an individual's overall aims, feelings, cognitions, and be- havior and are influenced by a wide variety of factors, including learn- ing, hormonal changes, and, it is important to note, the presence of external stimuli. By eliminating the Freudian concept of id, one does not eliminate or negate the importance of biological and instinctual factors. Rather, one places them in the proper context of ongoing inte- grated behavior.

12

DEVELOPMENTAL DEFECT
VERSUS DYNAMIC CONFLICT

One characteristic of recent developments in psychoanalytic theory, exemplified in the work of Kohut but present in other psychoanalytic writings, is a strong tendency to view at least certain classes of pathology in terms of developmental defects and arrests rather than in terms of dynamic conflict. This is presumably the main characteristic distinguishing the more severe pathologies, such as borderline conditions and narcissistic personality disorders, from the "structural conflicts" of the neuroses. The idea of developmental arrest is often employed literally in the sense that modes of behavior which were presumably normal at an earlier period of development are said to characterize the adults suffering from these more severe conditions. For example, according to Kernberg (1976) the borderline patient's continued use of primitive splitting as a primary defense indicates an inability of the ego (or self) to integrate good and bad, love and hate, because of its failure to grow beyond the developmental stage at which presumably gross affective and evaluative alternations are the rule. Kernberg tells us that the primitive splitting employed by the borderline patient is a normal defensive means of dealing with potential conflict at an early stage of development prior to the emergence of a stable ego structure.

In Kohut's writings one sees clearly the degree to which his self psychology is a psychology of developmental failure and structural defect rather than one of dynamic conflict. Kohut informs us that for the narcissistic personality disorder and others suffering primarily from self defects, the primary issue is not intrapsychic conflict, but lack of self-cohesiveness as a consequence of trauma-induced developmental failures. It is as if Kohut were positing a sort of "conflict-free" pathology of the self to parallel "conflict-free" ego autonomy. What Kohut and others (e.g., Stolorow and Lachmann, 1980) propose is that neurosis involves mainly dynamic conflict, while narcissistic personality disorders and other similar pathology consist primarily in structural defects, which develop and can be considered quite apart from dynamic conflict.

The general contrast between developmental arrests and defects on the one hand and intrapsychic conflict on the other is perhaps most fully articulated in a recent book by Stolorow and Lachmann (1980). As they note, "the crucial distinction is between psychopathology which is the product of defenses against intrapsychic conflict and psychopathology which is the remnant of a developmental arrest at prestages of defense. . . ." (p. 5). For example, in one patient presumably suffering from a developmental arrest, idealization and grandiosity involve mainly an "inability to register and affirm the real qualities of the self or objects . . . ." (p. 64), while for another patient, grandiosity "was defensive in nature. It served to deny his vulnerability and his realistic limitations" (p. 84).[56] Or, to take another example, in one case splitting is seen as a defense against intrapsychic conflict; while in the patient judged to be suffering from a developmental arrest, it is taken as an expression of an integrative incapacity. According to the authors, not only are there prestages of defense in developmental arrest, but also prestages of transference and of the therapeutic alliance. For example, while in classical transferences, the therapist "is experienced as a separate . . . whole object—a target of displaced affects and conflictual wishes," in pre-stages of transference, the therapist "is predominantly experienced as an archaic, prestructural self object" (pp. 173–174).

I do not believe that the above dichotomy between developmental and structural defects on the one hand and dynamic conflict on the other is entirely tenable. Let me indicate the reasons for this position. Most generally, structural defects and dynamic conflict are different aspects of and entail different perspectives on a continuing set of complex phenomena. This is always apparent in Freud's formulations in which dynamic considerations (i.e., of wishes, conflict, and defense) are never replaced by a structural perspective. Rather, both are different aspects of a single complex phenomenon. Thus, when Freud (1940) speaks of "splitting of the ego" in fetishism versus id-ego conflict in neurosis (what Kohut refers to as "structural conflict" between intact structures), he is not contrasting a structural defect with a dynamic conflict. For, in this view the "splitting of the ego" in fetishism is as dynamically determined as the id-ego conflict in neurosis. And for Freud, neurosis is not simply a dynamic conflict between fully intact structures (so that one could, practically speaking, ignore structural considerations) but is, from one vantage point, *also a developmental failure*. The presence of a neurosis bespeaks, among other things, some inherited, constitutional component, an earlier unresolved infantile neurosis, the persistence of infantile wishes, the presence of psychosexual fixations, and a failure of the ego to resolve conflict more adaptively.

While some people may be more disturbed than others and may show a greater degree and wider range of developmental failures, it does not follow that issues of intrapsychic conflict are irrelevant to them. For those with so-called self defects and developmental arrests, there are also conflictual wishes and aims defensively dissociated from the rest of the personality because of the anxiety they would entail. The wishes and aims may center on fantasies and themes of merging, engulfing, and being engulfed, symbiotic union versus separation, etc., rather than primarily oedpial themes, but they are nevertheless conflict-laden wishes. The general point is that developmental failures and structural defects have dynamic aspects. Indeed, to say that someone is developmentally impaired or has an ego or self-defect means, in part, that certain characteristic wishes (e.g., fantasies of symbiotic merging) are particularly intense and particularly prominent.

Part and parcel of early traumas which presumably led to developmental impairments and structural defects are *conflict-laden wishes, longings, and other affective reactions*. Clinically, one frequently observes that it is precisely the person deprived of love and empathy who is most conflict-ridden in regard to being loved. For example, very deprived children who are finally indulged (e.g., by a well-meaning child worker or "big brother") will often react with destructive feelings and behavior of one kind or another. (In one case with which I am familiar the mother forbade the trips to a restaurant with the child worker because she had to face the inevitably destructive behavior afterward). It is not uncommon to see children with a history of deprivation react with depression, tears, and rage following indulgence. One can also observe in adult patients who have had a battered and deprived childhood the strong tendency to re-institute conditions of misery and failure after a helpful and empathic relationship has been established, either in or out of therapy. In a recent paper, Bowlby (1981) describes a patient who did not seem to be content until her needling succeeded in making him irritable. This urge to needle became stronger after Bowlby had done something that she felt was kind. Her explanation for her behavior was that "I can't take kindness." Here is someone who was deprived of kindness and now reacts to being treated kindly with hostility because, as Bowlby notes, "in her experience, to become attached to someone could lead only to rejection and further suffering" (p. 19). Bowlby goes on to say, "Once I had become irritable any warm feelings that she might have felt in response to my kindness were snuffed out. Then she felt safe again, though of course terribly isolated" (p. 19). The point I am making by all these examples is, to repeat what I have said above, that early traumas, early developmental impairments, and early structural defects are always accompanied by intense and conflict-laden wishes and feelings. The fact is that we have intense reactions (e.g., rage) to experiences of trauma and deprivation and that we are most conflicted in the areas in which we are deprived. As I stated above, it is precisely the person deprived of love who is most conflicted about giving and receiving love. It is as if one of the costs and consequences of trauma is to develop an "allergy" to the very "substance" one needs and of which one has been deprived. Continuing the analogy, such an allergic reaction means that the therapeutic task will be far more complex than compensating for an earlier deficiency.

A subsidiary assumption that is part and parcel of the developmental defect–intrapsychic conflict dichotomy is that the former group of people pursue primarily self-cohesiveness, while the latter is concerned mainly with drive gratification (and the conflicts in which they are implicated). I suggest instead that Gedo (1979; 1980) and Klein (1976) are correct in their proposal that the integrity and continuity of self-organization is a superordinate aim for all people, quite independent of diagnostic category. For more disturbed people, who are prone to what Kohut calls "disintegration anxiety," this aim is often pursued at the level of sheer intactness of self. For others, the pursuit of this superordinate aim mainly takes the form of striving to resolve and integrate the incompatibilities and conflicts among various subordinate aims (Klein, 1976).

While satisfaction of basic drives and needs (which are not limited to sex and aggression) generally tends to be self-enhancing and deprivation tends to be self-diminishing, their psychological meaning and consequence cannot be divorced from superordinate issues of self-organization. A main consequence of inner conflict, which entails the experience of wishes and desires linked to basic drives and needs as "ego-alien" and their relegation to the realm of the dissociated, is *both* the failure to experience satisfaction of specific wishes and desires *and* the frustration of the superordinate aim of integrity and unity of self-organization. However, the frustration of a specific wish or need in a context of non-conflict will have different psychological consequences. Many people can endure serious frustration of certain basic needs without marked psychological consequences if the frustration is experienced in a context compatible with "self-values." And, as Klein (1976) notes, issues of sensual craving, gratification, and deprivation are intimately bound up with "self-values."

There is no logical or clinical incongruence between the structural point of view (of which notions of developmental arrest and self-defects are examples) and the dynamic. The integration of the two points of view is made possible with the recognition that whatever one's developmental level and structural limitations, the resolution of incompatibilities is a universal task and the failure to resolve incompatibilities or their attempted resolution through dissociative means weakens the integrity of the personality. Another way to make the same basic point is to say that a self psychology and a dynamic conflict psychology are congruent insofar as degree of self-integrity is intimately linked to the resolution and integration of incompatible aims and motives. What follows is that while the content and nature of conflicts may vary, resolution of conflict will be likely to be therapeutic for all levels of pathology (which is not to say that other factors, such as identification with the therapist, will not also be therapeutic or that other factors will not be especially relevant for certain classes of pathology).

Since the pre-psychoanalytic writings of Janet and Charcot, it has been recognized that both severe incompatibilities and the resort to dissociation as the solution to such incompatibilities weakens the personality. This basic point is echoed in current discussions of the use of "splitting" in borderline conditions. Kernberg (1975; 1976) who has written most extensively in this area, makes the explicit point that the use of splitting tends to erode ego strength.

I have noted above that according to most current writers, the essential factor in the etiology of developmental defects and arrests is early trauma of some kind. Thus, we have already noted that according to Kohut, early lack of empathic mirroring and opportunities for idealization are the primary etiological factors in accounting for lack of self-cohesiveness. Stolorow and Lachmann too, we have seen, link developmental arrests and failures to trauma and deficiencies in early care, including absence of empathic responsiveness, extreme inconsistencies, and "frequent exposure of the child to affectively unbearable sexual and aggressive scenes" (p. 5).

I have already noted (and will discuss again later in the chapter) that there is little or no evidence for these etiological claims. I want to highlight here the degree to which the emphasis on trauma and ensuing defect represent a return to the relatively static and exclusive structural emphasis of pre-psychoanalytic continental psychiatry and a giving up of the insights provided by the psychoanalytic emphasis on intrapsychic conflict.

One will recall that the pre-psychoanalytic emphasis was on constitutional factors in accounting both for extent of the incompatibilities and the inability to resolve them in non-pathological ways. It was Freud's contribution (and, in a sense, the beginning of psychoanalysis) that he essentially reversed the causal sequence. That is, it was not that constitutional weakness and relative incapacity for integration produced conflict and dissociation (and thereby, further weakened the personality—though Freud did allow some weight for such assumptions), but that incompatibilities and the use of repression in order to resolve them weakened the personality and left one prey to symptoms. By contrast, the current emphasis on developmental arrests and self-defects, in a somewhat different language, shares the same explanatory form as the pre-psychoanalytic concepts of Charcot and Janet. Thus, Kernberg, for example, wonders whether those characterized by borderline personality organization are handicapped by a constitutionally given, overly intense aggressive drive. And when constitutional factors are not invoked, one need merely substitute for constitutional weakness and hypnoid states the newer factors of arrests and defects which are held to be brought about by early trauma. In other words, what is invoked in the etiology of pathology is not intrapsychic conflict, personal meanings, and fantasied interpretations of ostensible events, but the direct *effects of supposed actual events* (usually maternal failure—e.g., lack of empathic mirroring—of some kind) upon psychological development, relatively unmediated by personal fantasies and meanings. This kind of etiological explanation is similar in form to early Freud's seduction theory and to pre-psychoanalytic accounts. It is a straightforward A causes B account, much as one would say that lack of vitamin D (A) causes rickets (B).

In short, whether the result of heredity or early trauma, what is proposed in much current literature as the core explanation of serious pathology is that one is dealing with a deficient and defective organism. I have referred elsewhere (Eagle, 1982a) to the tendency of some current psychoanalytic writers to depict their patients as so infantile and so defective that one wonders how they can function at all. The example I used was Giovacchini's (1981) description of a patient in the following terms: "Both visual and auditory modalities were fixated

at early post-symbiotic levels and did not undergo confluence as occurs during the course of psychic development and integration" (p.
422). As I stated there, "the synthesizing of . . . visual and auditory
modalities is a very early and primitive achievement. If Mr. R. has not
accomplished this basic developmental task, how is he able to function? However disturbed Mr. R. is, we know from Giovacchini's description that he holds down a job, is married, pays his therapy fees
and, generally speaking, carries out many functions expected of
adults. How is it possible for someone incapable of synthesizing visual and auditory modalities to do all these things?" (pp. 40–41).

As Levine (1979) points out, conceptualizations in terms of developmental arrests and self-defects tend to confirm the patients' fantasies that he or she is, in fact, defective. I would add that these sorts
of formulations also serve to preclude the analytic examination of
these fantasies, including their defensive function and their enmesh-
ment in conflict. This is a particularly important point to make insofar
as so-called defects and arrests are not necessarily transparent but
rather involve the theoretical interpretation and judgment that certain
behaviors are expressions, often indirect and subtle ones, of underlying developmental defects and arrests. What follows is that if one's
theoretical predilections are in a particular direction, one can view a
particular set of behaviors as indications of self-defects and developmental arrests, while someone with a different theoretical inclination
will give a different diagnostic meaning to these behaviors. I remind
the reader of Gedo's (1980) observation, noted earlier, that the Goldberg (1978) case book is replete with instances of self-defects and
hardly mentions oedipal conflicts, while the Firestein (1978) case
book dealing with seemingly similar phenomena has not a word about
self-defects, but much about oedipal issues. And, as Rangell (1980)
has noted, the kinds of patients described as narcissistic personality
disorders and as suffering from self-defects by Kohut and his followers
have long been observed by many analysts who viewed them as neurotic rather than as warranting a distinct diagnostic category.

Treatment Implications of the Defect Versus Conflict Dichotomy

Accompanying the developmental defect–intrapsychic conflict dichotomy are corresponding differential emphases in therapy. If one
conceptualizes pathology in terms of unconscious intrapsychic conflict, anxiety, and defense, then therapy consists in helping the patient
better deal with conflict through increased awareness and insight and

through increasing the ego's province and control. One's aim is to examine infantile wishes and the conflicts, anxieties, and defenses that surround them in the light of current reality so that one can consciously select such options as renunciation or gratification. If, however, one conceptualizes pathology in terms of developmental defects, then the therapeutic aim is some sort of repair of this defect—usually via the therapeutic relationship.

One sees this latter conception of psychoanalytic therapy with increasing frequency in discussions of work with more disturbed patients. In this latter conception, one can no longer say that the basic aim of psychoanalysis is either to make the unconscious conscious or to enlarge the scope of the ego ("where id was, there shall ego be"). One is not as likely to think of therapy as a process in which one gradually owns the wishes that one has disowned, in which one comes to claim as part of oneself "ego-alien" desires and aims that one has disclaimed (Schafer, 1976). Instead the patient-therapist relationship itself—whether described as a "holding environment" or as permitting mirroring and idealizing transferences—in some fashion helps repair the defect, facilitates the building of new structures and the resumption of developmental growth which was interrupted by early trauma. As Stolorow and Lachmann (1980) put it, "Kohut's treatment approach aims at permitting the arrested narcissistic configurations to unfold as they would have had the process not been prematurely, traumatically interrupted" (p. 86). As for their own approach to therapy with developmental arrests, Stolorow and Lachman consistently contrast the goal of analysis of intrapsychic conflict and defenses in neurosis with the goal of promoting "the structuralization of the self representations" (p. 143) in cases of developmental arrest. As to the specific means through which the latter is to be accomplished, to the extent that this issue is addressed, the authors refer to the therapists' empathic understanding and "empathic clarifications" of the patient's need to maintain his or her archaic state, including the use of the therapist as a self object, for the purpose of maintaining self-cohesiveness and stability. According to the authors, "the analyst's empathic clarification of the patient's specific need for archaic self objects promotes differentiation and structuralization" (p. 170). In general, the authors contrast intrapsychic conflict in which early experiences that are defended against are analyzed in the transference with developmental arrest in which the experiences the patient needed but lacked are understood. Finally, in Fairbairn's (1952) conception, therapy helps the patient dissolve the cathexis of the bad object through the good object relation represented by the therapeutic relationship. Whether or not therapy leads to all these desirable outcomes, the point is that this conception involves a basic alteration of the psychoanalytic theory of therapy. Furthermore, this alteration is based on the mistaken notion that in developmental arrests and structural defects (assuming that these are identifiable phenomena) intrapsychic conflict is not a primary issue.

Many recent conceptualizations of therapy suggest that treatment compensates for early traumas and the deficiencies they bring about. I have referred to this elsewhere as a "deficiency-compensation" model of therapy. However, it is likely that the salutary effects of therapy have mainly to do, not with eliminating developmental failures and structural defects, but with ameliorating the effects of the *unrealistic* anxieties and unresolved conflicts typically accompanying whatever failure and defects are one's lot. Furthermore—and this seems to me a critical point—whatever the level of one's constitutional or historically endowed degree of ego strength or self-cohesiveness, unresolved conflict and accompanying anxiety weaken the personality, and the resolution of conflict and decreases in anxiety strengthen the personality. For example, for someone who shows evidence of a thought disorder, the factors likely to be most relevant and most amenable to change in therapy will probably have to do with the role of anxiety and conflict in eliciting and/or intensifying the thought disorder and the defensive function of this symptom.

I share Gedo's (1980) skepticism toward talk about resumption of developmental growth and the claim that psychotherapy somehow directly repairs developmental impairments and structural defects— whether through "transmuting internalizations" or any other hypothetical process. Rather, as Gedo points out, the effects of such impairments and defects are more likely to be ameliorated through "new functions learned in the context of a satisfying and age-appropriate human relationship" (p. 378). For some patients the new learning consists in such things as more efficient tension regulation, the prudent avoidance of understimulation or disruptive over-excitement, and raising unrecognized biologically based needs (e.g., symbiotic needs) to the level of conscious awareness and attempting to meet them in a manner consistent with one's self-organization. For many patients, as noted earlier, the experience of the therapist as a supportive symbiotic partner sufficiently reduces anxiety to permit the learning of new functions. But I strongly suspect that for all patients help in the recognition and resolution of conflicts is a primary means of promoting increased feelings of intactness and self-cohesiveness.

As adults, we are not simply frozen at "arrested" points in child-hood. Hence, it is not at all clear as to what is meant by permitting arrested configurations to unfold as they would have in the normal course of development. No process, physiological or psychological, unfolds in an adult as it would have when we were 1, 2, or 3 years of age. What can such talk mean or refer to? After all, as Loewald (1979) reminds us, "the analysis of adults, no matter how much given to regression or how immature they are in significant areas of their func-tioning, is a venture in which the analysand not only is in fact, chronologically, a grown up, but which makes sense only if his or her adult potential, as manifested in certain significant areas of life, is in evidence" (pp. 163–164).

That we do not, as adults, simply resume a developmental growth that was arrested at an earlier period does not mean that growth in adulthood is not possible. As adults, we can experience a deepening and increase in self-understanding and self-knowledge; we can alter our attitudes and our irrational and grim unconscious beliefs; we can become more self-confident and less plagued with anxiety; we can become more forgiving and self-accepting and less self-castigating; and so on. Furthermore, many of these outcomes may follow a re-newed struggle with developmental issues which were left unre-solved. However, all these changes are age-appropriate ones that occur in the lives of adults. They do not, nor could they, constitute the resumption of a developmental growth process that is characteristic of a 2- or 3-year-old.

As for the "transformation" of archaic configurations . . . into more mature forms of self-esteem regulation" (Stolorow and Lachmann, 1980, p. 86), we are not told precisely (or even imprecisely) how such transformations occur in treatment. We are merely told generally that the analyst's empathic mirroring and understanding, his permitting the archaic configuration to unfold, and his availability as a self object all work to heal self-defects, promote structuralization and resumption of developmental growth, facilitate separation–individuation, and transform archaic self and object configurations into more mature ones. Given the remarkableness of these claims, it would be important to go beyond these vague generalizations and to learn something about the specific psychological processes which bring about all these changes.

In contrasting treatment of neurosis and treatment of develop-mental arrest, Stolorow and Lachmann observe that in the former, reconstruction of the past will alert the therapist to satisfactions the patient will *wish to repeat* in the transference, while in the latter, reconstructions will alert the therapist to traumata the patient *will strive not to repeat*. The point I raise here only briefly is the one more fully discussed in Chapter 9 in dealing with the work of the Mt. Zion group. That point is that the form of treatment which Stolorow and Lachmann reserve for developmental arrests is, according to the Mt. Zion group, applicable to *all* psychoanalytic psychotherapy. According to the Mt. Zion group, the assumption that patients seek to repeat or obtain in the transference the gratification of infantile wishes is simply not an accurate description of what goes on in treatment with *any* patient. Instead, they suggest and present impressive evidence for the idea that *all* patients seek "conditions of safety," one critical aspect of which is the assurance that the therapist (or perhaps more accurately, the patient–therapist interaction) will not repeat earlier traumata. In other words, what Stolorow and Lachmann suggest as specifically and differentially appropriate for developmental arrests, the Mt. Zion group highlights as an essential ingredient of *all* psychotherapy.

Etiological Claims and False Developmental Assumptions

I want to note some additional difficulties that characterize current discussions of developmental arrests and defects. The emphasis on early periods of development has led to unbridled speculations regarding supposed events and processes in infancy and childhood. Such speculations are often of an etiological nature or may simply refer to what presumably goes on in early development. What they all have in common is that, remarkably enough, they are entirely based on clinical work with adult patients and make no reference to empirical studies with infants and children, let alone long-term longitudinal evidence.

Consider, for example, the extraordinary fact that *all* the evidence Kohut and his followers adduce to support their etiological notions regarding defects in the self are derived from the production of adults in treatment. Or consider some examples from Stolorow and Lachmann (1980). First, "a . . . characteristic of the very young infant's experience is his inability to integrate or synthesize representations with different affective colorations" (p. 4). But there is not a word on the nature of the evidence that leads to this conclusion. We are not told how Stolorow and Lachmann have become privy to the nature of the young infant's experience. It is worth noting in passing that to the extent that there *is* reliable evidence available regarding the young infant's cognitive capacities, it indicates that he or she has a far greater integrative and synthesizing capacity than is suggested by all the recent speculations regarding early splitting and other related characteristics (e.g., see Stern, 1980).

As for the second example, in discussing traumatic deficiencies in early care having to do with absence of empathic responsiveness, extreme inconsistencies, and "frequent exposure of the child to affectively unbearable sexual and aggressive scenes," Stolorow and Lachmann conclude that "when traumata such as these interfere with the structuralization of the representational world, the individual remains arrested at, or vulnerable to regressive revivals of archaic, or more or less undifferentiated and unintegrated self-object configurations" (p. 5). To the extent that one can decipher the jargon, what is being proposed here is a causal proposition regarding the effects of early experiences upon subsequent development without a shred of evidence.

The question that arises in all these instances is the nature of the evidence regarding these supposed actual events, let alone their purported effects on subsequent development. One finds in the current literature all sorts of descriptions of early deprivations, parental pathology, etc., all based, as noted, on adult productions and accounts. But, as Rubinfine (1981) cautions, "under *no* circumstances are we ever justified in using our creative fictional 'constructions' about origins of pathology in the first year of life to serve as data for theorizing about early psychological development" (p. 394). As for the adult patients' memories about purported early events, I remind the reader of Freud's (1899) warning, after noting that certain memories may have been falsified, that "it may indeed be questioned whether we have any memories at all *from* our childhood; memories *relating* to our childhood may be all that we possess. Our childhood memories show us our earliest years not as they were but as they appeared at the latter period of arousal. In these periods of arousal, the childhood memories did not, as people are accustomed to say, *emerge;* they were *formed* at this time" (p. 321n.).

The first above example from Stolorow and Lachmann also illustrates another difficulty of much current writing, which is characterized by the tendency to conceptualize adult pathology in terms of presumably normal stages in infant and child development. Thus, in the above example, an adult's difficulty with positive and negative affective evaluations is taken to represent an arrest at a similar normal stage in infant development. One finds that this sort of thinking completely underlies Kernberg's (1975) discussion of splitting. Splitting, Kernberg tells us, is the infant's normal manner of coping with positive and negative affects, given his limited integrative capacity. It is the continued defensive use of such splitting, Kernberg goes on, which then characterizes the borderline adult. However, as Peterfreund (1978) so cogently points out in referring to those fallacies as the "adultomorphization" of infancy and the "tendency to characterize early states of normal development in terms of . . . later states of psychopathology" (p. 427), adult pathology is not simply the persistence of normal infant processes. Or, to state it in reverse fashion, infant behavior is not the same nor even essentially similar to adult pathological behavior. The normal infant is not an arrested or defective version of the completed adult, but an organism whose responses are highly adaptive, given its capacity and level of organization. This is perhaps the most basic and most serious problem with the conceptualization of adult pathology in terms of arrested development. It perpetuates the fallacious idea that certain adult pathology is essentially a "freezing" of, or regression to, a particular normal stage of development. It draws on vague analogies between purported infant states and adult pathology without shedding light on either.

Consider as a case in point the frequent analogy drawn between adult narcissistic behavior and feelings (e.g., self-centeredness, a feeling that everything is coming to them, an unrealistically grandiose view of their abilities and achievements) and presumed infantile narcissism. As Peterfreund points out, given the infant's world and capacities, his *seemingly* narcissistic behavior is *normal* behavior and bears little essential similarity to the narcissistic behavior of adults, which is characterized by its own motives and processes. To link the two represents superficial analogizing and "a confusing adultomorphization of infancy" (p. 436). Other examples of both adultomorphization and what can be called "pathormorphization" (Milton Klein, 1981) of infancy, cited by Peterfreund, include Mahler's (1968) characterization of early infancy as "normal autism" and Melanie Klein's (1932; 1948) positing of the "paranoid-schizoid" and "depressive" positions of infancy.

Similar superficial analogic and confused thinking often enter discussions of regression. As Peterfreund cautions, "when complex biological systems break down they do not necessarily retrace the steps by which they develop, and one must be cautious about viewing the products of a breakdown as representing steps in normal development" (p. 439). While a man who has suffered a cerebrovascular accident and is therefore unable to speak may be said to be suffering from aphasia, one would not want to say that he is in "the same state as an infant of two months who cannot speak." Nor would one "characterize a normal two-month old infant as in a 'normal aphasic' state of development." Nor would one describe the man who suffered the cerebrovascular accident as having "'regressed' to an earlier state of 'normal aphasia'" (Peterfreund, p. 439).

What is clearly suggested in recent discussions of developmental arrest is that the functioning of individuals so afflicted either remains at or, under appropriate precipitating conditions, regresses to states and stages of functioning which were normal at earlier periods of development. This state of affairs is a highly unlikely one. Rather than reflecting a particular earlier level or state of development, pathology is characterized by a particular dysfunctional *direction* of development, which may bear varying degrees of (mostly superficial) similarity to those earlier periods, but which is certainly not to be equated with these earlier states and which certainly entails radically different processes and capacities. The very concepts of developmental arrest and development defect, if they are to be theoretically coherent and meaningful, must be clarified and elucidated in their own right (e.g., the particular direction of development taken in specific areas; the specific nature of "defects" in ego functions) rather than rest on superficial and misleading analogies with earlier periods of development. I want to note my conviction, however, that even when that is accomplished one will still find that not only are considerations of dynamic conflict and structural defects not incompatible, but that they are simply different perspectives on the same general phenomenon.

I come to one final way in this discussion in which current formulations of developmental arrests do not represent accurate accounts of the nature of development. The implication in many clinical and theoretical descriptions is that problems and issues associated with later stages of development do not make their appearance until earlier stages are successfully negotiated. This is most frequently presented in terms of pre-oedipal and oedipal issues. For example, Kohut (1977) writes that oedipal issues and "structural conflicts" do not surface until earlier pre-oedipal concerns having to do with self-cohesiveness have been resolved.

I believe that this is an inaccurate conception of how development proceeds and I also believe that it is contradicted by clinical evidence. With regard to the latter point, it is a common clinical experience to observe in patients with a predominance of pre-oedipal constellations—whether these are described as self defects or schizoid or even schizophrenic—the presence of typical oedipal conflicts and anxieties (e.g., castration anxiety, guilt and anxiety regarding incestuous wishes, etc.). In such patients, oedipal conflicts often trigger and are saturated with unresolved pre-oedipal issues and concerns, but they nevertheless remain characteristically oedipal in nature. (It should be noted that in typically neurotic patients, too, pre-oedipal issues are re-aroused and re-intensified at later oedipal and post-oedipal periods—such as adolescence—albeit in less intense degree and although dealt with in a less pathological way.)

The point is that even in instances of developmental defects or arrests, it is not the case that psychological development on all fronts comes to a standstill as is implied in Kohut's descriptions and formulations. This is an inaccurate model of how development proceeds. Rather, what is more typical for people with developmental defects in certain areas is that they are more poorly equipped to deal with later developmental challenges (that is, challenges characteristic of later developmental stages) and later developmental issues are more suffused with earlier unresolved issues. But, and again this is the critical point, all of development in all areas is not held in abeyance awaiting the correction of the defect or arrest. For example, among severely disturbed adolescents (whether described as borderline, schizoid, or narcissistic disorders) issues and problems having to do with sexual gratification, reawakening of oedipal conflicts, intimacy, heterosexual and homosexual fears, independence, vocational choices, and so on, make their appearance and become prominent. After all, rapid physical growth, endocrinological and other physiological changes, altered social demands and pressures, and other radical changes are as characteristic of adolescents with self disorders as they are of normal adolescents.

I recently treated a very disturbed young man who reacted with thinly disguised castration anxiety whenever he engaged in behavior which could be seen as adult and as supplanting father (e.g., at mother's request, carrying out a chore at home which father typically did, but which the patient could now do) and reacted with a sense of entrapment whenever his girlfriend's behavior could be construed as a demand that he make a long-term commitment to her. Now, despite his severe pathology and developmental arrests, these above reactions are not unlike patterns one commonly sees in neurotic patients. *That* is not where the basic differences lie. What is distinctive about my patient is the way he reacted to his ambivalence toward and conflicts surrounding his relationship with his girlfriend, which included dissociation and feelings of depersonalization (i.e., chronic "fuzziness" and inability to remember and report), obsessive homosexual thoughts and fears, and a recurrent dream in which he is being "smothered" and is "slipping into black nothingness." The dream, in particular, reflects the saturation of oedipal conflicts with primitive, pre-oedipal fears and fantasies.

I also recall a hospitalized, actively schizophrenic patient I treated suddenly announcing in a group therapy session that he would volunteer for castration surgery if that was necessary to cure his illness. He then went on to make clear his belief that his incestuous wishes were the source and cause of his "craziness," that he experienced his craziness as a castration anyway, and that if he went directly to the heart of the matter by getting castrated he might get better and recover. Now, a good deal of this material is obviously oedipal in nature. The patient is not unique in this regard. What is striking, of course, is the blatant conscious and untamed appearance of incestuous wishes and the direct, undisguised link between such wishes and actual (not displaced or symbolic) castration expectations.

To return to the basic point, whether or not clinical accounts or pathology in terms of "structural defect" are correct, such a point of view is not incompatible with dynamic considerations. Recent emphasis on developmental arrests, self-defects, borderline conditions, and so on have highlighted certain considerations and certain dimensions of personality and of psychopathology which have tended to be ignored in traditional theory. Thus we are much more likely now to be aware of the overriding importance of separation-individuation and "narcissistic" dimensions, including differentiation between self and other, degree of self-integrity and self-cohesiveness, ability to relate to the other as a separate other, and regulation of self-esteem. And this, I believe, is a real contribution. However, these dimensions are likely to be important for all people, in varying degrees and in different ways. There are likely to be, for example, different forms of separation-individuation challenges at different periods in one's life. In short, it is not the case that one group of people is governed by a psychology of aims, impulses, and inner conflict, while another group is governed by a psychology of self and the pursuit of self-cohesiveness.[57] As I have argued, such pursuit cannot be divorced from issues of gratification of basic instinctual drives and needs, and for all people the integrity of self-organization is a superordinate aim and is pursued at different levels.

Further, whatever defects one has, whether constitutionally given or the result of early traumas, what further weakens the personality is the existence of excessively intense and pervasive conflicts and other incompatibilities which, through their failure to be resolved, threaten one's sense of self-coherence and self-integrity. This idea has been central to psychoanalysis from Freud's earliest writings to G. S. Klein's (1976) recent "exploration of essentials." Furthermore, recent apocalyptic claims notwithstanding, unresolved conflicts and incompatibilities and the defenses and anxieties accompanying them are the appropriate material for therapeutic intervention. That is, the resolution and integration of unresolved schisms in the personality is the major therapeutic means through which one strengthens the self and ameliorates so-called self-defects.

There is no need for a dichotomy, certainly not a radical one, between a psychology of developmental arrests and one of dynamic or structural conflict. Rather, at each developmental stage one is challenged by the need to resolve and integrate various kinds of incompatibilities, including the incompatibilities among adaptational modes appropriate to different stages. How well one faces these tasks as well as how successfully one integrates one's various needs and aims both reflects and determines the subsequent quality and integrity of one's self-organization. Of course, one's success in resolving incompatibilities reflects one's integrative capacity which, in turn, is undoubtedly influenced by, as noted earlier, constitutional predispositions and early experiences. But it is unlikely that a particular set of early experiences—whether consisting of failures of empathic experiences or opportunities for idealization—would have a determinative and decisive influence on something as complex as integrative capacity.

In any case, issues of conflict, self-organization, and ego functions, including integrative capacity, are all inextricably linked.

III

THE CONCEPTUAL STATUS
OF PSYCHOANALYTIC THEORY

Up to this point, I have been discussing and evaluating mainly the *content* of various formulations and theories. I turn now to the *form* of these formulations, their conceptual, methodological, and epistemological status. I will deal mainly with the following related issues: the clinical theory–metapsychology debate; the identification of psychoanalysis as a hermeneutic discipline; the status of data derived from the clinical situation; and the dual status of psychoanalysis as both a treatment and a theory of human behavior and personality development.

13

CLINICAL THEORY AND METAPSYCHOLOGY

In recent writings both within and outside the psychoanalytic community, an increasingly radical distinction has been made between the clinical theory and the metapsychology accompanied by the judgment that the former is the heart of psychoanalytic theory and the latter is to be rejected as, at worst, pseudo-science and at best, a mode of explanation inappropriate to the subject matter of psychoanalysis (e.g., see Klein, 1976; Rycroft, 1966; Gill, 1976). The most elaborated and highly developed presentation of this point of view is found in Schafer's (1976; 1978) writings.

The advocates of the clinical-theory-only approach reject *any* account or model which makes use of a causal, natural science mode of explanation, attempts to establish generalizations, and attempts to elucidate the mechanisms underlying observed behavioral phenomena.[58] What remains, then, is the implicit and explicit claim that the clinical formulations of psychoanalysis are both uniquely appropriate and self-sufficient in explaining the phenomena with which psychoanalytic theory is concerned. Also part of the cluster of attitudes which constitute the clinical-theory-only approach are the assertions that the clinical psychoanalytic situation is the ideal source, *sui generis*, for obtaining observations and data for the clinical formulations; and that psychoanalysis is a hermeneutic discipline—that is, clinical formulations (and therapeutic interpretations) are held to be more concerned with deciphering hidden meanings than with establishing empirical laws. Finally, some but not all advocates of the clini-

147

cal-theory-only approach maintain that the method through which human behavior is to be understood is qualitatively different from that
employed to understand inanimate phenomena in the former's reliance on empathic identification (Home, 1966).

Before commenting further on the position described above, it will
be useful to elaborate on what specifically is meant by clinical formulations in the present context. An examination of the writings of advocates of the clinical-theory-only approach indicates that essentially
what they mean by clinical formulations or clinical theory is an explanatory account in which a person's behavior or symptoms are explained by reference to his conscious or unconscious aims, wishes,
and goals. All behavior, no matter how bizarre or trivial, is to be
understood in terms of an agent's wishes and aims, what he is trying to
do. (I have referred to this in a previous paper [Eagle, 1980] as "motivational explanation.") This position is worked out most fully and
explicitly in Schafer's (1976) concept of "action language." (The reliance on explanation by way of reference to the agent's wishes and
aims has leaned heavily on the philosophical distinction between reasons and causes and on the philosophy of action.)

It seems to me that many of the criticisms offered and positions held
by this group are valid (as I will try to show, it is the *solutions* they
offer that are problematic). For example, they have pointed to the
reification and personification involved in many metapsychological
formulations. That is, they have quite rightly pointed out that the
translation of clinical observations into metapsychological language
hardly constitutes a deeper level of explanation. To borrow an example from Sand (1981), to translate "he fell in love with her" into "he
cathected her representation with libido" does not add anything of
explanatory value. It merely creates the illusion that one is being
more objective or more scientific or somehow providing a deeper
level of explanation. And one need merely scan psychoanalytic journals and books to learn just how widespread this illusion is. And
finally, I believe that the critics of metapsychology are partly correct
in maintaining that some clinical formulations largely rest upon their
own empirical evidence and are not logically derivable from the
metapsychology.[59] In general, I believe that Sand (1981) is correct in
identifying Freud's metapsychology as a model (or an analogy or
metaphor) intended to serve a heuristic function rather than a theory
which can account for the clinical phenomena, can be verified by
observation, and can generate predictions which can be confirmed or
disconfirmed by empirical evidence.

I believe that the advocates of the clinical-theory-only approach
have served a very valuable purpose in exposing the illusion that

metapsychological translations are explanatory in any meaningful sense. And they have been correct in noting that the gap between clinical observations and the *current* metapsychological model has never been bridged and probably will never be bridged. But these valid criticisms of metapsychology have, as Bowlby (1981) has pointed out, led to a despair of ever relating psychoanalysis to the traditional sciences and have been extended to positions which I believe to be totally incorrect and limiting.

Whatever the inadequacies of Freud's instinct theory or hydraulic model or any other aspect of his metapsychology, he was, I believe, correct in searching for a deeper level of explanation in the substrate and processes underlying the behavior we carry out and the goals we pursue. For Freud, instincts always represented the substrate of more observable psychic phenomena. But the larger challenge Freud was addressing—and this has always represented the central tension within psychoanalytic theory—was the need to understand the empirical relationship between something like, let us say, a hormonal secretion or hypothalmic stimulation or generally between the neurophysiological and biochemical level on the one hand, and a wish or plan or feeling or aim on the other, and to integrate these different universes of discourse. It is this search for a deeper level of explanation rather than the specific content that I take to be the significance of Freud's metapsychology. To limit psychoanalysis to the so-called clinical theory and reject *any* form of deeper theoretical account is to declare this central challenge irrelevant and, as I have argued elsewhere (Eagle, 1981), to accept an inadequate and truncated form of explanation as well as to isolate psychoanalysis from an enriching body of facts and perspectives. It is one thing to insist on the legitimacy, even centrality, of explanation by way of motives and aims, including unconscious motives and aims. It is another thing to declare such accounts as final and to limit a discipline to such explanatory accounts. As I have argued previously, while from one perspective motives, reasons, and aims represent explanatory accounts of behavior, from another, broader perspective, they constitute the very data which themselves require deeper explanation. As the philosopher Max Black (1967) has observed, "As soon as reasons for action have been provided, an inquiring mind will want to press on to questions about the provenance and etiology of such reasons" (p. 656).

The very idea of a purely clinical theory untainted by any trace of metapsychology is illusory. For example, the very notion of unconscious wishes and aims, so central to the clinical theory of psychoanalysis, inevitably entails metapsychological assumptions and considerations. Rubinstein (1976) has shown that the conception of an unconscious wish, although treated as a conscious wish from a common sense point of view, can be seen, upon critical analysis, to represent only an "as-if wish" and is a concept which "exists *only* in the world of natural science, namely, in the form of . . . processes of a certain type in the brain of the organism . . ." (p. 255). He has also argued that the very notion of derivatives of an unconscious wish, which is essential to clinical confirmation, rests on Freud's energic hypotheses (Rubinstein, 1980). I have also tried to show that the notions of universal unconscious wishes and motives entails assumptions regarding species-wide instincts and "is more a statement of our biopsychological nature than a description of motives and reasons for our actions" (Eagle, 1980, p. 369).

Kohut too has claimed that his self psychology is limited to concepts which are experience-near and are based on empathic introspection, presumably in contrast to Freud's mechanical and experience-distant metapsychological formulations—surely a distinction which parallels the clinical theory-metapsychology dichotomy. An examination of the degree to which Kohut's program to avoid metapsychological assumptions and to limit itself to experience-near and empathically derived concepts is successful should be quite instructive.

Aside from the problems attendant upon the fact that the empathic processes of Kohut and his followers and, for example, analysts from the New York Psychoanalytic Institute seem to result in different diagnostic and dynamic conclusions (Gedo, 1980) (a point I will pursue later), one finds additional difficulties with this program of stressing empathically derived formulations.

His claim to rely entirely or mainly on empathic introspection notwithstanding, an examination of Kohut's writings will reveal that they are filled with straight causal formulations and metapsychological concepts and speculations (e.g., the concept of "narcissistic libido"; presumed developmental stages of "autoerotism" and "primary narcissism"; the idea that lack of early mirroring contributes causally to self defects; and the very central concept of "self-cohesiveness"). I make this point in order to demonstrate how difficult it is to remain within the bounds of a strictly clinical, phenomenological, experience-near, and empathically derived explanations of human behavior—even for someone whose avowed aim is to remain within such limits. Also, as noted earlier, the attempt to employ experience-near concepts when they are not appropriate and the illusion that one is using such concepts when one is, in fact, not doing so leads only to the production and proliferation of "hybrid concepts" (Slap and Levine, 1978).

Kohut's central formulations and concepts are no more experience-near or empathically derived than other psychoanalytic concepts. For example, Kohut's genetic and etiological assumptions regarding the importance of adequate "mirroring," and opportunities for parental idealization could not possibly be primarily based on empathy, but rather are based on something like the following implicit inference: Because the adult patient now establishes mirroring and idealizing transferences in his analysis and because he seems to need and benefit from the analyst's mirroring and from his opportunity to idealize the analyst, one can infer that he wasn't provided adequate mirroring and opportunities for idealizing in his infancy and childhood. This is merely an inference relating the nature of the transference to alleged earlier events and clearly has nothing to do with empathy.

To take another example, Kohut's etiological statements and speculative diagnoses of the patient's parents surely could not be based on empathy, but rather constitute an implicit inference concerning a causal relationship between alleged parental behavior and pathology and the patient's current difficulties. This etiological-causal claim may or may not be correct (that is obviously an empirical question), but it is entirely unrelated to the issue of empathy. To clothe these formulations in the garment of empathy constitutes, I believe, a subtle claim for a kind of immunity from prosecution. That is, if one explicitly presents an etiological claim such as that A is causally related to B, then it is immediately apparent that in order for one's claim to merit serious attention, one must produce meaningful empirical evidence, preferably of a longitudinal-prospective kind. However, if one maintains that one's formulation is based on "clinical evidence" empathically acquired, there is a tendency for others to be less critical and less demanding.

What especially confuses matters in this area is the fact that psychoanalysis is both a form of therapy and a theory of human behavior and that psychoanalytic writings often conflate therapeutic and theoretical aims and contexts. Formulations and forms of explanation deemed appropriate to the clinical context are also legislated for all of psychoanalytic theory. For example, the clinical-theory-only position is partly based on the belief that it is uniquely appropriate to and sufficient for the clinical context (while the metapsychology is held to be inappropriate to the clinical context). While we have seen that this belief is illusory, it nevertheless has provided a rationale for insisting on the self-sufficiency of the clinical theory.

As another example, consider the premium placed on "empathic introspection" discussed above. Certainly, any psychotherapeutic approach (as contrasted to somatic treatments or perhaps behavior therapy) places a high value on the therapist's empathy with the patient during the course of treatment. Similarly, one can readily understand the importance of employing experience-near locutions and avoiding metapsychological language in clinical work with patients. But it is another matter to elevate and apply these considerations to methodological and epistemological principles which are to serve as guides and boundaries for the construction of theory. Indeed, however plausible, the claim that empathy and the use of experience-near formulations are more therapeutically effective than non-empathic responses and experience-distant formulations does, itself, need to be tested through empirical data that are themselves not merely empathically derived. And a theory of why the former is therapeutically effective (assuming that this is the case) need not itself be limited to empathically derived and experience-near terms and conceptualizations.

The brief account of Kohut's formulations demonstrates how difficult it is to remain within the bounds of a strictly clinical, experience-near, and empathically derived explanation of human behavior—even for someone whose avowed aim is to remain within such limits. The fact is that those who attempt any kind of theoretical explanation of what they are observing, however much they might espouse empathy and claim to rely on it for knowledge, soon go beyond empathically derived concepts in their explanatory accounts.

Perhaps in the therapeutic context there is a form of distinctly clinical explanation that facilitates the kinds of therapeutic goals (e.g., insight, avowal of certain aims and wishes) especially characteristic of psychoanalysis. But explanations given to patients in the clinical context have, at best, a very complex bearing on the form that theoretical explanations of clinical phenomena will or should take. While interpretive explanations in the clinical context may use the personal language of wishes, aims, and feelings, there is no good reason to expect that a theoretical explanation of these wishes, aims, etc., needs to use the same language and the same kinds of concepts.

Let us say that one has a complete empathic sense of what another is experiencing (or even what another has experienced). As soon as one goes beyond that point, however, and wants to understand and explain why he is experiencing what he does, one has exhausted the possibilities of empathic accounts. Would one want to limit one's explanation to an (empathic) identification of what another is experiencing? The point is similar to the one I have made regarding the limitations of motivational explanation—that is, one wants to know the "provenance and etiology" of experience as well as motives.

The impulse to develop an account that would explain observed phenomena on a more theoretical and abstract level is the impulse behind all scientific-theoretical endeavors to find the order and reality underlying appearances. The problem with Freudian metapsychology lies not in the impulse, but in the empirical and theoretical emptiness of the result—hypotheses which cannot be refuted, concepts which are pseudo-quantitative and pseudo-physicalistic (see Holt, 1976), formulations with referents and meanings so imprecise that they can explain everything and therefore nothing, etc. *These* are the problems, not the search for a more abstract, theoretical, and comprehensive level of explanation. The clinical theory versus metapsychology is really a pseudo-issue. It is not a question of two theories in psychoanalysis, the clinical theory and the metapsychology. Rather, it is a question of a continuum of levels of abstraction, comprehensiveness, and depth and power of explanation.[60] (See also Holt, 1972, on the tension within psychoanalytic theory of Freud's mechanistic and humanistic images of man.)

14

THE EPISTEMIC STATUS OF CLINICAL DATA

From the beginning, the conflation of and tension between therapeutic and theoretical aims has been a central characteristic of psychoanalysis. Although psychoanalysis is a treatment, Freud nevertheless believed that its place in history would be secured because of its contribution to an understanding of the structure of the mind. And through the years we have been told and have told ourselves that the clinical psychoanalytic situation is a unique source for generating data which will contribute to a psychoanalytic theory of human personality—a happy convergence between therapeutic and theoretical-explanatory aims.

But what is the epistemic status of clinical data derived from the psychoanalytic situation? And what are the uses to which they are put? As we have seen, Kohut does not hesitate to base etiological formulations on clinical data although, quite obviously, adult patients' reports of early events are nothing more than *current* reconstructions and impressions of what occurred in the past—with all the possibilities of selection, construction, and distortion to which such memory reports are subject.

Just as reports of early memories are not an adequate basis for etiological claims and formulations, neither is therapeutic outcome. To consider a concrete example from Kohut's writings, that the provision of empathic mirroring on the part of the therapist promotes therapeutic improvement (and let us assume, for the sake of the argument, that this has been demonstrated) does not vouchsafe the etiological conclusion that lack of early parental mirroring played a critical causative role in the patient's current difficulties. There are all sorts of other reasons that the therapists' empathic mirroring could play an ameliorative role. To employ an analogy: if one could show that the therapists' suggestion that the patient will improve has an important therapeutic function, would one want to conclude that it was the early lack of such suggestions which are etiologically implicated in the patient's current problems? In general, as far as that sub-set of clinical formulations which has to do with etiology is concerned, clinically derived data are woefully inadequate. They are simply no substitutes for longitudinal, developmental, and prospective studies.

The fact is that there is remarkably little reliable evidence regarding the general effects of early experience upon later development or even regarding the question of whether early experiences have a special and irreversible determinative role in personality formation, let alone evidence for the effects of specific factors such as lack of empathic mirroring (e.g., Clarke and Clarke, 1976). It is at least possible that a belief in the special role of early experiences is partly mistaken. Because it is so strong and ingrained a belief, going back at least as far as Plato, it is likely that clinical data *reflect* that belief rather than provide meaningful support for it. When one looks at the data systematically from reasonably well designed studies, one does not find much clear-cut evidence supporting this belief. One sees indeed such findings as the fading effects of early experience over time; a lack of impressive stability of certain psychological characteristics over lengthy periods of time; an absence of neurotic disorder in adolescence for more than half the children who had shown an emotional disorder at age 10 (Rutter, 1976); and in general, one finds that the area is a complex one in which, in order to achieve some order, one must clarify such things as the nature of the early experiences being investigated, the area of behavior or personality one is studying (e.g., temperamental traits vs. traits of motivational content [Kohlberg, La Crosse, and Ricks, 1972]) and whether one is actually studying the effects of prolonged or early experiences.

In addition, even in well-controlled studies, the conclusions one is likely to draw regarding the importance of early variables for predicting later behavior will vary with whether one is carrying out a follow-up study or what Kohlberg *et al.* call a follow-back investigation: For example, in a follow-back study, Robins (1966) found that 75% of adult alcoholics studied were truants as juveniles (as compared to 26% of the control group). However, employing follow-up data, he found that 11% of children who were truants as juveniles were diagnosed as alcoholics as adults (compared to 8% of the control group). Obviously, this comparison has implications for the etiological limitations of clinical data which are derived from an informal follow-back procedure. However, the general point I want is make is that understanding and determining the effects of early experiences upon later personality development is an incredibly complex matter and requires, among other things, the teasing out of different variables and reliable and systematic data. Clinical data from the psychoanalytic (and other therapeutic) situation(s) do not even begin to meet these requirements. Therefore, however much certain formulations, such as the relationship between early empathic mirroring and the establishment of a cohesive self, may capture the imagination of the psychoanalytic community, they are at best hypotheses and speculations which, at present, are totally unsupported by meaningful evidence.[61]

In view of the complexity and uncertainty of the effects of early experience and of the relationship between early experiences and adult personality development, it is distressing to come across assured assertions in this area without any evidence. For example, Stolorow and Lachmann (1980) inform the reader that "absence of empathic responsiveness to the child's developmental requirements, extreme inconsistencies in behavior toward the child, and frequent exposure of the child to affectively unbearable sexual and aggressive scenes . . . interfere with the structuralization of the representational world, the individual remains arrested at, or vulnerable to regressive revivals of archaic, more or less undifferentiated and unintegrated self-object configurations" (p. 5). What is striking about this passage is not only the use of jargon and vague, undefined terms, but the assertion, *without any evidence,* that such and such traumata have particular developmental effects. I cannot resist observing that the use of jargon and vague terms is not merely, so to speak, fortuitously unfortunate but *necessary* in the sense that it permits assertions without evidence—insofar as it allows to remain unclear the kind of evidence that would support or fail to support the claim regarding the purported relationship. That is, as long as one does not know precisely what is meant by terms such as "structuralization of the representational world" and "regressive revivals of archaic undifferentiated and unintegrated self-object representation," one cannot say what kind of phenomena and observations would constitute evidence for or against the assertions.

What is also distressing about much of the recent literature is that so-called characteristics of the infant are asserted and described without any reference to the body of research on infants or any other evidence (we have already seen some consequences of this tendency in the earlier discussion of Mahler's work). For example, Stolorow and Lachmann claim that "a . . . characteristic of the very young infant's experience is his inability to integrate or synthesize representations with contrasting affective colorations" (p. 4). No evidence is offered that supports this view. What is presented is a reference to Kernberg. But if one looks at the source, there is no supporting evidence presented there, either. Rather, what one finds is the *assertion* that "splitting processes probably begin around the third or fourth month of life, reach a maximum between the sixth and twelfth months, and gradually disappear in the second and early part of the third year" (Kernberg, 1976, p. 7). As Spence (1982) has observed, much psychoanalytic writing is characterized by continued and frequent references to other "authorities" where claims similar to the one being made are also made—and also without evidence. After some time, the claim is taken as demonstrated fact. It is as if the implicit conception of evidential support were simply repetition and frequency of assertions.

Etiology aside, what about general theoretical formulations which have to do with *current* diagnoses and *current* dynamics? Here, too, I believe it can be shown that, quite contrary to the claims of most psychoanalytic writers, data derived from the clinical psychoanalytic situation represent, at best, problematic evidence. That is, while they may have heuristic value and, as Kubie (1975) has noted, may represent a rich source for generating hypotheses, they have little probative value with regard to testing these hypotheses (see Grünbaum, 1980; 1982). I begin with a recent observation made by Gedo (1980) that while followers of Kohut "found" extensive evidence of self-defects in patients' productions, analysts from the New York Psychoanalytic Institute, dealing with cases which seemed to present very similar constellations, found equally extensive evidence for the presence of oedipal conflicts and no apparent indications of self-defects. One can find other similar examples in the psychoanalytic literature. Since the data in the clinical situation are most often opaque with regard to such matters as the unconscious motives, conflicts, and self-defects they presumably reveal, and require interpretive clarification, it is apparent that the therapist's theoretical persuasion will be a critical determinant of how these data are interpreted.

The influence of theoretical persuasion upon the meaning and significance given to observations is certainly not unique to the psychoanalytic situation. But what compounds the problem in the clinical situation is the special, epistemically contaminated status of the data. That is, through suggestion and a variety of subtle and selective reinforcement cues, the therapist may be instrumental in *generating the very data cited to support this or that theoretical interpretation.* How else to account for the fact that each therapist seems to produce data congruent with his theoretical bias? And how else to account for the fact that, as Marmor (1962) and others have pointed out, patients seem to experience the kind of "insight" which corresponds to their therapist's theoretical orientation? Speaking of "radically divergent theories" of psychoanalysis, Marmor writes: "The fact is that patients treated by analysts of all these schools . . . believe strongly in the insights which they have been given . . . depending upon the point of view of the analyst, the patients of each school seem to bring up precisely the kind of phenomenological data which confirm the theories and interpretations of their analysts! Thus each theory tends to be self-validating. Freudians elicit material about the oedipus complex and castration anxiety, Jungians about archetypes, Rankians about separation anxiety, Adlerians about masculine strivings and feelings of inferiority, Horneyites about idealized images, Sullivanians about disturbed interpersonal relationships, etc." (p. 289).

As Masling and Cohen point out in a recent unpublished paper, "from the very beginning of therapy, some content areas are reinforced explicitly and implicitly, and some not" (pp. 6–7). They report a series of studies which demonstrate that the patient's productions are markedly influenced by the therapist's subtle and most often unwitting reinforcements. For example, Murray (1956), in an analysis of a tape of Rogers as the therapist, showed that 68 client statements about independence were met by subtle approval, while none were disapproved. By contrast, 16 client statements about sex were met with disapproval, while only 2 were approved. By the end of the therapy the client was concerned with independence and seemed unconcerned with sex. Truax (1966) essentially replicated Murray's findings.

Greenson (1967) reports an interaction with a patient which illustrates the same sort of reinforcement:

> He had been a lifelong Republican (which I had known), and he had tried, in recent months, to adopt a more liberal point of view, because he knew I was so inclined. I asked him how he knew I was a liberal and anti-Republican. He then told me that whenever he said anything favorable about a Republican politician, I always asked for associations. On the other hand, whenever he said anything hostile about a Republican, I remained silent, as though in agreement.

Whenever he had a kind word for Roosevelt, I said nothing. Whenever he attacked Roosevelt, I would ask who did Roosevelt remind him of, as though I was out to prove that hating Roosevelt was infantile.

I was taken aback because I had been completely unaware of this pattern. Yet, the moment the patient pointed it out, I had to agree that I had done precisely that, albeit unknowingly (p. 273).

Such ostensibly supportive data are then taken as confirmations of the very same theoretical position which, a broader view reveals, has contributed importantly to generating these data. That is, a consideration of the above phenomena indicates that reinforcement, suggestion, and compliance, however subtle and complex, are critical factors in generating these supposedly *confirming data*. Furthermore, the more ambiguous productions, if interpreted in accord with one's theoretical bias, are also taken as confirmatory data. Therefore, if the productions are sufficiently ambiguous, each therapist, whatever his or her theoretical persuasions, can reach the verdict that they constitute confirmation.

One can reply to the above difficulties by arguing that all observations of facts are, to use Popper's (1972) term, theory-impregnated. However, this is not an adequate reply for a number of reasons. In other disciplines, the data are not as opaque, thus rendering the limits of interpretation of observations narrower. Observers of different theoretical orientations are more likely to agree on such basic matters as whether or not *x* occurred. For example, in a memory study, there will be universal agreement among observers as to whether or not a particular stimulus item was recalled, although these observers may have radically different conceptions of memory processes.

In the non-clinical situation, there is a fuller recognition of the problem of selective bias and, most important, the consequent implementation of standard safeguards (e.g., double-blind studies, control groups) represent reasonably effective means for dealing with this issue. Such safeguards are not present in the typical clinical situation. A distinctive feature of human interaction is that one can often, wittingly or unwittingly, *elicit* from others the responses one wants to elicit—that is, reactions that are in accord with one's expectations and desires. The evidence on experimenter bias suggests that this is a ubiquitous problem even in the experimental situation (e.g., Rosenthal, 1963) and must be dealt with in various ways. Imagine how much more likely it is to characterize the rich, affect-laden interaction of the clinical situation.

While one cannot, perhaps, avoid theoretical biases, as von Eckardt

(1981) has argued, in citing the work of Sheffler (1967) and Giere (1979), "the ideal of objective data is possible at least to this extent: that data relevant to a given theory T can be collected by someone whether or not he or she believes in T or, even, whether or not he or she has knowledge of T" (p. 572).[62] She then goes to note Giere's point that a good scientific test "must be a statement that can reliably be determined to be true or false using methods that do not themselves presuppose that the hypothesis in question is true" (p. 95). But these are precisely the conditions violated by most clinical data—certainly those collected, interpreted, and evaluated by the therapist himself. This is true despite all the talk about therapists' forming and testing hypotheses within the therapeutic session. When has a Freudian analyst tested the hypothesis that a neurotic patient has no oedipal conflict or when has a Kohutian analyst tested the hypothesis that a narcissistic patient has no significant self defects or had adequate empathic mirroring as an infant? When has a Jungian analyst tested the hypothesis that his patient has no collective unconscious? Even if all these hypotheses could be tested, the fact is that such tests in the clinical situation employ methods and entail assumptions which, precisely contrary to Giere's description, indeed, do themselves "presuppose that the hypothesis in question is true." Concepts such as oedipal conflicts, self defects, and collective unconscious are all *assumed* to be true by their respective adherents and are employed to interpret ambiguous and non-transparent data.

In view of the above considerations, I question Sand's (1981) assertion that the clinical formulations of psychoanalysis are, like similar formulations in the natural sciences, inductively established empirical generalizations and, hence, entirely independent of metapsychology and any "higher theory" insofar as the latter "has not power to alter generalizations based upon the observation of actualities" (p. 178). Since at least some of the generalizations of the clinical theory are based on contaminated data, it is not at all clear that they are inductively established or "based upon the observation of actualities." Indeed, they are often metapsychology disguised as clinical formulations.

Consider the central clinical concept of an unconscious wish. As is suggested by Holt (1976), the link between unconscious wish and the notion of instinct or drive does not derive directly from clinical experience, but is based upon theoretical presuppositions regarding the nature of the organism. Further, since, as noted earlier, overt behavior is opaque as to underlying unconscious wishes (if it were transparent, interpretation would not be necessary), it is likely that the operative unconscious wishes posited in any particular case will, in part at least, be a function of one's theoretical conceptions regarding human nature and one's conceptions regarding the kinds of wishes any person is likely to have. Thus, the sensitivity of Freudian analysts to unconscious sexual and aggressive wishes is intimately linked to a superstructure of theoretical concepts and ideas, including instinct theory, repression, psychosexual development, sublimation, and an excitation-discharge model of the nervous system. It is not simply a matter of observing sexual and aggressive behavioral "actualities," but of *interpreting ambiguous or opaque behavior as sexual and aggressive.* Indeed, at times, as in the case of sublimation, patently *non*-sexual and *non*-aggressive behavior is nevertheless linked to transformed sexual and aggressive wishes.

Similarly, the sensitivity to and "observation" of self-defects on the part of Kohut and his followers is also not simply a matter of observed "actualities," but is based on interpretations which themselves rest on an entire set of theoretical assumptions regarding the nature of psychological development (which, by the way, includes a rejection of those very assumptions which permit Freudian analysts to "see" ubiquitous sexual and aggressive wishes in behavior).

Continued insistence on the primacy of the clinical psychoanalytic situation as the primary source of data and a reluctance to go outside this situation may have had a deleterious effect not only on the construction of psychoanalytic theory, but on the development of psychoanalytic therapy. I know that this is contrary to the predominant view, but let me explain my reasons for taking this position. As stated, traditionally, the psychoanalytic situation has been valued as much for its research as for its therapeutic value. It purportedly represented a unique source of data for understanding the structure of human motives, wishes, defenses, indeed for understanding the structure of the human mind and of personality functioning.

The belief that the psychoanalytic situation represents a unique source of data (and, for some, the only legitimate source) for assessing psychoanalytic formulations can lead to ambiguity concerning the justification of psychoanalytic treatment. Is it to be justified mainly for its therapeutic efficacy or because of the unique data it purportedly yields?[63] Is it possible that an interest in the latter is rationalized by a claim regarding the former? If psychoanalysis *as treatment* is to be justified for its therapeutic efficacy (rather than for its research value), should it not be evaluated by rigorous outcome studies?

Some psychoanalytic authors write as if their primary foci of interest are the phenomena generated by the psychoanalytic situation. They often justify this position by noting that the psychoanalytic situation is a unique one, unlike, in important respects, most other human interactions. What seems to be lost is the fact that the psychoanalytic situation is or should be of interest only insofar as it sheds light on such matters as psychopathology, personality functioning, and treatment. If they are unique, the heralded uniqueness of the psychoanalytic data is as likely to be a limitation as a virtue. For the psychoanalytic situation and the data it generates are of significance only in terms of the broader context to which they point.[64]

It seems to me that it is time to make some simple and clear judgments of the "emperor has no clothes" variety. The psychoanalytic situation is, above all, a therapeutic situation rather than a source of data for etiological formulations or even for theories of personality development. The most pertinent questions to be addressed to that situation have to do, first, with outcome—what kinds of changes and effects does this form of intervention produce?—and second, with the processes underlying the various outcomes. It is as subject to systematic evaluation as any other form of intervention and cannot, *a priori*, be *assumed* to be more effective, more lasting, and more profound than other therapies.

Persistent contrary claims notwithstanding, there is no convincing evidence for the variety of assertions that classical psychoanalysis is the "pure gold" of psychotherapy, that it is the only form of therapeutic intervention which avoids symptom substitution and produces structural personality change. Instead, there are mainly unsubstantiated assertions based on the implicit logic that, of course, psychoanalysis is the only therapy which produces structural change because the underlying theory (regarding repression, insight, making the unconscious conscious, etc.) says it is. Well-controlled outcome studies are eschewed in favor of continued assertions and claims. It seems remarkable that through the years conferences and publications on the "curative factors in psychoanalysis" are offered with precious little systematic evidence—beyond personal experiences and impressions presented in case reports—regarding outcome.

Beginning with the Marienbad conference in 1934, debate has raged as to the relative curative roles of insight, introjection, and other factors without any seeming recognition that in order to study curative factors, one must first reliably demonstrate that a cure (or its equivalent) has occurred. It is as if the debate stops at the question—and here one observes an example of a confounding of therapeutic and research interests—of what would be or should be the curative factors, according to this or that theory, without a concern for the empirical issue of whether or not cure occurs. This focus is scholastic to the point of being medieval. It reminds one of the illustrative stories (told by Francis Bacon?) of monks arguing, on purely theoretical grounds, about the number of teeth in a horse's mouth. When a novice suggests that they look in the horse's mouth, he is thrashed soundly for his blatant disrespect.

Broadly speaking, what is most important for psychoanalysis as a therapeutic situation is the development of a coherent *theory of therapy* which rests, not merely on the psychoanalytic theory of personality or psychopathology, but also on reliable empirical data identifying the interactions and interventions that are effective for particular goals, and the processes accounting for whatever effectiveness is achieved. Whatever the accompanying theory of personality and conception of human nature, one's psychotherapeutic approach must stand or fall on its pragmatic accomplishments.[65]

Psychoanalysis as a therapy cannot be justified on the basis of its links to the psychoanalytic theory of personality (and this point holds for any other therapeutic approach), nor can it be justified on the basis of the uniqueness of the psychoanalytic situation or the unique data it generates. As a therapy, and like any other therapy, it can only be justified on the basis of its accomplishments and on the basis of its contribution to a theory of how people change. And, most importantly, data from the therapeutic situation can make a primary contribution, not to an etiological theory of psychopathology or to a theory of personality development, but to a theory of therapy, that is, an understanding of the relationship between certain kinds of operations and interventions and the occurrence or failure of occurrence of certain kinds of specific changes.[66] It seems to me ironic that psychoanalytic writers attempt to employ clinical data for just about every purpose but the one for which they are most appropriate—an evaluation and understanding of therapeutic change.

15

PSYCHOANALYSIS AS HERMENEUTICS

I want to turn briefly to the currently popular conceptions of psychoanalysis as a hermeneutic discipline concerned only with interpretation and deciphering meanings (see, e.g., Ricoeur, 1970; Radnitzky, 1973; Schafer, 1976; Steele, 1979). I have yet to see in descriptions and defenses of the hermeneutic position any successful treatment of the mundane, but inescapable, problem of reliability and the associated one of criteria for knowledge. That is, if my interpretation or deciphered meaning or empathic grasp is radically different from and even contradicts yours, on whose empathy or interpretation does one rely for knowledge? If, as we have seen, a follower of Kohut and a New York Psychoanalytic Institute analyst each claims that, on the basis of empathy, he has achieved the knowledge that the primary bases for his patients' difficulties are, respectively, self-defects and oedipal conflicts, on what basis is this dispute evaluated?

Such failure to address adequately this simple but very basic question plagues all those positions—whether described as hermeneutics or *verstehen*—that have in common emphasis on interpretation, meaning, and empathic or intuitive means of knowing. Indeed, it seems to me that the recent embrace on the part of some psychoanalytic writers of hermeneutic, perspectivist (e.g., Schafer, 1976; Steele, 1979), and other related positions is based partly on a despair regarding the ability of psychoanalytic formulations to deal with this issue. It is as if the implicit reasoning were that if one cannot develop adequate criteria for evaluating the accuracy of clinical interpretations and formulations, the next best thing is to declare the issue irrelevant by virtue of adopting a hermeneutic or "perspectivist" position. For, according to this point of view (at least the extreme relativistic version of it), since different interpretations or formulations are only constructions, are only intended to provide different and helpful perspectives, the issue of reliability can be bypassed.[67]

Let us assume that in the clinical-therapeutic context the issue of reliability can indeed be bypassed insofar as a wide range of interpretations or, to use Fingarette's (1963) phrase, "meaning-schemes," receive confirming "insights" (Marmor, 1962) and are likely to be equally effective. It is also possible that the practice of offering any interpretations is partly or mainly, as Bergin and Lambert (1978) suggest, merely a congenial medium for the operation of the truly therapeutic factors (which, according to them, have to do with personal and relationship factors).

This is of some comfort to those taking the perspectivist or hermeneutic position insofar as it seems to support the argument that psychoanalytic interpretations merely provide a new perspective or "meaning scheme" and that different perspectives and different interpretations may be equally "valid" with regard to certain (therapeutic) aims.

If one probes further, however, and asks about *what* substantive matters the patient is being offered a new perspective, whether it is possible to evaluate different perspectives, and, if so, on what basis it is possible to do so, the difficulties of the perspectivist position become more apparent.

An attempt to answer the above questions returns the issues of validity and effectiveness through the back door. That is, one is often told that different interpretations offer different perspectives on some *larger truth* (enter the validity criterion) and/or that different perspectives also differ in how *helpful* they are (enter the effectiveness criterion). Neither claim is systematically addressed, only asserted. That is to say, whether or not different interpretations have *any* claim to *any* truth, large or small, is precisely the issue to be determined. And as for how helpful the interpretation is, that too is obviously a matter to be determined. Merely providing a new perspective does not guarantee that it will be helpful at all. Furthermore, that different interpretations from different theoretical perspectives all yield confirming "insights" does not necessarily argue they all constitute aspects of a large truth. It is as good an argument for the importance and operation of such factors as patient compliance and would suggest that the clinical situation and clinical data are inappropriate for the evaluation of the validity of interpretations.

However, even if the perspectival position were to assume a certain limited validity in the context of a discussion of the *therapeutic effectiveness* of interpretations, the main thrust of hermeneutic and perspectivist arguments has focused on claims that hermeneutic disciplines (of which psychoanalysis is purportedly an example) constitute distinctive means of *arriving at insights and truths* about human behavior and experience. They are meant to comprise a structure of "human sciences" or, in Dilthey's (1961) term, *Geisteswissenschaften*, which have the same relationship to knowledge of man that the natural sciences or *Naturwissenschaften* have to knowledge of nature. The fact that alternate perspectives or different interpretations, including perhaps demonstrably and blatantly false ones, can be therapeutically effective could hardly be of comfort or even of relevance to those with these larger ambitions.

Furthermore, remaining entirely within the therapeutic context, a determination of the therapeutic effectiveness of different perspectives and interpretations (indeed, a determination of whether they have *any* degree of effectiveness) requires the very kind of controlled studies generally eschewed by hermeneuticists.[68] Further, data yielded by such studies would contribute to a *theory* of therapeutic effectiveness (the autonomous theory of therapy I referred to earlier) which would then be as subject to evaluation (i.e., to refutation, to degrees of confirmation) as any other theory. One would direct to it the same questions one directs to any other theory, whether in the natural or social sciences—questions having to with the theory's ability to predict, to compete against other theories, to elucidate basic underlying processes and thereby account for a wide range of phenomena. Now, to the extent that one is carrying out such an evaluation and to the extent that one has developed a theory precise enough to be susceptible to such evaluation, *one has left behind and rendered the hermeneutic position irrelevant.* Or, to put it somewhat differently, while different perspectives and interpretations may be equally effective, theoretical explanations of why they are equally effective (or of why they are not equally effective if that is the case, or of why they are irrelevant to the issue of effectiveness if that is the case) and evaluation of these theoretical explanations already go beyond the issues raised by the hermeneutic argument.[69] Hence, neither as a theory or as a therapy (or as a theory of therapy), neither in terms of veridicality or effectiveness (or a theory of effectiveness) is it useful to conceptualize psychoanalysis as a hermeneutic discipline.

Returning to the clinical context for a moment, the argument that practically any plausible "meaning scheme" or "story" is effective suggests a paradox or at least an irony that should be confronted. For whatever one may say in theoretical papers about "stories" and "constructions," the fact is that most therapists make a genuine effort to understand their patients, that is, to grasp what is really going on and what is the case. Furthermore, I suspect that most therapists, whatever their philosophical persuasion, *believe* that their interpretations and formulations are validly descriptive of their patients rather than merely plausible "stories." I also strongly suspect that were those who take a perspectivist position (and therefore profess not to have this belief) to carry their philosophical position into the context in which they function as therapists, their therapeutic effectiveness would be impaired.

It should be noted that the idea that a wide range of plausible "meaning schemes" or "stories" are equally effective is a hypothesis yet to be tested. Although all patients may report "insights" confirming their therapist's particular theoretical orientation, it does not necessarily follow that all interpretations are equally effective. Nor does it follow that an elaborate "narrative" which fits all the pieces of the patient's life together (Sherwood's [1969] comprehensiveness criterion) is necessary for therapeutic effectiveness. My own guess is first, that more accurate interpretations are more likely to be effective—that is, that some version of Freud's claim that interpretations which "tally with what is real" is likely to be the case; and second, that the importance of elaborative "narratives" has been overemphasized. I should make clear, however, that the accuracy of interpretations is not so much defined by the patient's response (e.g., confirmation versus rejection, nature of subsequent associations, etc.) as by such criteria as whether the interpretation is in accord with what is known about the syndrome from which the patient is suffering, is in accord with certain central issues facing many patients, and more in accord with the nature of the human condition. For example, as discussed earlier, on such grounds I believe that interpretations of agoraphobia in terms of separation-individuation are more likely to be both accurate and effective than interpretations in terms of prostitution or street-walking fantasies.

The individual or personal "flavor" of the interpretation, in my view, comes not from the cleverness or uniqueness or comprehensiveness of the "narrative" or "construction" (that is, the "narrative's" success in linking together a wide range of events or dynamic hypotheses), but from the attitude and style of the therapist—that is, from such factors as the ability of the therapist to listen, to state his interpretations in terms of patients' concrete experiences and feelings, to express authentic caring and concern while retaining a technical neutrality which avoids taking sides in a conflict. The fact is that, as Levenson (1982) points out, every communication has its pragmatics as well as its semantics. Particularly in therapy, we communicate as much by who we are, and the manner and style emanating from who we are, as by what we say. It would be useful, it seems to me, to adapt Winnicott's (1965) concept of "good enough mothering" to the therapeutic situation and accept the idea of a "good enough interpretation."

A "good enough interpretation" is in accord with what is generally and reliably known about a syndrome, doesn't conflict with what is known about human nature, is embodied in references to the patient's specific and concrete experiences and concerns, and is presented in a manner which authentically conveys at least some level of concern, interest, and caring. While many—perhaps most—interpretations offer coherent "meaning schemes," "stories," "constructions," and interesting "perspectives," they are not "good enough" if they do not meet the above criteria. For example, I believe that a therapeutic interpretation in terms of "archetypes" or the "collective unconscious," while it provides a "meaning scheme," etc., is not "good enough" because it is *inherently* impersonal and *necessarily* has more to do with a broad intellectual construction than a particular person's experiences, concerns, and struggles. In that sense, it has more to do with the therapist than with any particular individual patient. Also, it is utterly isolated from what is reliably known either about any particular syndrome or about human nature.

A central point I want to make in suggesting the concept of a "good enough" interpretation is that it is possible to draw on reliable data and knowledge which are external to the clinical situation in order to develop clinical interpretations which are veridical to a "good enough" degree. As to whether such interpretations are more effective—that is, whether there is support for Freud's conviction that truth and efficacy have an integral connection is, I repeat, yet to be empirically tested.

Psychoanalysis and History

One variant of the hermeneutic argument is that psychoanalysis is a historical discipline in Collingwood's (1956) sense of the nature of such disciplines. I want to examine briefly here the validity of that argument. In a recent fascinating paper, Blight (1982) has acknowledged, or perhaps I should say conceded, that psychoanalysis is an historical discipline insofar as there is an analogy between the analyst's attempts to reconstruct the patient's life experiences and the historian's attempts to recreate the motives and experiences of historical figures. He then argues against the traditional idea of a "Great Divide" between historical disciplines and the natural sciences (between *Geistewissenschaften* and *Naturwissenschaften*), trusting that the discovery and awareness of commonalities among all critical inquiries will discourage the turn to hermeneutics on the part of psychoanalytic theorists. I am certainly in sympathy with Blight's goals, but he has conceded too much. For one, his readiness to classify psychoanalysis as an historical discipline is based on an implicit equation of psychoanalysis with psychoanalytic *therapy*. It is not at all clear that psychoanalytic *theory* is an historical discipline as that is conceived of by Collingwood. Its ambition is *not* simply to elucidate *individual* events without regard for the question of generalizability. On the contrary, the structure of psychoanalytic theory can be described as a body of propositions which, in general form, is not unlike other theoretical formulations in the social and natural sciences.

Even if one limits one's consideration to psychoanalytic therapy, there are important differences as well as similarities between psychoanalysis and historical disciplines. It is true that both in historical inquiry and psychoanalytic therapy there is an attempt to reconstruct events, to understand the experiences and motives of individuals, to construct a "narrative," and to decipher meanings. But psychoanalytic therapy constitutes a practical treatment and intervention and, as we have seen, thereby immediately confronts the issues of effectiveness and accountability. In this context, whatever understanding is achieved is (or should be) in the service of therapeutic effectiveness and in the service of developing an adequate theory of therapeutic effectiveness. Furthermore, in the clinical context, *it is the response of the subject of one's interpretations to these interpretations* that defines the issues of accountability and effectiveness. This consideration makes it immediately apparent that, in contrast to historical inquiry, in the clinical context interpretations are above all *interventions.*[70]

The original discussion began with a distinction between the clinical-therapeutic context on the one hand and theories of pathology (including etiology) and personality development on the other. I have tried to show that the conflation of the two contexts has led to certain confusion. What emerges from a discussion of the clinical-therapeutic context is still another distinction, the neglect of which has also led to a degree of confusion. The latter distinction I refer to is that between the interpretations given in the clinical situation (or the "narratives" developed to guide those interpretations) on the one hand and, on the other hand, both an evaluation of the effectiveness of these interpretations and a theoretical account of whatever degree of effectiveness is achieved. While interpretations may be like historical accounts or hermeneutic activities in certain respects, the measure of their effectiveness, as well as theoretical explanations of whatever degree of effectiveness is achieved, are not at all like historical accounts or hermeneutic activities. Rather, they are like other theoretical accounts in the natural and social sciences.

Another example of an attempt to characterize psychoanalysis as essentially an historical discipline is found in Sherwood's (1969) *The Logic of Psychoanalytic Explanation.* Sherwood tells us that psychoanalytic explanation is best thought of as a "narrative" (of a patient's history and dynamics). Sensitive to the issue of reliability of knowledge, Sherwood suggests adequacy, comprehensiveness, and accuracy as the criteria by which psychoanalytic "narratives" should be evaluated. In a highly revealing comment, Sherwood notes that the adequacy, comprehensiveness, and accuracy of the "narrative" need not bear any systematic relationship to general psychoanalytic theory. I have attempted to discuss in detail the soundness of Sherwood's scheme elsewhere (Eagle, 1973). The point to which I want to call the reader's attention here is the confusion between therapeutic and theoretical perspectives evidenced in Sherwood's formulations. On the one hand, the basic descriptive unit he suggests—the psychoanalytic "narrative"—is obviously appropriate to and, indeed, taken from the clinical–therapeutic context. On the other hand, the criteria he suggests for evaluating these "narratives" have little to do with the clinical context and are more appropriate to evaluating theoretical accounts. Furthermore, and this is most striking, the criterion most appropriate to the clinical context—therapeutic effectiveness—is not even included among the evaluative criteria.

Why would one want to construct an adequate, comprehensive, and accurate "narrative" about a person if not for the belief that such an account will somehow play a critical role in the therapeutic situation? (We have already been told by Sherwood that the individual "narrative" bears no necessary systematic relationship to the general theory of psychoanalysis.) Sherwood, following Freud, seems to make the implicit assumption that a veridical "narrative" will also necessarily be a therapeutically effective one and is, therefore, concerned with the accuracy of the "narrative." But, of course, efficacy cannot just be presumed. Furthermore, in order to determine whether or not effectiveness and veridicality are closely related, one would, of course, need to determine veridicality and effectiveness independently of each other.

Psychoanalysis is a peculiar therapeutic discipline in that historically the *truth* of an intervention has been a relevant and even primary consideration (for example, consider insight and making the unconscious conscious as therapeutic goals of psychoanalysis). From the beginning, psychoanalysis has been bedeviled by this question of the validity of interpretations. Freud's response to this issue is characterized by Grünbaum (1980) as the "tally argument." That is, Freud (1916–1917, pp. 448–463) assumed and insisted that only interpretations which "tally with what is real" are therapeutically effective. Hence, therapeutic success vouchsafed the validity of interpretations (and the theory of personality from which the interpretations are derived). Of course, as Grünbaum has shown with great clarity, this argument does not hold. But the "tally" assumption continues to be made implicitly. As I have tried to show above, Sherwood is concerned, for example, with the accuracy of psychoanalytic "narratives" in the clinical context because he implicitly assumes that is *relevant* in that context.[71]

The belief that under appropriate conditions the truth is not only enlightening but freeing is a value that has always informed psychoanalysis. And it is a value that many of us share. In my view, it is ultimately this value that is rejected and negated by the hermeneutic position. However, this value is not upheld by a confusion or conflation of veridicality and effectiveness. I explore this issue further in the next chapter.

16

PSYCHOANALYSIS AS THERAPY AND THEORY:
Veridicality and Effectiveness

I believe that from the beginning psychoanalysis has confused its therapeutic and "research" (that is, theoretical-explanatory) goals. As noted, Freud believed that psychoanalysis should be remembered more for the truths it yielded than for its therapeutic effectiveness. This is perhaps a legitimate aspiration, but a serious problem arises when one considers that these truths are being offered to patients in treatment rather than research subjects. The profound moral dilemma is resolved if one makes the comforting assumption that because suffering and illness are relieved when one gains insightful understanding of certain truths about oneself, the therapeutic and "research" goals can be pursued simultaneously. Quite happily, with this assumption, the accuracy of the analysts' formulations, the patient's insights, and the furtherance of psychoanalytic knowledge all converge and can all be pursued simultaneously in the normal clinical psychoanalytic situation.

This harmonious picture and fortunate convergence of purposes is dramatically upset by some considerations and questions which analysts have tended to avoid. For example, what if insight and self-knowledge are not all that therapeutic? And what if what has been presumed to be insightful self-knowledge turns out to be, in part at least, compliance with the therapists' expectations and theoretical persuasion? It will be noted that in order to answer these (and other similar) questions, one must have independent measures of effectiveness and veridicality of interpretations. Quite remarkably,

172

psychoanalysis has not addressed itself systematically to either issue. It has assumed veridicality on the basis of presumed effectiveness (Freud's "tally" argument) and has assumed effectiveness on the basis of presumed veridicality (insight and making the unconscious conscious are therapeutic—the truth that "shall set ye free"). But neither effectiveness nor veridicality have been independently and systematically demonstrated.

To a certain extent, psychoanalysis has been able to escape rigorous accountability because of a widely shared value that the pursuit of insight, awareness, and self-knowledge, even if it does not lead to specific therapeutic gains (e.g., the removal of symptoms), is nevertheless a legitimate, even noble, endeavor. Indeed it may be, but, as I have tried to show, this begs the question just as long as we do not know to what extent that which is called insight or self-knowledge is just that or is rather the product of compliance and suggestion. (I remind the reader once again of Marmor's (1982) observation regarding the Freudian "insights" of Freudian patients and the Jungian "insights" of Jungian patients).

One can respond to the difficulties inherent in the veridicality issue by dispensing with it altogether and justifying it entirely on pragmatic grounds of effectiveness. One does not ask, for example, whether a drug is true or whether systematic desensitization is true or whether a trusting therapeutic relationship is true. One only asks to what degree and in what ways they are effective and how accurate are the theoretical accounts of whatever degree and kind of effectiveness they may have. To a certain extent, this picture is implicit in recent discussions of psychoanalytic therapy. That is, much less emphasis is placed on insight-producing veridical interpretations and much more on other factors, such as mirroring empathy and, in general, the therapeutic relationship. The issue of veridicality obviously is relevant only to interpretations and not to these other factors. Hence, to the extent that those other factors are stressed, the issue of veridicality does not apply.[72]

But the point to be noted here is that if psychoanalysis is to be justified entirely on the pragmatic grounds of effectiveness, it takes its place alongside other therapeutic interventions in which veridicality of the intervention also does not apply. In taking this place, issues of accountability and cost-effectiveness become paramount. For one can no longer justify as easily one's interventions on the grounds that they provide self-knowledge or on the basis of the simple faith that "the truth shall set ye free." One can only justify them on the basis that they are effective.

Is it the case, however, that psychoanalysis needs to dispense entirely with the question of the veridicality of its formulations and interpretations? Insofar as psychoanalysis is a theory of human behavior as well as a therapy, one would expect that, like any other theory, it would be concerned with the veridicality and validity of its formulations whatever their relationship to the therapeutic situation. How is that issue to be met? It seems to me that what has emerged from the prior discussion (as well as from other sources, such as Grünbaum's [1980] demonstration of the epistemically contaminated status of the clinical data) is that, contrary to the long-cherished belief on the part of the psychoanalytic community, the psychoanalytic situation is not the appropriate arena for testing the validity of psychoanalytic theoretical formulations.

While, in common with many interpersonal encounters, the clinical situation is an appropriate arena for empathic understanding of and even (partial) identification with a given individual patient and is certainly an appropriate arena for attempting to help that individual, and can be an important heuristic source for generating hypotheses, there is little in that situation that can yield reliable criteria for the systematic determination of validity of formulations. As we have seen, empathy and "cognitive identification" do not represent such criteria.

It seems to me that there is no alternative to the conclusion that the validity of psychoanalytic formulations are best determined outside the consulting room. Only outside the clinical situation can one obtain the proper controls and the proper degree of rigor which permit reliable conclusions and reasonable generalizability. The fact is that, like any other theory, psychoanalytic theory consists of a body of propositions (however informal or imprecise) *generally* applicable to human behavior. The individual patient represents an occasion for the individual application of this general body of propositions. Hence, quite contrary to the commonly held view in the psychoanalytic community, if one is interested in validity or veridicality, as opposed to effectiveness or something like the therapist's or patient's feelings of understanding or being understood, then it is degree of confirmation of the general hypothesis from which the particular interpretation has been tested that lends probabilistic support to the particular interpretation or formulation in a given individual case.

Critical judgment is essential in deciding *which* general hypotheses are most pertinent to the individual phenomena under consideration. It is in this area as well as in the elaboration of case-specific qualifications that the intuitive, even artistic, components of clinical judgment are most apparent. I am not minimizing the importance of these factors in ongoing clinical formulations and treatment in individual cases. But their importance should not blind one to the role of general propositions as the foundation of these individual clinical formulations.

The most substantiated psychoanalytic formulations are so by virtue of solid support from outside the clinical situation; and conversely, those least substantiated or even refuted have also been so rendered by extra-clinical evidence. Consider a few examples from the latter category: We have already seen that evidence from infant research throws into serious question theoretical assumptions that the infant goes through a period of "normal autism" (Mahler, 1968) or, early on, is in a state of primary narcissism or totally incapable of differentiation between self and other (see Klein [1980] and Stern [1980] for further discussion of this issue). We have also seen that general "secondary drive" theories of infant-mother attachment (of which Freud's "anaclitic" theory is an example) have been essentially refuted by the classic Harlow (1958) experiment and other related evidence. Other examples of psychoanalytic hypotheses refuted by evidence originating from outside the psychoanalytic situation include the symptom-substitution hypothesis and the claim that all dreams are generated by wish-fulfillment. With regard to the first, there is now considerable evidence that the therapeutic amelioration or removal of a symptom (via a behavior therapy technique, for example) presumably without resolution of the underlying conflict does not necessarily lead to the substitution of a new symptom. As for the wish-fulfillment hypothesis, the extensive recent research on REM sleep indicates that in human sleep dreaming occurs approximately every 90 minutes, that all mammals dream, and that dreaming is a psychological aspect of a complex and basic physiological state which certainly does not require a push for wish fulfillment as a trigger for its initiation.

As for examples of psychoanalytic formulations that find support from outside the clinical situation, consider Fairbairn's basic assumption that libido is "object-seeking" and Balint's (1937) claim that "primary object love" is a more accurate characterization of the infant than "primary narcissism." As we have seen, there is abundant evidence that human infants reach out for and begin processing stimuli almost as soon as they are born, show selective preferences for certain kinds of external stimulation, and are extremely responsive to objects that yield, in Harlow's (1958) language, "contact comfort" (tactile stimulation) and kinesthetic stimulation. (As noted earlier, all this evidence decisively refutes any notion of innate "primary hatred" of objects.)

The above "object-seeking" propensities can obviously be linked to an inborn attachment system, as posited by Bowlby (1969). The infant is born with a behavioral repertoire which both provides signals (e.g., smiling, vocalizing) and more directly and actively (e.g., sucking, clasping) accomplishes the "set goal" of achieving proximity to the caregiver. The evidence for an inborn attachment behavioral system obviously does not come from the clinical situation, but from observations of infant behavior and infant-mother interactions across a wide range of species. The embeddedness of the attachment concept in a broad biological evolutionary context gives it a solidity which cannot be provided by clinical data alone.

Although these formulations do not derive from the clinical situation, they do, indeed, carry implications for that situation. Let me add, however, that even if there were absolutely no immediate or evident therapeutic implications, the refutation and confirmation of psychoanalytic formulations regarding human nature and human behavior would still seem to me to be an essential task. I reiterate the reminder that psychoanalysis is a theory of human nature as well as a therapy. However, I believe these refutations and confirmations carry therapeutic implications (even if not with regard to specific techniques), some of which have already been absorbed. For example, the increasing emphasis on the relationship itself as a primary therapeutic vehicle reflects a theoretical shift in the image of human nature from an instinctual gratification-driven and tension-reducing organism to an object-seeking and object-needing one.

I would be surprised if the relinquishment of the symptom-substitution hypothesis did not have obvious concrete implications for treatment. At the very least, it would suggest that one need not automatically frown upon as futile those therapeutic methods and goals which focus primarily on symptom relief and amelioration. At most, it is possible and perhaps, in certain situations, even likely that symptom relief can itself serve as a vehicle for further personality growth. As for the implications of dream studies, the weakening of the wish-fulfillment hypothesis (or at least that aspect of it which argues that wishes are the necessary motive forces for the occurrence of dreams) plus other positive findings seem to support the very hypothesis considered and rejected by Freud to the effect that dreams are sleeping cognitions which reflect our preoccupations, our unfinished business, and are essentially attempts at problem-solving and mastery.

Finally, as an example of findings outside the clinical context which have direct implications for clinical formulations (and interventions), I refer once again to the syndrome of agoraphobia. Here, findings and concepts from a number of diverse areas converge on the conclusion that most frequently agoraphobia essentially represents a crisis in separation-individuation or, as Fairbairn (1952) put it, a "conflict between the progressive urge towards separation from the object and the regressive lure of identification with the object . . ." (p. 43). This conclusion is supported by as wide a range of evidence as the relationship between security of attachment and degree of exploratory behavior; the relationship between a "safe base" and exploration; prior incidence of school phobias; family history; and nature of the marital relationship. As I argued earlier, these findings then contribute to a more secure base for the development of specific and idiosyncratic clinical formulations and interventions in the individual case.

Many psychoanalysts, with their exclusive emphasis on case histories, appear to have made the assumption that the acquisition of psychoanalytic knowledge moves only in the opposite direction—that is, from individual case to theoretical propositions. However, the assumption that psychoanalytic explanation is, above all, concerned with the individual case has led to much confusion. It has led, for example, as we have seen, to Sherwood's (1969) suggestion that the individual psychoanalytic "narrative" be judged according to criteria that are more appropriate for evaluating general theoretical explanations. This may strike one as a naïve question, but why should one want to know everything possible about an individual patient? What therapeutic purpose does it serve? Or is it to be justified mainly or solely on the "research grounds" of furthering psychoanalytic knowledge? If so, we are back to the original issue of veridicality and Sherwood's proposal that "accuracy" serve as one of the validity criteria for evaluating "narratives" helps us not at all, since we are not told how accuracy is to be judged and that is precisely the question with which we started.

"Privileged Access"

Part of what underlies the focus on the individual case is the assumption that the patient's acknowledgment is a central, and for some (e.g. Mischel, 1963; 1966) necessary criterion for evaluating the validity of psychoanalytic interpretations. Quite obviously, this criterion is inextricably linked to the clinical situation, insofar as the reference is to the acknowledgment of an analytic patient and insofar as the argument is elaborated to refer to "delayed" acknowledgment following insight and the lifting of repression. The central role given to acknowledgment, either immediate or delayed, in turn rests on the philosophical assumption that the individual has "privileged access" regarding what he experiences, desires, wants, wishes, etc. Hence, in the final analysis, it is held that only the individual's acknowledgment of what he wants, desires, etc., can validate an interpretation or formulation in which attributions of want or desire are attributed to another. In this scheme, unconscious wishes and desires are treated as extensions of their ordinary counterparts and hence, "privileged access" is held to continue to apply, even if in a delayed sense.

I have dealt with this issue at greater length elsewhere (Eagle, 1982c), but I want to repeat the following points here: While a strong case can be made for the "privileged access" argument in regard to ongoing phenomenal experiences, the strength of the "privileged access" case is inversely related to the distance from immediate experience of the phenomena in question. The more distant from immediate experience, the more fallible an observer's reports of "inner events." For example, a report of a past event or past experience is as subject to error and distortion as any other report. Or, as another example, a life pattern of actions may be incongruous with or even contradict what one says one's motives, wishes, and aims are. Hence, there is only the weakest case for applying the "privileged access" doctrine to phenomena removed from direct experience. But it is precisely such phenomena—unconscious wishes and motives, for example—with which psychoanalysis is mainly concerned.

Some aspects of the psychoanalytic conception of insight are based on an implicit and modified version of the "privileged access" doctrine. In its simplest form, the idea is that after repressions are lifted, the patient directly and consciously experiences those wishes, desires, ideas, etc., which were hitherto unconscious. Hence, the patient's acknowledgment has a special privileged status insofar as he is reporting what is now a direct conscious experience. However, as we have seen, the fact that patients tend to "experience" and report the "insights" in accord with their therapists' theoretical persuasion upsets this simple notion of insight and suggests a much more complex and "constructional" process in which expectations, suggestion, and compliance are all operative. Furthermore, the kinds of things about which patients report insight often involve subtle formulations which are not directly linked to immediate experience. (For example, awareness of a pattern of behavior or awareness of subtle factors implicated in anxiety.) Hence, there is no good reason to assign such insight the status of "privileged access."

The very notion of unconscious wish (and allied concepts) as simply a conscious wish plus repression (or as a latent or potential wish) seems to me a naïve and inaccurate understanding of that concept. Such an understanding treats the concept as essentially an experiential one rather than as a theoretical and inferential construct designed to account for certain (difficult to explain) behavior (see Rubinstein's [1976] discussion of this concept). The placing of unconscious wish as a quasi-experiential concept then leads to the proposal that delayed acknowledgment is a critical criterion and to the bestowal of "privileged access" upon such acknowledgments.

Another factor that casts doubt on the primacy of acknowledgments as a criterion is defense. Given the ubiquitousness of defensive processes, why should one insist on acknowledgment? What if acknowledgment is never forthcoming? What if the general clinical formulation on which the interpretation is based has been well established, and what if the interpretation accounts for all the facts, is predictive, etc.? Would one still insist on acknowledgment before judging the validity of the interpretation? If an explanatory account of a person's behavior is adequate according to the usual criteria by which explanations are evaluated, why should it necessarily require that person's agreement and acknowledgment? It seems to me that insistence on the necessity of the patient's acknowledgment in determining the veridicality of interpretation is but another example of the confounding of therapeutic and explanatory aims. While the patients' acknowledgment may be critical in the therapeutic context, why should it play a special role in the explanatory context? This is a particularly apt question when one considers psychoanalytic explanations outside the clinical context where there is no patient to do any acknowledging (or disowning).

Once one recognizes that the individual patient's acknowledgment is neither a necessary nor sufficient condition for the validation of psychoanalytic interpretations (and certainly not a necessary or sufficient condition for the testing of general psychoanalytic propositions), still another basis for the epistemic value of the individual case history is undercut. And we are forced from still another point of view to face the conclusion that we must rely mainly on extra-clinical sources for the testing and validation of psychoanalytic interpretations and propositions. Interest in the individual case and individual "narrative" can only be justified on therapeutic grounds or on the grounds that it contributes to general psychoanalytic theory. As for the latter, there is no obvious justification for an elaborate and comprehensive individual "narrative." Whether the individual case history provides reliable knowledge and makes a reliable contribution to psychoanalytic theory is open to serious question. Given all the earlier discussed problems associated with that method—for example, the epistemically contaminated status of the clinical data—I do not believe that it is a reliable source for the testing of general psychoanalytic formulations and hypotheses, however useful it may be heuristically. Hence, I reiterate my earlier conclusion that data from outside the clinical situation are likely to constitute the best source for rigorous and systematic evaluation of psychoanalytic formulations.

Many recent formulations in psychoanalytic theory which continue to be based on the individual case history are taken as indications of progress in psychoanalytic knowledge. It is not clear in what sense they constitute progress. It seems to me that, rather than constituting progress, they are illustrative of the futility of relying wholly or primarily on data derived from the clinical situations and of the necessity of measuring one's formulations against more rigorously developed extant knowledge. My impression is that much current psychoanalytic theorizing is more saturated with jargon than earlier traditional psychoanalytic writing. Indeed, much current psychoanalytic literature includes formulations so vague and so jargon-filled that there is serious question as to whether they have any clear empirical meaning. Often, the necessary initial step in the approach to this material is to unravel what is really being said and thereby recover whatever empirical content resides in these formulations.[73] Is this to be viewed as progress?

I am under the impression that many current psychoanalytic writers and theorists pay far less attention to the body of extant knowledge outside psychoanalysis than did Freud. This tendency is partly encouraged by promulgation of the belief that psychoanalysis relies on distinctive methods (empathy and "cognitive identification," as we have seen) for acquiring knowledge and hence need not concern itself with the question of whether such knowledge is congruent with what is known outside psychoanalysis. The almost studied neglect and ignorance of research information and knowledge outside psychoanalysis also seems to me to be related to the conception of psychoanalysis as a hermeneutic or interpretive discipline and to the almost exclusive concern with the individual "narrative" and case history. We have seen earlier how the neglect of infant research, for example, permits developmental formulations which are not only unsupported by evidence, but which indeed are contrary to what has come to be known about the nature of infancy. Are we to view these formulations and the elaborate theoretical edifices to which they lead as indications of progress?

We have seen striking examples of how the case history can be employed by adherents of different theoretical schools to provide selective evidence for their particular point of view. I remind the reader of the point noted by Gedo (1980) to the effect that while the analysts in the Goldberg (1978) casebook found extensive evidence of self-defects and practically none for oedipal conflicts, New York Psychoanalytic Institute analysts, working with seemingly similar patients, found repeated instances of oedipal conflict and sufficiently little evidence for self-defects to justify complete failure even to refer to such pathology.

As noted earlier, given the fact that behavior is often opaque with regard to underlying motives and determinants, it is often possible to interpret a given behavior as providing evidence for one's theoretical point of view. The case history exquisitely lends itself, not only to selective interpretation, but to selective culling of evidence. After all, it is not verbatim accounts that are reported, but renditions that reflect the analysts' conception of what is important and what is worth reporting. It is naïve to believe that analysts are somehow immune to the influence of all those selective and distorting factors in cognitive organization and memory that afflict the rest of mankind. It seems clear that while the case history may have rich heuristic value in generating ideas and hypotheses, only very rarely, if ever, does it have probative value. That one can cite mirroring and idealizing transferences in analysis and, in general, adult patients' reports to support an etiological theory concerning the causal effect of lack of early mirroring on the development of self-defects is just one blatant example of the improper use of case history data and the attempt to employ such data probatively. Given such grossly inadequate conceptions of the nature of evidence, one must again ask whether recent changes in psychoanalytic formulations constitute progress.

It seems to me that it is time that psychoanalytic writers recognized that the use of the case history to confirm a particular theoretical point of view is simply inadequate. I entirely agree with recent comments by Holzman (1976): "It is therefore noteworthy that our 80-year-old discipline never developed further canons for research [than case vignettes] or for judging the worth of contributions. Large segments of what we teach can neither be confirmed nor proved false. New ideas in psychoanalysis provoke some essays for and against, but these are not sufficient. Unlike . . . literary criticism, we require more than such essays. We need proposals to test the ideas systematically, and unfortunately there are too few calls for such tests" (p. 269).

PART
IV

COMMON THEMES

If one takes a broad perspective and asks whether there are common elements in the different perspectives presented, what answers emerge? Are there common themes discernible in the different formulations I have discussed throughout this book?

17

INDIVIDUATION AND SELF-DIFFERENTIATION

A salient theme that is clear in the work of Mahler, Kohut, and Fairbairn is that *the* central dimension of psychological development is the move from a state of complete dependence and relative lack of differentiation between self and other to increasing definition of self and to increasing independence (or, as Fairbairn prefers, mature dependence). Although different terminology is used and although there are different emphases and elaborations, all three seem to be talking about the same basic dimension. For Mahler, it is the move from symbiosis to separation-individuation; for Kohut, it is the move from complete reliance on the self-object for self-definition and self-esteem to self-cohesiveness and to pursuits fueled by one's own ambitions, values, and ideals; and for Fairbairn, it is the move from infantile dependence and primary identification to differentiation and mature dependence.

All three seem to be saying that the main psychological significance of the object lies, not in the fact that it provides the occasion for the instinctual investments and gratifications emphasized by Freud, but in its role in making possible the development of self-integrity and independence. And all three also seem to share the view that at least the most serious and recalcitrant psychopathology is linked, not to conflicts centering on instinctual wishes (that is, id-ego conflicts), but to failures to negotiate successfully the development of separation-individuation.[74] Or, to quote Loewald (1979), "Problems of self-object differentiation, with its inherent issues of the polarity between indi-

185

viduation and emerging union, probably are not less but more universal and deep-seated than psychosexual conflicts of the oedipal nucleus
of neurosis" (p. 161).

If one translates Kohut's structural language into a motivational one,
he is implicitly saying in his writings that so critical and all important
is the need for self-cohesiveness and for self-esteem that when this
need is disrupted or somehow unmet, the prepotent motivational aims
of behavior, including compensatory and defensive behavior, become
increasingly directed toward these issues. Thus, according to Kohut,
destructive aggression, infantile sexual aims, and various kinds of infantile and pathological object relations—for example, the wish to
merge with an omnipotent self-object—are all reactions to and
motivated by the failure of an "enfeebled and fragmentation-prone
self" to achieve self-cohesiveness and reliable self-esteem. In effect,
Kohut is proposing a hierarchy of motivational aims in which it is
impossible to pursue more developmentally advanced assertive and
sexual aims (characteristic of the oedipal period) until the more basic
and elementary needs for self-cohesiveness and self-esteem have
been met to a reasonable degree. To the extent that these basic needs
are not adequately met, sexual and aggressive aims become subordinated to them.

One can view the development of self-cohesiveness or, in Mahler's
(1968) terms, of separation-individuation as a natural outgrowth and
line of development from the attachment instinctual system. One
takes for granted in animal and human development that the young of
the species become increasingly independent of mother, first engaging in play and exploration and later participating in all the adult
activities of the group. While in animals this development can be
viewed primarily in terms of physical and mental growth, of acquisition of behavioral repertoires, of various skills, and of establishing
one's place in a social hierarchy, human psychological development
must also include the development of a separate sense of self.

As Fromm (Munroe, 1955, p. 365) has noted, a sense of self is the
product of an evolutionary trend toward increasing individuation. A
sense of identity and of self is not present on lower phylogenetic
levels and may make a rudimentary appearance only with primates
(e.g., Gallup, 1977; 1979).[74A] Given the evolutionary "selection" of
this property, there is good reason to believe that it serves important
adaptive functions. One can speculate that pursuit of the superordinate aims of self-esteem and self-integrity is an efficient hierarchical
way of "guaranteeing" the pursuit of other needs and aims necessary
for survival. That is, psychological development in humans would not

be complete without the development of a sense of who one is and without the capacity to generate self-initiated plans, intentions, aims, and projects which, although implemented through the exercise of one's developing skills and abilities, are relatively meaningless without the former capacity. Clearly, Mahler *et al.* (1975) have in mind such phenomena as a sense of separate self and the capacity to initiate and pursue aims and plans. In short, the move from symbiotic dependence to individuation and independence is, above a certain phylogenetic level, a universal story. Most animals are genetically programmed to follow this line of development and survival of the particular species depends upon it. In humans, the universal story takes on a particular twist in that the move from attachment to individuation also involves the development of selfhood and all that it implies. This is truly an invariant and ubiquitous aspect of human development, certainly as universal and as biologically based as sexual and aggressive impulses and behavior.

While the development of individuation, autonomy, and selfhood may be a universal story, it is legitimate to wonder about the reasons for what seems to be increased pathology in this general area and for what seems to be a recent special sensitivity to both these dimensions and to the related issue of narcissism. One point that needs to be made is that the general sensitivity to these issues is not all that recent. As far back as 1945, Fenichel wrote that "our present society seems to be characterized by conflicts between ideals of individual independence . . . and regressive longings for passive dependence" (p. 464). Also the concern with issues of self in the writings of Sullivan (e.g., 1953, and with the importance of dependency needs in the work of, for example, Horney [1945]) were viewed as superficial and excessively 'cultural' because they were not viewed in the context of instinct theory and psychosexual development.

However, while the concern with these issues may not be all that recent, they are distinctly modern, as Fenichel suggests when he writes about "our present society." Furthermore, such concern has become more extensive and more systematized. That the issues of individuation and self-differentiation and the related ones of passivity and infantile dependence are cross-cultural ones is clearly suggested in an interesting study of *The Anatomy of Dependence* in Japanese culture written by a psychodynamically oriented Japanese psychiatrist (Doi, 1973). He defines the Japanese noun *amae* as roughly referring to the emotion felt by the infant at the breast and to infantile behavior which is based on the assumption that one will be indulged. He also notes that "the *amae* mentality could be defined as the attempt to deny the fact of separation" and that "the *amae* psychology works to foster a sense of oneness between mother and child" (p. 75). Interestingly, what controls or checks *amae* is *jibun*, which can be roughly translated as ego or self. Doi writes that a person who has *jibun* can control and cope with *amae*, while one with no *jibun* is at the mercy of *amae*. Also, people who have not adequately dealt with *amae* or who suffer from frustrated *amae* (one patient complains that he wants to experience *amae* with others, as he did with his parents, but "nobody lets me") are over-sensitive to separation and stranger anxiety (*hitomishiri*)—in short, what is observed is a relationship between adequacy of symbiotic gratification and security of attachment on the one hand and capacity to experience security and pleasure in separation and separate functioning. Especially interesting is Doi's speculation that increased pathology of *amae* is a function of a shift in Japanese society and in social relationships broadly described as a shift from *Gemeinschaft* to *Gesellschaft*, which, in turn, increases the likelihood and the incidence of frustrated *amae*. In other words, the shift from a society in which community, intimate bonds, a feeling of belonging (*Gemeinschaft*) are the rule to a society in which more distant and formal associations, as, for example, obtain in business transactions (*Gesellschaft*) are typical, results in the greater frustration and pathology of *amae*.

What is especially interesting about Doi's explanation is its contrast with psychoanalytic attempts to account for seeming shifts in the nature of pathology and in today's modal patient and perhaps, in less extreme form, today's modal personality. While Doi's account leaves room for the influence of factors at the social-cultural level, psychoanalytic explanations tend to reduce the social-cultural to the level of child-rearing practices and influences. Thus, Bader and Philipson (1980) suggest that because contemporary women tend to raise their children in isolation and are cut off from extended adult relationships and meaningful work, they seek satisfaction of their psychological needs in their children, which, in turn, leads to the undesirable consequences of maternal anxiety regarding separation-individuation and the child's emotional conviction that his or her own moves toward autonomy caused mother's frustration and unhappiness. And Kohut (1977) ventures the speculation that "the understimulation due to parental remoteness that is a pathogenic factor in disorders of the self is a manifestation of a disorder of the self in the parent" (p. 274). Kohut does not appear to recognize that his "explanation" merely pushes the question one step and one generation back.

Why are we suddenly witnessing an increase of parental disorders of the self? I have strong doubts that shifts in character formation and character type, including their pathological expressions (if such be the case), can be explained adequately by remaining entirely at the level of child-rearing.

I want to note, finally, that even if it is true that pathological disturbances in the area of separation-individuation and self-integrity are a particularly modern phenomenon, it may nevertheless be the case that separation-individuation and related *dimensions* are universal and that their importance for development is not limited to a particular historical era.

18

OBJECT-SEEKING AND OBJECT RELATIONS

Beyond the shared basic theme regarding self-differentiation discussed in the last chapter, there appear to be important divergences, at least between Fairbairn and Kohut. For Fairbairn, object-seeking is a basic propensity and the need for objects and object relations is a lifelong one. If this need is not met by relationships with real external objects, one substitutes relations with internalized objects. By contrast, Kohut often writes as if he believes that while objects are developmentally necessary for the establishment of self-cohesiveness, once one has achieved "healthy narcissism," one can enjoy the "luxury" of object instinctual investments and pleasures, but can a live and rich and meaningful life without them. For Kohut, it appears to be the pursuit of ambitions, values, and ideals and the self-esteem accruing from these activities rather than the establishment of satisfying object relations that makes life worthwhile. (I have referred earlier to Kohut's belief that traditional psychoanalytic theory overemphasizes object relations and views narcissism pejoratively and to his intention to correct what he believes to be an imbalance). I suppose that Kohut may have considered that for an adult to believe that the object is necessary for psychic intactness or survival bespeaks a lack of self-cohesiveness and a continuing relation to a self-object rather than a fully separate other.

Despite this important difference, it seems to me that it may be possible to reconcile to some extent Kohut's and Fairbairn's views in this area. If one accepts the proposition that I have put forth elsewhere (Eagle, 1982a) that interests, values, and ideals serve vital object relations functions, it becomes possible to view these activities, not simply in terms of "healthy narcissism," but as expressions of the universal object-relational needs and tendencies stressed by Fairbairn. This is not an arbitrary proposition which simply labels as object-relational a set of activities Kohut views as narcissistic. There is a good deal of evidence which I have summarized in the earlier paper referred to above and in Chapter 6 attesting to the fact that the cognitive-affective links provided *both* by interpersonal relations and by interests and values make possible psychological intactness under stressful and dire circumstances. Indeed, in these circumstances in which normal interpersonal relations are disrupted or not available (e.g., solitary confinement), the role of internalized interests and values in maintaining psychic integrity becomes all the more critical. Thus, it has been shown that among the factors which make for survival among prisoners of war are not only psychological links to others (e.g., one's family or countrymen), but interests of one kind or another. Strassman *et al.* (1956), in writing about United States prisoners of war repatriated by the Chinese and North Koreans in 1953, noted that "two things seemed to save the man close to 'apathy' death: getting him on his feet doing something, no matter how trivial, and getting him interested in some current or future problem" (p. 99). (See also Nardini, [1952], who reports similar findings.)

A common theme in autobiographical accounts of people under the dreadful conditions of imprisonment and concentration camps is the role of interests and values in increasing the likelihood of survival and in maintaining psychological integrity. This is true of people with as wide a range of backgrounds as Malcolm X (1964) and Victor Frankl (1962), George Jackson (1970) and Bruno Bettleheim (1960). One finds in their autobiographical accounts of physical and psychological survival striking similarities regarding the sustaining role played by connections to people as well as to interests and values. In a recent review of Bettleheim's (1979) book entitled *Surviving and Other Essays,* Robinson (1979) writes that "Bettleheim makes what is perhaps the finest point when he notes that the prisoners who did in fact survive were those who lived not for life's sake but for some ideal— cultural or religious—that transcended them" (p. 7). A similar account is given by Cohen (1953), a Dutch physician who both describes his own concentration camp experiences and summarizes many other accounts. Cohen poses the question, "What individuals were best fitted to adapt themselves, so that there was at least a possibility of their surviving a concentration camp?" (p. 147). He answers that "many writers, . . . agree that it was of the greatest importance that a person had some spiritual life" (p. 148). And he adds that "the conception 'spiritual life' is here used to comprise all spiritual values in their widest sense, such as morality, knowledge, emotion, intellect, character, religion, etc." He cites another writer, DeWind, who observes that "generally speaking, we see in the camp that anyone in whose life there are certain religious bonds (using the term in its most comprehensive sense, so as to include the devotion to a political system or a humanist view of life), manages the most quickly, after the initial stupor. It is therefore no mere accident that convinced Christians as well as the Communists, who would seem to be their psychological opposites, should have shown the greatest power of resistance in camps, and even managed to set up certain forms of anti-Fascist organization" (p. 148). There is also evidence that under conditions of sensory deprivation, isolation, and various forms of stress, activities which contribute "stimulus nutriment" (e.g., composing a poem) help preserve psychic intactness. It is in their contribution to "stimulus nutriment" that interests and values play an adaptive role in maintaining ego functions under conditions of sensory deprivation.

Rapaport (1958) proposes that the ego requires "stimulus nutriment" in order to function adequately and cites as evidence for this hypothesis the finding that ego functions are disrupted by sensory deprivation (e.g., Bexton *et al.*, 1954). He proposes further a dual autonomy such that autonomy of the ego from the id is facilitated by "stimulus nutriment" from the environment, and autonomy of the ego from the environment is facilitated by "stimulus nutriment" from the id (e.g., affective signals). And, indeed, Rapaport's hypothesis is supported by Goldberger and Holt's (1969) finding that subjects who are capable of "regression in the service of the ego" (as expressed, for example, in capacity to engage in reverie and fantasy) are better able to withstand the cutoff of environmental stimuli entailed by the sensory deprivation experience.

Although Rapaport emphasizes drives as the "ultimate guarantees" of the autonomy of the ego from the environment, he also discusses the "proximal guarantees" deriving from ego and superego structures which would include ideologies, values, and interests. If one can reformulate Rapaport's ideas into nondrive terms, one can say that the presence of a rich inner life facilitates the autonomy of the ego from the environment and that a diverse and engaging environment, plus an interest in and ability to respond to it, facilitates the autonomy of the ego from inner demands.

Of course, the first half of the above statement is precisely what

Cohen and other survivors of imprisonment and ordeals have reported—namely, that a rich inner "spiritual life" permitted some independence from the harsh and intolerable environment and thereby facilitated survival. Put in Rapaport's language of "stimulus nutriment," one can say that people without "nutriment" from inner sources of interests, values, fantasy, etc., are more dependent upon input from environmental stimuli. Hence, they are in greater difficulty when environmental stimulation is either disrupted or intolerable. By contrast, those people who receive "nutriment" from inner resources are more independent of environmental vicissitudes.

One may ask why "stimulus nutriment" should be so crucial for maintenance of ego intactness. Miller's (1962) interpretation of the isolation and stress data is that some kind of "mental exercise," which he describes as "the very essence of ego-activity," is the critical element in preserving ego intactness. This explanation may be appropriate to isolation situations (e.g., sensory deprivation experiments or solitary confinement), where environmental input is severely reduced and inner input can be seen as compensating, on a strictly quantitative basis, for reduced environmental input. It does not, however, seem to apply to other stress situations (e.g., concentration camps) where the issue is not reduced environmental input, but the intolerable quality of the environment. Even in the former case, however, Miller fails to note a critical nonquantitative aspect common to all forms of "mental exercise" used in preserving intactness. And that is the fact that all such activity involves a relationship to either objects or mnemic representations of objects in the world. This is true of all the activities mentioned by Miller, ranging from counting pebbles to composing poetry to becoming attached to spiders and cockroaches. In short, influenced by an ego psychological conception, Miller is led to ignore the object-relational aspect of the "mental exercises" that enhanced intactness.

Cohen's (1953) description of the survival-enhancing value of ideologies and cultural life will again be recalled. As Cohen and others have shown, these "cultural interests" permit escape from a harsh and intolerable environment into an inner life (in Rapaport's terms, they permit autonomy of the ego from the environment). But because the very inner life into which one escapes, by its very nature, is characterized by (internalized) cognitive and affective links to others, one's retreat is personal and yet not autistically personal. Although isolated from the current environment, the individual finds sustenance and support from "silent" links to an internalized cultural world. Because interests and values are structures which have internalized the cultural world, they permit autonomy both from the external environment and from the more idiosyncratic and autistic aspects of one's inner preoccupations.

Object Relations and "Transitional Objects"

The relationship between object relations and interests, values, and ideals is further elucidated by Winnicott's (1958) discussion of "transitional objects" and their importance during an intermediate stage in the movement toward individuation and autonomy. I spoke earlier of the child's early moves toward separation and autonomy and of the mother's role in facilitating this process. However, as Winnicott has shown (and, as reported above for the "blanket-attached" toddlers), at a certain stage in the child's development, objects other than mother are also called upon to facilitate this process. We are all familiar with the soothing and security-providing properties of the raggedy blanket or teddy bear and the particular role they play in situations of anxiety and psychological danger.[75] Winnicott has directly related these "transitional phenomena" to the establishment of culture and cultural interests and it would, therefore, be useful to trace and draw upon Winnicott's subtle and complex formulation in this area.

According to Winnicott, transitional phenomena are transitional in a number of senses. One, as noted above, at the most apparent level, phenomena are transitional because they occur at a transitional stage in which the child is moving from symbiosis to independence. Two, more subtly, transitional phenomena are transitional in a formal and cognitive sense. That is, as a *representation*, a transitional object is not actually taken to be the mother and yet is also not fully an abstract symbolic representation of her. The transitional object, then, is also transitional in the movement from concrete representation to the achievement of a true symbol. The child knows that the blanket or teddy bear is not the mother and yet he reacts *affectively* to these objects and derives comfort from them as if they were mother. Giving external objects the capacity to soothe and comfort permits a freer and safer exploration of and interest in the external world.

This suggests still a third important sense in which the transitional object and earlier transitional phenomena are transitional. The child is not called upon to decide whether the meanings experienced in the object are entirely his creation or whether they exist in the external world. In this sense, these meanings are intermediate between the subjective and the objective. In Winnicott's (1958) words, "Of the transitional object it can be said that it is a matter of agreement between us and the baby that we will never ask the question, 'Did you conceive of this or was it presented to you from without?' The important point is that no decision on this point is expected. The question is not to be formulated" (p. 239–240).

In the course of development the transitional objects of childhood are given up and "there is a gradual extension of range of interest" (p. 232). Although the specific transitional object loses meaning, it becomes "spread out over the whole intermediate territory between 'inner psychic reality' and 'the external world as perceived by two persons in common,' that is to say, over the whole cultural field" (p. 233). In other words, a process that began with external transitional objects becomes internalized as cultural interests and values.

As Winnicott notes, in the cultural areas of art, religion, etc., we also allow the question of subjective or objective, of whether it is my creation or part of the external world to be deferred. In this sense, cultural phenomena reflect both inner and outer reality. That is, because they are internalized, they are deeply personal and so to speak, can be carried around. And because they are consensually validated and communally shared, they speak to our need for connections to objects in the world.

Implied in Winnicott's posited link between transitional phenomena and later cultural activities and interests is the idea that a groundwork for cultural interests is the need to develop symbolic supportive substitutes for early sources of security and safety. In a sense, they represent internalized home bases which one must periodically return to before setting out again. In a very advanced manner we do what Harlow's monkeys and young children do when confronted with strange, complex, and novel situations. This is surely close to what Winnicott had in mind when he referred to certain cultural activities (e.g., music, poetry) as periodic therapeutic regressions and as similar to transitional phenomena.[76]

Finally, Winnicott's (1965) discussion of the "capacity to be alone" sheds light on the relationship between self-cohesiveness and object relations. The critical point made by Winnicott is that both the internalization of environmental ego supports and a sense of ego relatedness permit one to be alone without undue anxiety and without a sense of psychological isolation. That is, because one *feels* related to people (including images or symbols of them), one can be physically alone without feeling psychologically bereft. Just as the child feels related to his transitional object, which permits him to be soothed and comforted by its actual presence, so we, as adults, can feel related to "cultural interests," ideologies, and value systems, all of which constitute cognitive and affective links to the world and all of which permit us to feel related rather than isolated.[77]

The above discussion points to the conclusion that self-intactness or self-cohesiveness and object relations are inextricably linked, not only developmentally, but as an ongoing dynamic process. The very activities and abilities Kohut sees as narcissistic and as relatively autonomous of object relations—ambitions, values, ideals—are inherently object-relational in nature. They entail stable and internalized cognitive and affective links to objects in the broadest sense of the term.

19

THE PURSUIT OF SUPERORDINATE MOTIVES

Both Kohut and Fairbairn seem to view sex and aggression as entirely subordinate to issues of self-cohesiveness and object relations, respectively. Indeed, both, for example, refer to hostility as essentially a "deterioration" by-product of disturbances in the areas of self and/or object relations. The irony here is that while in Freud's formulations, the object and object relations are subordinated to sex and aggression, Kohut and Fairbairn reverse the process and tend to subordinate sex and aggression entirely to the vicissitudes of self development and object relations. It seems difficult for psychoanalytic (and other) theorists to resist the conviction that all behavior can be reduced to one or two basic and superordinate motives and aims. What tends to be overlooked by uncritical enthusiasts of self psychology and object relations is that reductionism can work in both directions—that is, while object relations and self can be reduced to sexual and aggressive motives, it is possible to reduce sexual and aggressive motives merely to transformations (including "deterioration" products) of self- and object-relational pursuits. They seem to find it too difficult to accept the reality of a multiplicity of motives and aims (or behavioral systems) which, while interacting with each other in complex ways, cannot be reduced to this or that presumably more basic, superordinate motive.[78]

While sexual and aggressive behavior and feelings are undoubtedly intertwined with object relations and with what Klein (1976) calls "self-values," they undoubtedly constitute distinct behavioral systems and are regulated by distinctive environmental and internal (e.g., hormonal) influences. While sexual and aggressive behavior and feelings are often elicited by situations and cues which have "self-value" and object relational significance, they are also elicited by other distinctive cues. For example, while it may be true, as Rochlin (1973) claims, that aggression is often released in response to threats to self-integrity and self-esteem, it is also facilitated by a wide range of factors, including modeling, observational learning, vicarious reinforcement, hypothalamic stimulation, testosterone level, and social contagion. Also, there are such simple facts as the widespread enjoyment derived from slapstick comedy or watching a boxing match. What are the relevant object-relational and self considerations in regard to such phenomena?

Similar considerations apply to sexual behavior and feelings. They are also elicited by a wide range of situations and internal events which are not necessarily and obviously linked to issues of object relations and self-integrity. Lust and hatred are both common human feelings and inform a good deal of behavior. It is arbitrary to assume that they are necessarily subordinated to and/or transformations of motives primarily linked to object relations and self-cohesiveness.

What *does* seem to be a legitimate question to ask is whether the sexual and aggressive behavioral systems are as critical for early personality development as is assumed by traditional Freudian theory. Here is where the criticisms and doubts raised by object-relations and self theorists are germane and receive support from recent evidence. Generally, the evidence supports the conclusion that factors such as degree and nature of sensory stimulation (including tactile and kinesthetic), infant-mother coordination, security of attachment, nature and degree of separations, and degree of "sensitive responsiveness" shown by the caregiver have a more critical role in early personality development than matters of aggression and sex, including the vicissitudes of deprivation and gratification at different psychosexual stages.

It is important to note that infant and childhood research has led to the discovery of such phenomena as the infant's remarkably complex cognitive abilities, his need for and responsiveness to sensory stimulation, his early attachment needs and responses, his response to separation, his struggles for separation-individuation, his dependence on an emotional "safe base" during early exploratory behavior, and so on. It has led to remarkably little additional discovery or solid information regarding the role of infantile sexuality. And I do not believe that this can be explained simply as a function of selective *direction* of research or defensive neglect of this area of behavior (a case of re-repression of the importance of sexuality). Rather, the early clinical formulations on infantile sexuality have virtually exhausted the subject and have not been especially heuristic in pointing to further findings and formulations.

The one interesting emendation I have come across during the last few years is G. S. Klein's (1976) suggestion that infantile sexuality is more accurately designated as infantile *sensuality*. All the evidence indicates that the infant is truly a sensual creature in the sense of being exquisitely sensitive to and requiring sensory stimulation in all modalities. However, this sensual propensity is inextricably linked to objects (how can one receive sensory stimulation without objects?) and object relations and is *not* accurately captured in talk about instinctual impulses seeking discharge. That is to say, it is not especially adequately captured in traditional formulations of libido theory and psychosexual development.

I have argued above that our behavior is characterized by a multiplicity of motives and aims which cannot be reduced or subordinated to one or two presumably basic and underlying motive systems. How does this argument jibe with the position which, as we have seen, is taken by a number of recent psychoanalytic theorists to the effect that self-integrity or self-unity is a superordinate motive in behavior? In order to answer this question, one needs to take a closer look at the concept of superordinate motive.

It seems clear that from the beginning of psychoanalysis, some variant of self-unity and self-integrity has served, in some sense, as a superordinate motive. Thus, from the very beginning, Freud (1893–1895) proposed the basic idea that certain traumatic memories and ideas are kept from conscious awareness because they are inimical and even repugnant to one's self-conception. That is, repression works to keep a particular self-conception intact. This basic idea is retained in all psychoanalytic conceptions of dynamic conflict and defense and is obviously what Klein (1976) is referring to when he talks about "fractionating" methods employed in an attempt to resolve incompatibilities and thereby protect self-integrity. However, even if the preservation of self-unity and self-integrity becomes a prepotent motive when it is threatened, it does not follow that it is *the* underlying motive in *all* or most of behavior or even that it is a ubiquitous and necessary component in all or most of behavior. To make this assumption is to duplicate Freud's thinking, merely substituting self-integrity for sexual motives.

Another difficulty with the positing of self-integrity as a superordinate motive is that, again similar to Freud's error in this context, it appears to confuse function with motive (see Moore, 1980). For example, while a wide range of behaviors may contribute to survival, it does not follow that survival is a *motive* for these behaviors. We may carry them out for a host of specific reasons and motives. Survival is likely to constitute a prepotent motive for behavior only when it is threatened.[79] Similarly, while a wide range of behaviors may contribute to self-unity and self-integrity, it does not follow that *that* is the aim or motive for these behaviors. Rather, it is likely that each of these behaviors is being pursued for a variety of specific reasons and motives. In fact, as with survival, it seems highly likely that self-unity and self-integrity cannot be pursued directly and are always by-products of other specific motives and aims. Even in the earliest psychoanalytic formulations and retained in the various developments of psychoanalytic theory is the basic idea that one's self-conception is kept intact (later referred to in terms of ego intactness), not because that aim is directly pursued, but through defensive operations which are generated by anxiety and the desire to avoid unpleasure.

It seems to me that only in some very limited senses can one legitimately speak of self-integrity as a superordinate motive. First, the achievement of self-cohesiveness may be, as Kohut argues, a basic developmental issue. Hence, pathology in this area may result in a lifelong need to pursue self-cohesiveness and a lifelong sensitivity to relevant threats (of course, even here it would not mean that all behavior is dictated by such pursuits). Secondly, as noted above, it is likely to be a prepotent motive when threatened or, perhaps, when competing with other motives. A mechanism which makes the pursuit of self-intactness a prepotent motive when it is threatened is highly adaptive and "efficient" insofar as subsumes a wide range of possible situations. But, of course, it will be recognized that what is essentially being described is a defensive mechanism sensitive to experiences of anxiety and "ego-threat," a mechanism which is activated by an internal message which says something like: "drop everything and give priority to doing something about my experienced anxiety and threat."[80] Hence, I would conclude that the most meaningful sense in which one can understand the pursuit of self-intactness as a superordinate motive is essentially in terms of anxiety and defensive coping with anxiety, concepts long an essential part of psychoanalytic theory.

The positing of superordinate motives such as the need for and pursuit of self-cohesiveness or self-integrity is, wittingly or unwittingly, essentially a new metapsychology to replace the Freudian metapsychology. As I noted earlier (Footnote 50), Freudian instinct theory, which is the heart of his metapsychology, represents an attempt to establish uniformity and regularity as the basic reality underlying the diversity and specificity of different behaviors and motives. It seems to me that the new self psychology essentially attempts the same thing, with pursuit of self-cohesiveness and self-integrity as the new version of the basic motivational reality underlying a wide range of behaviors. Freud's attempt to find uniformity understandably required him to develop a causal (or, at least, quasi-causal) theory in which uniformity is found in underlying basic instincts, psychic energy, and other presumably universal dimensions and mechanisms (including someday, he hoped, biochemical brain mechanisms). Many current theorists, however, who eschew any metapsychology or any resort to causal or natural-science models, are trying to find (I should say, construct) a similar uniformity in human behavior, while remaining entirely with the motivational mode of discourse, by positing a superordinate motive which somehow underlies the myriad of specific motives which we pursue and which inform our behavior.

There is a double irony here. The first irony is the image of those who eschew metapsychology being drawn into what is really a metapsychological stance (as, in a somewhat different context, Rubinstein [1976] has pointed out); and the second irony is that in attempting to avoid the metapsychological and presumably remain close to the level of the clinical and the experiential, they end up doing more violence to that level than is done by an outright metapsychological or causal approach which claims, not to be describing a person's motives and experiences, but only to *explain* them. That is, it is one thing to claim that underlying a range of diverse behaviors, motives, and experiences are certain causal mechanisms. The behaviors, motives, and experiences remain intact at that level of discourse. It is another thing to claim that necessarily and invariably, while seeming to pursue the specific motives a, b, c, . . . , one is all the time, either instead or also, pursuing this or that superordinate motive. This latter approach attempts to find uniformity in the motivational realm; given the diversity of aims, that cannot legitimately be done. It then takes the next step of reducing and transforming the diversity to a superordinate motive, a step which, I maintain, deforms the specific motives and experiences (usually, in the service of a particular pet conception of psychological development or of human nature).

Perhaps the simplest way of stating the point here is to say that it is one thing to be told that underlying all your diverse experiences and motives are certain basic causal (or quasi-causal) processes. It is another thing to be told that underlying all your diverse experiences and motives is a superordinate motive for self-cohesiveness or self-realization or whatever. The former leaves your diverse experiences and motives intact. The latter, because the superordinate motive is presumably at the same level of discourse as the concrete experiences and motives, substitutes one for the other, and thereby violates and entails the transformation of what you are actually experiencing and desiring. In short, a legitimate concept of superordinate motive does not entail a reduction of all behavior to that motive or the presence of that motive as a necessary component of all behavior.[81] We are, so to speak, stuck with the more complex situation of a multiplicity of specific motives and aims interacting with each other in various ways. The uniformity underlying the surface diversity will be found, not at the same level as the very surface phenomena to be explained (that is, at the level of motives and aims), but at another level of discourse (at the level of processes and mechanisms).

20

ID-EGO REVISITED

The basic idea expressed in Freud's "where id was, there shall ego be" is that psychoanalysis helps the ego appropriate to itself portions of the id. However, this can be understood in at least two ways, as a function of how one conceptualizes the terms "ego" and "id":

(1) In the context of the conception of id as instinctual drive and ego as apparatus or controlling structure, Freud's dictum means that where the "seething cauldron" of instinctual drive was, there shall greater control and delay be. According to this interpretation, the goal of psychoanalysis is to increase the ego's control, even to the point of renunciation, over certain instinctual impulses implicated in intrapsychic conflict. This has been the dominant interpretation of Freud's dictum and is what is clearly implied in the version of Freudian theory represented by Hartmann and other psychoanalytic ego psychologists (and this is the version to which Apfelbaum [1966] and Klein [1976] direct their cogent criticisms).

(2) In the context of the conception of id as impersonal "it" and ego as personal "I," the idea of the ego appropriating to itself portions of the id can be understood to mean that what was impersonal and disowned comes to be owned and experienced as part of oneself (see Schafer, 1976). This meaning is closer to the literal rendering of the German "Wo es war, soll Ich werden" (where it was, there should I become). (See Brandt [1966] and Bettelheim [1982] for discussions of the English translations of Freud's terms.) According to this latter version of the id-ego concepts, the ego's appropriation refers, not to

greater control over the inherently chaotic and "ego-alien," but to the transformation of an impersonal "it" (e.g., an unbidden obsessive thought; an hysterical or phobic symptom) into the personal realm of "I desire," "I want," etc.

In this latter meaning, the disclaimed is dealt with, not merely by exerting control over it or by continuing to split it off from one's self-organization, but by *enlarging* one's self-conception so as to *include* the hitherto disclaimed. (G. S. Klein [1976] uses the term "identification" to describe this means of dealing with aims incompatible with one's self-organization). This does not imply that one *acts* on or has a uniform attitude toward all that is now avowedly aimed for, desired, and wanted. It means rather, in Fingarette's (1969) terms, that one "spells out" what one has already aimed for, desired, and wanted, as revealed all along in one's behaviour (including dreams, symptoms, and free associations). At the very least, this "spelling out" lessens the degree of self-deception or, in Sartre's (1956) phrase, "bad faith" characterizing one's life. At the very most, it permits a glimpse of the distant and age-old spiritual ideal that one will do the "right and the good not through obedience to the law and self-discipline, but as the issue of [one's] spontaneous response to the situation and moment" (Fingarette, 1969, p. 97).

This issue is a classic one and has been addressed by others—for example, Kierkegaard's (1956) contrast between "purity of heart" and "double-mindedness"; and Sartre's (1956) contrast between the freely chosen projects of (pre-reflexive) Consciousness and a Self which is a product of "impure reflection" and, in Fingarette's (1969) words, "biased towards a fixed conception." If we take id and ego to refer generally to disowned versus owned, one may, without doing too much violence, understand Sartre's pre-reflexive consciousness as at least partly analogous to Freud's id and his Self of "impure reflection" to the defensive aspects of the Freudian ego engaged in dissimulation and disavowal of the projects in which pre-reflexive consciousness (unconscious aims) is engaged. The question that Sartre poses—and it is a variation of a classic question which is also of central interest to psychoanalysis—is how to achieve congruence between pre-reflexive consciousness and the Self of "impure reflection." This question breaks down into two further questions: one, how is it possible to escape self-deception and achieve true self-knowledge; and two, how can "the freely chosen projects of Consciousness coincide with the enduring system which is the Self?" (Fingarette, 1969, p. 97). In the psychoanalytic context, the first question is traditionally dealt with through insight into and understanding of one's unconscious wishes and aims (which is analogous to Fingarette's notion of "spelling out," making explicit, and avowing the nature of one's engagements in the world).

As for the second goal of achieving harmony between spontaneously and freely chosen projects and the "enduring system which is the self," according to the id-ego conception of drive versus controlling structure, it is essentially unattainable. For if one accepts as inevitable the "ego's primary antagonism to instincts" (A. Freud, 1966, p. 157), then it is difficult to envisage a coincidence or even real reconciliation between one's "spontaneous response to the situation and the moment" and the dictates of law and self-discipline. As Apfelbaum (1966) points out in the context of a critique of ego psychology, according to the id-ego conception which underlies ego psychology, increased ego control over id impulses and/or weakening of the strength of instinctual impulses are the main salutary outcomes of therapeutic change, growth, and increases in self-knowledge. Id impulses, themselves, are held to be timeless, statically infantile, and not subject to growth and change. One cannot look forward to saying, with Confucius, "At seventy I could follow the dictates of my own heart; for what I desired no longer overstepped the boundaries of right."

This version of the id-ego model overlooks the possibility that increases in self-knowledge and the rendering of the formerly impersonal into the personal through avowal leads to modifications of the aims and impulses themselves. As Apfelbaum (1966) suggests, it is not simply that unacceptable infantile impulses are repressed and disavowed, but that repression and disavowal work to keep wishes and aims infantile and maladaptive insofar as they are not subject to the modifications and corrections made possible by experience and self-reflective awareness. Hence, one can set as a goal of therapy, not simply increased control over or even sublimation of timeless and statically infantile instinctual impulses, but the ownership and avowal of disclaimed wishes and aims in the faith that for most people the relationship between the life of spontaneous impulse and the life of self-reflection is not necessarily one of ultimate incompatibility and "primary antagonism."[82]

If the above view is correct, it follows that increases in self-knowledge and claiming the disclaimed permits not simply a greater understanding and control over one's wishes and aims (that is, a greater capacity to operate according to the dictates of law and self-discipline), but a kind of transformation of the wishes and aims themselves which, in the long run, renders less necessary the constant exercise of self-reflective awareness and control. That is, if one's "spontaneous response to the situation and the moment" is identical to "the right and the good," or in Confucius's terms, if the "dictates of the heart" no longer overstep "the boundaries of right," then, indeed, one has achieved the spiritual ideal in which the "freely chosen projects" of pre-reflective Consciousness coincide with an authentic Self. It is important to note that this congruence is brought about by enlarging experience and joining the Self to the functions of critical knowledge and self-reflective awareness. That is, as is the case in learning any skill, what begins as the insistent, willed exercise of the self-reflective function ends in a decreased need for the exercise of that function. Or, to put it somewhat differently, because one has confidence that one *can* spell out one's engagements and because the projects in which one is engaged are less at variance with one's sense of who one is, there is less need for the vigilant exercise of the self-reflective function. It is this state of affairs which is essentially described in the age-old spiritual ideal of which Fingarette speaks.

Until now, I have contrasted two versions of the id-ego model, id as instinctual drive and ego as controlling structure versus id as impersonal "it" and ego as personal "I." I have argued against the notion that instinctual drive is inherently antagonistic to the ego and necessarily equated with the disavowed and the impersonal. In arguing for the greater usefulness and accuracy of the id and ego defined as disavowed versus avowed, I have suggested that the id should be defined as referring to *any* set of aims and wishes which are disclaimed and thereby rendered an impersonal "it." I believe that this latter rendering of the "Es-Ich" distinction is, indeed, more useful and accurate. However, I now want to soften that position in a particular sense and for a particular purpose.

I noted previously my conviction that Freud was correct in identifying biologically laid down imperatives as the source of universal desires and wishes.[83] I would add that the self-conception and self-organization one developmentally achieves is the product of an interplay between these universal desires and wishes and one's particular history which leads one to endorse one set and one version of these desires and to reject another set and another version. Certain needs, desires, and wishes, whether or not endorsed by the self, are universal, and can, therefore, be assumed to be part of everyone's personality structure, even though not necessarily part of everyone's self-organization. If this is true, the dictum "where id was, there shall ego be" or the notion of the ego as appropriating to itself portions of the id can also be understood to mean that every cultural being, that is, every person, must meet the challenge of finding a way to represent psychologically the biologically rooted universal needs and desires that make up a large part of our human nature.[84] That is, in order to live reasonably harmoniously and in accord with our human nature, these universal needs must find their way into our psychological and experiential world of everyday aims and desires. In this sense, saying that the ego must appropriate to itself portions of the id means that one must find a place in one's everyday and experienced world of personal desires and aims for those aspects of our vital biological nature and needs which, for whatever reasons, remain unrepresented or poorly represented (for example, represented by symptoms).

Ideally, the pursuit of consciously experienced wants and aims would be fully congruent with one's organismic needs. Indeed, the pursuit of wants and aims experienced as self-maintaining and self-enhancing would be a highly efficient way of meeting the full range of one's organismic needs. In this sense, self-organization can be seen as a biologically evolved adaptive hierarchical structure coordinating a wide range of subordinate functions. In as complex a system as a person, one would expect the evolution of a superordinate structure whose main functions would include the coordination and fulfillment of a wide range of the person's interests and needs. And a superordinate structure or a self-organization which excludes and dissociates a wide range of strivings and aims does not adequately reflect one's welfare and is therefore carrying out its adaptive functions poorly. In this conception of the id and ego one can identify as a central feature of pathology the failure of the ego to appropriate to itself and render into personal aims vital biologically based needs. It would be as if one's physiological nutritional needs were unrepresented or poorly represented on the psychological level of experience, wants, and desires. One could say in such a case that these physiological needs are not appropriated by the ego in the sense that they are not rendered into personal aims, wants, and desires (as is the case in severe anorexia nervosa).

In the above I am suggesting that there is one sense in which the conflation of id as impersonal "it" and as biological substrate *is* legitimate. And that is contained in the idea that there are certain universal and vital biologically based needs and propensities (which are *not* best conceptualized as instinctual drives) that need to be represented in and "transformed" into personal aims and desires. These needs and propensities include sexual and sensual experience, attachment, object-seeking and object relational needs and tendencies, including the need for communion (Bakan, 1966), and experiences of self-integrity and self-esteem. In optimal development, this representation and "transformation" is successful and in pathology it is not. As Gedo (1979) points out, one goal of psychoanalysis is to raise to the level of conscious awareness certain universal, vital biological needs which are poorly represented. (Note that this is another way of saying that where id was, there shall ego be.) The reasons for the unsuccessful psychological representation of these vital needs include developmental trauma, inner conflict, repression and dissociation, and possibly a non-facilitating or interfering broader social context.[85] It should be noted once again that these failures in representation are *not* a function of an *inherent* antagonism between the biological substrate and the ego. Indeed, it is highly likely that in the course of evolution a system would have evolved and been selected out as adaptive in which, for the most part, experienced aims and desires are congruent with and adequately represent vital needs in contrast to a system in which biologically based urges constitute an inherent threat to one's self-organization.

When the id is defined as "seething cauldron" and the relationship between id and ego is conceptualized as one of "primary antagonism," it is understandable that emphasis would be placed on the controlling function of the ego and that the necessary fate of the id is to be repressed. But as we have seen, one must not assume that only the irrational and the infantile comprise the repressed. One must entertain the alternative idea that that which is repressed *becomes and/or remains* infantile and antisocial. Similarly, it is not that the universal bodily needs and functions which are experienced as alien and threatening are inherently and truly so, but that the loss of, in Winnicott's (1958) words, the "intimate relationship" between mental functioning and the soma renders them so.[86] But, as Winnicott tells us, this isolation and antagonism between mind and soma is a pathological rather than a natural state of affairs. If so, then the version of the id-ego relationship which posits a "primary antagonism" between them is essentially a description of a deep-seated pathology rather than an accurate description of the human personality.

It seems to me that the core of truth in Reich's (1973) concept of "orgastic potency" and in certain aspects of therapies which are related to Reich's work, such as bioenergetics and perhaps primal therapy, is the recognition that at least for some patients what is necessary is not even greater ego control, but increased possibility, when appropriate, to relinquish ego control—that is, to reverse the popular Freudian dictum ("where id was, there shall ego be") into "where ego was, there shall id be" (at least when id and ego are understood as impulse versus control). Psychoanalytic theory which early on began with a primary recognition of the pathogenic effects of repression of sexuality (as expressed, for example, in concepts such as dammed-up libido and "actual neuroses"), more and more came to view sexuality and the instinctual life in general as inherently antagonistic and inimical to the ego. Ego psychology, with its emphasis on ego functions and apparatuses, with its interpretation of id-ego as impulse-control, with its talk of *neutralized* energies, and with its implicit equation of conflict-free with autonomy from the instinctual, is the natural end product of this basic conception of the id-ego distinction. As such, it does violence to the early and most vital aspect of psychoanalytic theory and the psychoanalytic spirit. It has led to a certain sterility, resulting, in Conrad Aiken's (1964) words, in the:

> withholding what's most precious to ourselves
> Some sinister depth of lust or fear or hatred,
> The somber note that gives the chord its power;
> Or a white loveliness—if such we know—
> Too much like fire to speak of without shame.

What must be clear from the above is that certainly not the "white loveliness," but even the "sinister depth of lust of fear or hatred" are not *inherently* threatening, but "most precious to ourselves."[87]

Rather than the instinctual being threatening and inimical to the ego, a broader and more adequate conception of the biological and the instinctual, which includes such phenomena as the attachment behavioral system, the unfolding of separation-individuation, and the object-seeking propensities of which Fairbairn spoke, indicates an inextricable interdependence between the instinctual and ego functions. This is obviously what Modell (1975) is trying to convey by his notion of object relational instincts associated with the ego. Once one drops the seething cauldron and drive discharge conception of instincts, eliminates the structural division of personality into an id which is entirely cut off from reality and an organ meditating reality, and accepts the revised and broader conception of instinct argued for here, there is no longer any need to posit autonomy of ego functions from the instinctual in order to understand reliable reality-testing behavior. Instinctual propensities (e.g. early attachment responses) already include responses to objects in reality.

Finally, that our most vital psychological needs are biologically rooted—a recognition central to Freud's thinking—is the ultimate guarantee against a "socially enslaved" conception of human nature. There are, of course, enormous cultural variations in human behavior, but the limit to the range of these variations is set by our common biologically rooted human nature. We cannot be endlessly varied and modified and still remain human. Recognizing this fact permits the judgment that certain cultural and social manipulations and conditions are either not adequately responsive to or do violence to this common biological heritage.

Of course, at its best, the social and cultural can *transcend* the instinctual and the biological without doing violence to it. That is, social and moral ideals—for example, the idea of justice—can transcend the instinctual, not because the two are in an inherent antagonistic relationship, but because these ideals are simply not within the province of the instinctual. Thus, there is nothing in evolutionary development which makes the advocacy of equal rights, for example, an inevitable outcome. It is truly a cultural achievement which, in a certain sense, transcends biology and evolution.

Generally speaking, we transcend the instinctual by aligning ourselves with social and spiritual ideals, thereby expanding the personal. If it is true that we expand the realm of the personal, so to speak "from below" by appropriating "portions of the id," it is also true that we expand the personal "from above" by appropriating social and moral ideals and experiencing them as part of oneself. In an important sense, the superego can be experienced as an impersonal "it" just as much as the instinctual (still another reason for not fully equating the impersonal with the instinctual). As noted earlier, in discussing the concept of internalized object, the superego can be and is often experienced as an ego-alien introject, as indicated by such popular images of conscience as a homunculus inside one's head dispensing "do's" and "don'ts." Hence, it is just as legitimate to speak of the ego as appropriating to itself portions of the superego and it may be just as valid to aim for "where superego was, there shall ego be" as to aim for "where id was, there shall ego be."

The expansion of the personal "from below" and "from above" are not as unrelated to each other as might appear. Thus, the ability to appropriate social and moral ideals and truly experience them as part of oneself will undoubtedly be influenced by the vicissitudes of the attachment system, the capacity for what Winnicott (1965) calls "ego relatedness," and other factors which are embedded in an affective-instinctual matrix. When the social and moral ideals adopted are severed from and unrelated to this affective-instinctual matrix, they are likely to shade into an untempered coldness, harshness, and cruelty. They are likely to lose their link, in Unamuno's (1931) words, to "flesh and bone" and to lead to what to Kant was the cardinal moral failure—treating others as objects (and obviously, not in an object-relational sense).

I believe that as far as locating the source of our greatest social peril is concerned, Kant's insight was more profound and more accurate than Freud's. That is, cataclysmic social evil in such forms as nuclear war and other forms of genocide do not reflect the unbridled expression of an aggressive instinct freed from the restraints of civilization. Rather, such evil reflects the unbridled expression of social ideals which entail the objectification and dehumanization of others and which are freed from their connection with the affective and the instinctual. An individual whose instinctual impulses (as defined in traditional theory) have run rampant may rape and kill, but only a handful of people. But the large-scale slaughter made possible by modern technology requires and entails such qualities as affectlessness, indifference, and a kind and degree of rationality which is so devoid of and divorced from other considerations that it turns around on itself and becomes a form of madness. One sees in this behavior, not the instinctual run wild, but functions which are the province of the ego and superego—ideology, national goals, planning, etc.—severed from all feelings and run wild. Thus it is undoubtedly true that in the modern era, such a mundane property as social conformity has far more to do with the possibility of mass warfare than any seething cauldron of aggression, anger, and hatred.

There is probably no phrase that sheds greater light on the nature of social evil in our modern era than Hannah Arendt's (1963) term, "the banality of evil." She points out in *Eichmann in Jerusalem* that rather than being a monster of inhuman and gargantuan proportions, Eichmann was an ordinary and unimpressive civil servant whose job happened to be shipping people to their deaths rather than, let us say, cars. Here was not someone of obvious madness in whom rage, hostility, sadism, and hatred had run wild and had shed all its restraining social controls. Instead one confronted a prosaic little man, a good husband, a decent father, a patriotic citizen, a man with petty ambitions who kept talking about simply doing his job. What is truly frightening, as Arendt tells us, is the juxtaposition of an evil which is almost unimaginable with the utter banality of the perpetrator. It reminds us that, in appropriate circumstances, great evil can be committed by ordinary people doing the ordinary things of choosing not to know, remaining indifferent, and simply doing their jobs.

To return to the original issue, transcending the instinctual is, in itself, no guarantee of goodness. Both on an individual and a social level, it can be a destructive or a constructive force. Somewhat paradoxically, only a transcending which continues to keep certain roots in the instinctual—that is, a social ideal which at least does no violence to our common biological human nature—is likely to be a truly mean-

ingful and constructive one. The human response to ideals and values
which are unattainable and experienced as too distant from one's human makeup has always been either to pay lip service or to ignore
these ideals and values. For example, the Christian teaching to turn
the other cheek has not prevented Christian nations and peoples from
being warlike.

As I argued previously, if universal social and moral ideals are not
to be merely empty abstractions or worse yet, objectifications of hu-
manity, they will have emerged organically from and will have retained their links to concrete and parochial experiences. The adult
who has become capable of a true universal spirit was once an infant
embedded in a biological-affective libidinal matrix of a quality unique
to him—parochial in its very essence. If his universalism is truly human, it will have emerged organically from this early matrix and will,
in very subtle ways, reflect its early roots and early ties. The relationship between mother and child is always concrete and parochial, and
so is, I believe, any human relationship between man and man. Any
universalism which overlooks this fact has permitted ideology to dom-
inate flesh and bone and usually leads to the treatment of man as an
object and his subjection as a means to an end.

In *Hadrian's Memoirs,* Margaret Yourcenar (1965) attributes to
Hadrian the comment that the Jews are a strange people, up to their
eyes in a cloaca, with their brows touching heaven. I have always
found that description extremely moving and profound. I believe it
captures with poetic irony the insight of the necessary and vital link
between the cloaca and heaven—between the bodily/instinctual and
the spiritual/ideal.

A psychology which posits an inherent "primary antagonism" between id and ego, which contrasts a seething cauldron of instinct with
a controlling and delay structure, which sees as its primary therapeutic task the subjection of the former by the latter, and whose perspective leads to the view that this seething cauldron and its derivatives
represent the primary source of individual and social evil is simply
not faithful to human nature or to the facts of individual and social
behavior. If we are to retain the id-ego conception as the cornerstone
of psychoanalysis, then we must recapture the early psychoanalytic
and even pre-psychoanalytic emphasis on the disclaimed versus
claimed, the impersonal "it" versus the personal "I," the dissociated
versus the integrated, and, in G. S. Klein's (1976) words, the "frac-
tionated" versus the fuller self.

NOTES

1. The most recent example of this tendency I have come across is found in Kaplan's (1981) review of Gedo's book, *Beyond Interpretation*. In raising the question of "whether such a revision is worth undertaking," Kaplan wonders whether "the sorts of things Gedo deals with, and deals with quite well, are not already present in . . . traditional psychoanalytic theory. Surely one can find in many places in Freud the idea that disorganization or organization as responses to interpretation of illusion is a diagnostic index. Nor did Freud neglect the problem of a hierarchy of defensive functions" (p. 287). The point is not whether one finds (or thinks one finds) this or that specific idea somewhere in Freud's writings, but whether Gedo's reformulations are logically consistent with the central assumptions and propositions of traditional theory.

2. The idea that behavior is to be understood in terms of its survival function is also a central characteristic of the more recent ethological approach to behavior. A basic assumption of ethology is that *behaviors* and behavior systems as well as organ structures have been selected out on the basis of their adaptive value. Hence, one important way of understanding a given behavior is to clarify its adaptive function. But what distinguishes Freudian instinct theory from ethology is the former's assumption that sex and aggression exhaust the possible basic adaptive motives of behavior. What further distinguishes the two approaches is, as is discussed below, Freud's conception of instinctual drive in terms of excitation and his equation of survival or adaptive value with avoidance of the danger of excessive excitation. From this point of view, any behavior which results in drive discharge is to that extent adaptive insofar as it avoids the danger of nervous system damage resulting from excessive excitation. By contrast, most contemporary ethologists (Lorenz is an exception) do not employ a drive discharge model. Finally, while ethologists are concerned with understanding only species-wide behaviors, Freudian theory is also intended as a guide for clinical understanding and intervention in the individual case.

3. As late as his 1940 publication, Freud wrote that the "id is a source of . . . . danger and that for two different reasons. In the first place, an excessive strength of instinct can damage the ego in the same way as an excessive 'stimulus' from the external world" (p. 111).

213

4. Note the similarity between Freud's view and those of McDougall (1948) who stated that "the instinctive impulses determine the ends of all activities and supply the driving power by which all mental activities are sustained; all the complex intellectual apparatus of the most highly developed mind is but a means towards these ends, is but the instrument by which these impulses seek their satisfaction . . ." (p. 38). I don't believe that this similarity in views reflects Freud's influence on McDougall. Rather both reflect the prevailing quasi-evolutionary assumption that all behavior, including mental activities, are in the service of instincts which serve survival functions.

5. Note the link between development of thinking on the one hand and the psychological existence of external objects on the other. In Freudian theory, it is the need to come to terms with the reality of objects and the way they operate (in particular, the role they play in drive gratification) that makes necessary the development of secondary process thinking. I say secondary process thinking because it is in primary process thinking that one attempts constantly to ignore the realistic operations of objects and bend them to one's wishes. In any case, what is of interest here is Freud's insight regarding the link between the possibility of thinking and the availability of objects. As we shall see, it is not, however, frustration of drive which turns us toward objects, but our innate propensities. The unfolding of such propensities, in turn, provides the primitive schemas for the development of thinking.

6. That even the provision of "contact comfort" is not sufficient for normal development is shown by the serendipitous finding that monkeys raised by *any* inanimate surrogate mothers showed severe behavioral disturbances when they reached adulthood (Harlow, 1974).

7. Uncritical extensions from animal findings to human behavior is often perilous. However, in the present case the extension seems warranted for at least two reasons. One, converging evidence from observations of human infant-mother interactions points in the same direction as the Harlow findings (e.g., see Stern, 1980). And two, the role of factors other than hunger and thirst in contributing to the development of infant-mother attachment is likely to be greater rather than less as one moves up the phylogenetic scale.

7a. Harlow & Harlow (1972) have also demonstrated the effectiveness of other variables in mediating infant-mother attachment. For example, infants prefer a moving to a stationary surrogate, and warmth is so important that for the first 15 days infant monkeys prefer a heated wire surrogate over a room temperature cloth surrogate. After 15 days, this preference is reversed. Finally, it is practically impossible for an infant monkey to become attached to an icy cold surrogate. It is to be noted that the features that the infants prefer and that facilitate attachment—movement and warmth—are precisely those that are properties of natural mothers.

8. It should be noted that the origin of these concepts is found in the writings of Ferenczi (1950) and Hermann (1933, 1936). Michael and Alice Balint (M. Balint, 1937; A. Balint, 1939) acknowledge their indebtedness to both, in particular Frenczi's concept of "passive object-love" and Hermann's positing of an instinct to cling (which, in a remarkable way, presages such concepts as Harlow's "contact comfort"). Hermann was one of the first analysts to make use of what might now be seen as a comparative and ethological perspective. He observed certain similarities between the early clinging of infant apes and clasping and grasping responses of human infants and, on that basis, proposed an instinct to cling. Only recently has psychoanalysis begun to take seriously and indeed, make central the emphasis of the Hungarian school upon early object relations, independent of psychosexual considerations.

9. Here is an example of what I referred to earlier. An attempt to correct a blatant

deficiency of traditional theory—its neglect of the facts of maturation of cognitive functions and controlling structures—is hailed as a major theoretical advance and breakthrough.

10. In 1950 Dollard and Miller published their book, *Personality & Psychotherapy*, which was an attempt at translating Freudian concepts into the terms of Hullian learning theory. This perceived affinity between Freudian and learning theories was undoubtedly based largely on their sharing what Cofer and Appley (1963, 1972) has referred to as a "homeostatic drive" model of human behavior. Of course, no such affinity exists between Freudian theory and current behavior theory which, reflecting the Skinnerian influence, has no prominent concept of drive in its theory.

11. Terminology is an issue here. What the English object-relations theorists refer to as schizoid personalities, Kohut is likely to describe as narcissistic personality disorders, and Kernberg could well describe as borderline conditions.

12. Alternative, non-optimal patterns include a premature push into independence by virtue of being unavailable and an over-anxious, hovering presence which discourages independent behavior.

13. These are not to be confused with Freud's (1914) ideas of ego instincts which have to do with self-preservative behavioral tendencies. The distinction Modell is proposing is actually closer to White's (1963) "viscerogenic" versus "neurogenic" motives.

14. It is obvious that Modell is trying to find room in traditional psychoanalytic theory for phenomena such as attachment responses, the "object-seeking" emphasized by Fairbairn (1952) and "primary object love" referred to by Balint.

15. I would note in passing that when one observes the difficulties Modell encounters in his attempt to fit "object relations instincts" into an id-ego framework, one is once again impressed with the advantages of Bowlby's (1969) more sophisticated concept of relatively separate but interacting behavioral systems which are influenced by different stimulus configurations and different internal conditions.

16. If increased intensity of instinctual demand is involved, it is, as Apfelbaum (1966) points out, just as likely that it is already a consequence of repression rather than simply the cause of repression.

17. In *Inhibitions, Symptoms, and Anxiety*, Freud (1926) describes the agoraphobic's need for companionship in terms quite similar to current views: as due to "a temporal regression to infancy (in extreme cases, to a time when the subject was in his mother's womb . . .)" (p. 127).

18. Whether the development of self-cohesiveness and an intact sense of self is best described as a specifically narcissistic line of development is questioned by Gedo (1980). That is, one can examine the development of self and recognize the centrality of self-organization for personality in a context quite independent of the concept of narcissism. (See, for example, G. S. Klein [1976] and Gedo [1980], both of whom view the continuity and integrity of self-organization as a superordinate aim independent of a theory of narcissism.) This conceptual distinction between a narcissistic line of development and the growth of self highlights the fact that Kohut is not simply introducing the importance of the self into psychodynamic self psychology, but is presenting *a particular theory of the self*, a theory which states that the development of the self is equivalent to the development of narcissism. It is that equivalence which helps explain the positing of such presumably developmental phenomena as the phase-specific emergence of a grandiose and exhibitionistic self. One can lose sight of the fact that Kohut's theoretical point of departure is Freud's theory and discussion of narcissism. What remains as an interesting and important theoretical task, is an analysis of the precise transformations Freud's concept of narcissism undergoes as it emerges in Kohut's self psychology.

19. It is difficult to understand, given Kohut's conception of development, why the earliest stage of narcissistic development should be called "autoerotism."

20. An example of this is offered by Slap and Levine (1978). In discussing the case of Mr. B., Kohut relates that after the male patient's female analyst referred to him as "lovable and touchable," "he became excited and anxious, had difficulty sleeping, and reported a variety of alarmingly blatant aggressive, sexual, and oral fantasies about women, including the analyst" (Slap and Levine, 1978, p. 511). Slap and Levine note that Kohut does not discuss the patients' fantasies, but interprets the patient's reaction in the following way. "The childhood wish (or rather need) for his mother's empathic physical response had suddenly become intensely stimulated . . . . In the last analysis, however, it was the patient's basic psychological defect which accounted for the excitement . . ." (Kohut, 1971, p. 234). The point of this example is that it suggests that Kohut can interpret and will find evidence for the presence of self defects and the need for the maternal empathic response in behaviors which do not, in any obvious way, suggest these features and which many other analysts would not interpret in this manner. Hence, if almost any behavior can count as evidence for self-defects and need for empathic response, it becomes obvious that Kohut is proposing a new way of looking at just about all pathology.

21. It will be recalled that this is precisely the logic employed by Spitz (1960) when he attributes the damaging consequences of maternal deprivation to the fact that the unavailability of the mother prevents the discharge of libidinal and aggressive drives.

22. This is particularly true in the case of the infant whose "stimulus barrier" and other coping mechanisms are not yet sufficiently developed.

23. The formulation that the essence of anxiety is excessive excitation indicates that Freud never fully relinquished the core idea of his first theory of anxiety. In that theory, Freud proposed that anxiety was the result of the toxic accumulation of undischarged sexual tensions. Such tensions became transformed into anxiety. Or stated more formally, anxiety is the result of the transformation of the affect of a repressed impulse. Thus, Freud believed that certain sexual practices which interfered with libidinal discharge, such as coitus interruptus, were instrumental in causing anxiety. This first theory of anxiety was presumably dropped, partly because Freud could not envisage a process by which libido could be transformed into anxiety. As most summaries of Freudian theory are fond of stating, this first theory was replaced by Freud's second, signal, theory of anxiety, the essentials of which are the concept of signal anxiety and the idea that, rather than repression causing anxiety (as the first theory states), repression precedes and is instituted by (signal) anxiety. That is, a small quantity of anxiety acts as a signal to alert the ego to danger and consequently, to the necessity of instituting repression and other defensive action.

But what is the nature of the danger to which the ego is alerted? As noted, the ultimate danger (including the dangers inherent in castration anxiety, loss of the object, etc.) is ego-damaging excessive excitation emanating from drive. In other words, what is retained from the first theory of anxiety is the basic idea that accumulation of excitation from undischarged drive tensions represents a basic threat to the organism and is linked to anxiety. What is relinquished is the idea that such drive tensions are automatically *transformed* into anxiety. The link between drive tensions and anxiety is retained, but now resides partly in the fact that the organism responds to the danger inherent in the former with signal anxiety, an attenuated quantity of anxiety which indicates the anticipation of danger and which initiates defensive actions to avoid the danger. The other, more dramatic, link between drive tensions and anxiety is that the essence of *massive anxiety* (in contrast to signal anxiety) is a traumatic situation in which one is helpless in the face of overwhelming endogenous stimulation emanating from drives. In other words, implicit in this formulation is the idea that *massive anxiety is the affective, experiential component of overwhelming excitation.* What follows from this is that in an important sense, anxiety is not the *transformation* of drive tensions, but the *affective experience* of excessive excitations coming from drives (just as, in an appropriate situation, it would be the affective experience of excessive excitations coming from external stimulation).

This idea that anxiety is related to excessive excitation is quite consistent with current theories and findings which link anxiety to physiological over-arousal. For example, Lader and Wing (1966) cite evidence that there is a genetic component to habituation rate, a finding that is of interest in light of their theory that a low habituation rate combined with a high level of central nervous activity leads to positive feedback with increasing neural activity—a phenomenon which, according to them, "represents a danger to the organism" in that it results in "excessive excitaion in the central nervous system" (p. 142). They go on to state that "morbid anxiety is the experience of abnormally prolonged excessive activity" (p. 143), a statement remarkably similar to Freud's basic view of anxiety.

One issue which emerges from this brief discussion of Freud's theory of anxiety is the role of defense in reducing anxiety. Why and how does defense reduce anxiety? Freud has given a number of answers to this question. In his early clinical papers (e.g., *Studies in Hysteria*), he described the operation of defense in terms of keeping an idea morally repugnant to oneself out of conscious awareness. One can say that here defense succeeds in reducing anxiety because it leaves one's self-image intact. A later answer given (e.g., Freud, 1926) is that insofar as a particular idea or wish has been associated with threats of castration, of loss of love, etc., the removal of the idea from conscious experience will reduce the anticipated threat associated with the idea. Note that this is a relatively straightforward conditioning explanation (see Dollard and Miller [1950] for a translation of certain Freudian concepts and formulations into learning theory terms.)

What is dealt with partly in the second answer is the relationship between defense and excessive excitation. That is to say, if, as noted earlier, the ultimate threat represented by loss of the object, loss of the object's love, and castration is that one is helpless in the face of overwhelming endogenous stimulation, then any maneuver which reduces this threat will thereby also reduce anxiety. Thus, if thinking or wishing X is associated with anticipation of certain dangers, then removing X from consciousness will reduce the anxiety associated with these dangers.

What the above answer does not deal with is the question of a more direct relationship between defense and excessive excitation. Yes, the removal of an idea or wish from consciousness can attenuate the expected punishments associated with this idea or wish and thereby reduce anxiety. But can defense more directly reduce excitation? And in answering this question, we come upon other ways in which defense reduces anxiety. For one, most, if not all, defenses other than repression permit some instinctual discharge, that is, some degree of entertainment and/or realistic or fantasied carrying out of the instinctual wish and idea. For example, rationalization permits one to pursue an instinctual aim under the guise of pursuing a more socially acceptable aim. Or, as another example, undoing also permits some instinctual gratification as long as it is followed by undoing behavior. Now, the point is that to the extent that these defenses allow partial drive discharge or gratification, they reduce the danger of the accumulation of excessive excitation and thereby serve to minimize anxiety potential.

A more abstract and basic conception of how defense reduces the danger of excessive excitation was developed by Freud (1895) in the "Project" and essentially proposes the idea that "side-cathexis" as it were siphons off potentially excessive excitation by redirecting excitation from the "memory-motive structure . . . away from its major pathways . . ." (p. 323). These "side-cathexes," which represent Freud's earliest conception of the ego, can be said to *inhibit* excitation from being fully directed to certain neurones.

24. Of course, as Levine (1977) questions, why should an oedipal fantasy develop *de novo* in an adult who is no longer in the original oedipal-inducing situation? As Levine notes, this is only one specific example of the kind of difficulties one encounters with the general uncritical view that chronological adults resume and complete long-interrupted developmental tasks.

25. Kohut does point out that with the development of self-cohesiveness one can relate to others as separate persons rather than as self-objects and one can value them for their own qualities. This implies that with the development of self-cohesiveness one is more able to experience intimacy (as contrasted with symbiotic merging) with another. But this does not contradict the implication that someone with an oedipally derived incapacity for intimacy could nevertheless lead a full and satisfying life so long as a certain degree of self-cohesiveness and "healthy narcissism" were achieved.

26. In fact, it is optimal doses of frustration which, according to Kohut, lead to the building of psychic structures in therapy.

27. By contrast, Mahler (1968) does provide some idea of the processes mediating the failure to develop an intact sense of self in, for example, symbiotic psychosis.

28. Although Kohut criticizes traditional psychoanalytic theory for its failure to recognize the positive aspects of narcissism, it seems likely that the starting point for Kohut's concern with "healthy narcissism" is Freud's (1914) idea that excessive cathexis of the object carries the risk of depletion of the ego and his statement that "a strong egoism is protection against falling ill." (He also adds, "but in the last resort we must begin to love in order not to fall ill".)

29. The emphasis on self-maintenance and self-enhancement as basic motives is clearly related to the non-psychoanalytic self psychologies of Fromm (1947), Rogers (1959; 1961), and Maslow (1954; 1968) for examples. It is also related to Freud's early discussion of self-preservative tendencies and to his concept of "ego interests." Hartmann (1964) has also discussed the latter concept, but it has never played a prominent part either in traditional theory or in later ego psychology (see Eagle, 1981).

30. One can accept the recent arguments of Klein (1980) and Stern (1980), for example, that some degree of self-other differentiation is already present at birth and continue to maintain that normal psychological development is marked by an *increasing* degree of such differentiation.

31. "Healthy narcissism" becomes the equivalent of sublimation, save that in Kohut's scheme what is sublimated is not instinctual drive aims, but archaic grandiosity and exhibitionism. Thus, what the narcissistic perspective and the perspective from the point of view of instinct theory have in common is a reductionism by which the multifarious nature of behavior and its accompanying motives are reduced to this or that specific set of motives.

If self psychology replaces traditional psychoanalytic theory, I can envisage the day when a new version of ego psychology will come along which essentially argues for the possibilities of activities autonomous of narcissistic motives.

32. A similar point is made by Arlow and Brenner (1964), who dispute Freud's view of schizophrenia as essentially a narcissistic disorder and who note that many schizophrenic patients are often intensely involved with other people.

33. If the narcissistic personality disorder were, in fact, someone who had presumably not moved beyond the early stage of the fragmented self, it would be difficult to understand how therapy of any kind—concepts such as "transmuting internalization" notwithstanding—could be of significant help. I share Gedo's (1980) skepticism in this

regard. After all, therapy does not transform someone who, developmentally speaking, is a psychological infant, and who, in the central area of development of self, has not moved beyond a stage of fragmentation into an adult. If therapy does help, it does not mean that this transformation has taken place. It simply means that Kohut's conceptions, particularly the implicit claim that the patient is at the same psychological stage as perhaps a two-year-old infant, are in error.

34. By *inherently* incongruent I mean that the incongruence will not be simply a function of the patient's defensive distortions or elisions or of the different perspective (e.g., inclusion of unconscious wishes) taken by the therapist.

34a. As Rubinstein (1980) points out, as basic a psychoanalytic concept as unconscious motive or wish is also used as if it belonged to the world of persons when, in fact, it is part of the world of organisms. Such practices can be heuristic as long as one knows that one is using terms in an "as-if" manner. As noted earlier, what makes Kohut's use of "hybrid concepts" especially ironic is his insistence that, in contrast to traditional psychoanalytic theory, his self psychology is based on empathy and experience–near concepts.

35. Gedo is, of course, aware that Kohut does not refer to symbiotic wishes as such, but instead uses such descriptions as relating to the therapist as a "self-object" and fantasies of "narcissistic union." But I think he is correct in his assumption that Kohut's talk about "self-object," "narcissistic union," and "mirroring transferences" is equivalent or very close to what others describe in terms of symbiotic wishes and fantasies.

36. Rangell (1980), in questioning the recent popularity of diagnoses such as narcissistic personality disorders, has argued that the kinds of problems and symptoms described by Kohut and his followers have long been presented by patients who are diagnosed as neurotic by many other analysts. In any case, it appears that today's modal patient presents somewhat different kinds of problems than patients of an earlier period.

37. While the above account is consistent with clinical experiences in which an individual experiences aspects of himself as alien, at times as a demon to be exorcised, it is not consistent with other clinical phenomena—for example, ego-syntonic low self-esteem, guilt, or hostility.

38. Although Schafer speaks of ones feeling assailed or gratified by introjects, the logic of Fairbairn's formulations would cover only the former. That is, as noted above, according to Fairbairn, only "bad" objects are internalized, under the impact of deprivation and in order to control the apparent badness of the object. (For a further discussion of this issue, see Guntrip, 1968.)

39. As Meissner (1981) points out, under certain circumstances introjection can be transformed into identification.

40. I once treated a patient whose presenting symptom was dyspereunia. She reported that invariably before sexual intercourse the thought, "if they could see me now" popped into mind. The "they," she was clear, referred to her parents, who believed that she was a virgin and a "good girl." This seems a clear example of an internalized object relation rather than a successful identification.

41. What Fairbairn could mean by internalization of the "exciting object" is that the child continues to yearn and long for fulfillment of the needs excited by the object. But if this is so, then internalization of the "rejecting" and "exciting" objects would have different meaning. The former involves an internalization of an attitude that was once external toward oneself, while the latter refers to continued expectations from the representations of an external object.

42. Note the similarity between Fairbairn's "pristine unitary ego" and Kohut's concept of the early state of "absolute perfection" of the infant. Both concepts are not only

hopelessly vague, but also seem to involve, to use Peterfreund's (1978) term, an "adultomorphic" and romanticized conceptualization of infancy. See Peterfreund for some perceptive comments on psychoanalytic conceptions of infancy.

43. Because for Fairbairn, excessive identification ("primary identification") is the very pathology to be eradicated, he would hardly be likely to posit identification and internalization as therapeutic mechanisms. Since Kohut, on the other hand, sees lack of self-cohesiveness as the primary issue, identificatory processes which strengthen such cohesiveness are viewed as constructive.

As Schafer (1968) points out, terms in psychoanalytic writing like "internalization," "identification," "incorporation," and "introjection" are beset with confusions and ambiguities. I do not plan to discuss the issue here, but merely want to point out that some differences between theorists (e.g., between Fairbairn and Kohut) may, at least in part, be a function of differences in terminology and definition: For example, what Fairbairn refers to as "primary identification," many theorists today discuss in terms of lack of differentiation between self and non-self and do not invoke the concept of identification at all. One question that arises is whether "primary identification" can lead to the kind of accretions in self structure discussed by Kohut; and if not, how does it differ from the kind of identification that does lead to such accretions?

Another important question that arises in Fairbairn's work is how the internalization process involved in the internalizing of objects differs from the presumably normal identification process which facilitates the formation of identity and contributes to accretions in self-structure. One is particularly interested in asking this question in view of Fairbairn's description of internalization. For example, the child's taking on the "badness" of the object seems to fit the general description of identification in terms of the assumption into oneself of characteristics of the object. In what specific ways, if any, does such internalization differ from identification? This question is related to the question of how the internalization involved in the internalizing "bad" objects differs from the kind of internalization in object constancy, interests, and values, all of which contribute to rather than detract from one's inner resources. This, too, is a variation of the larger question of the differences between internalizations that disrupt and disturb the personality (e.g., function as "internal saboteurs") and those that contribute essentially and positively to the formation of self structure and inner strength. I cannot discuss it here, but I can say, in passing, that I don't believe that the latter is simply a matter of internalizing "good" rather than "bad" objects.

44. It would appear that for Fairbairn an ideally good environment would be one which fully meets the infant's basic object-relational needs. It is worth noting, in passing, that Fairbairn is implicitly proposing a rudimentary instinct (implied by his use of "libido") which centers on object seeking tendencies and object relational needs. I mention this because Bowlby (1969) has criticized object relations theory on the ground that it appears to leave no room for instincts. While there is obviously no explicitly developed concept of instinct in Fairbairn's formulations, it seems to me that there is an implicit and rudimentary one which, in some respects, is similar to Bowlby's attachment concept.

It should also be noted that a basic difference between Freud's concept of instinct and what I am referring to as Fairbairn's implicit and rudimentary concept of instinct is that the former basically involves a build-up and discharge of endogenous excitation, with external stimuli serving mainly a sort of "releasing" function. By contrast, in Fairbairn's concept, the organism actively seeks stimuli and, in general, exemplifies what Modell (1975) was trying to convey with his comment that for object relational instincts, "a fitting in of specific responses from other persons" constitutes the gratification.

Finally, it should be noted that these different conceptions of instincts parallel, to some degree, differences within ethological theory—for example, between Lorenz's (1965, 1966) formulation of instincts and the formulations of Hinde (1959). In a symposium on psychoanalysis and ethology, Kaufman (1960) states in commenting on this difference that, "evidence has accumulated which throws great doubt on the validity of the reservoir concept of behavior, according to which discharge of energy in an act brings that behavior to an end. It has become abundantly clear that most behavior is brought to an end not by the performance of an act but by the presence of certain stimulus situations" (p. 321).

45. I am aware that other conflicts and dynamic themes are relevant—for example, the oedipal theme in which mother's punishment or the patient's pain during intercourse could be unconsciously construed as punishment for sexual wishes toward father.

46. The patient did verbalize some limited insights. For example, her recurrent thought, "But he didn't say anything" following her angry outburst suggests some awareness that the personal meanings of the event to her were deeply involved in her reaction. This represents some shift to a more inward looking attitude. And the interpretation of her symptom linking defiance and ensuing pain was meaningful to her. However, as I noted, this meaning and understanding was not applied to the transference situation and to what I am referring to as the "enactment." And, after all, it was after this critical event that the symptom disappeared.

47. There are also important differences between the concept of "corrective emotional experience" and current views. For example, as far as I know, no current therapist would accept Alexander and French's technique of adopting a role intended to fit the patient's particular conflicts and anxieties. In general, Alexander and French tended to reduce many complex processes to the simple factor of "corrective emotional experience" and tended to ignore or not sufficiently emphasize other factors involving the patient's active role in formulating unconscious plans, presenting tests to therapists, determining whether tests have been passed or failed, judging whether or not conditions of safety obtain, and deciding whether or not to bring forth warded off contents.

48. Both Klein and the Mt. Zion group take this concept from Freud's (1920) observation of a child attempting to cope with mother's departure by playing a game in which he repeatedly has objects disappear and then finds them. Freud interprets this game as the child's attempt to turn the passive traumatic situation into an active one for the purpose of mastery.

49. The idea of a natural antipathy between instincts and ego, which is expressed in some of Freud's writings and certainly in Anna Freud's writings, seems to contradict the view expressed in *Civilization and Its Discontents*, that society is a necessary component in neurotic conflict.

50. Those rejecting any semblance of metapsychology for psychoanalysis are, in effect, ruling out as inappropriate for psychoanalysis a further consideration of the nature of the link between our biological structure and the kinds of wishes, motives, and aims we are likely to have. I will discuss in a later section the general position of those who would limit psychoanalysis to the so-called clinical theory.

51. This conception may be partly obscured in the work of Fairbairn because of the use of such locutions as "*libido* is object seeking" and "*ego* has its own aims." One must remember, however, that such locutions were developed in the context of and in response to pre-existing psychoanalytic formulations. Thus, Fairbairn disputed the claim that libido is pleasure seeking, while remaining in the same context and in the same universe of discourse, by arguing that libido is object-seeking. Similarly, with Apfelbaum's argument that the ego has its own aims. It is a response to the conception of ego solely as structure and function. In other words, both Fairbairn's claim that libido is

object-seeking and Apfelbaum's claim that the ego has its own aims are metaphors arising out of a particular context. However, as these examples show, not all metaphors are equally valid or equally useful. Thus, if one can translate the metaphor "libido is object seeking" to refer to such phenomena as an innately based interest in objects, it becomes clear that this metaphor is more accurate, more in accord with the facts, and therefore more useful than the drive discharge "libido is pleasure-seeking" metaphor it is meant to dispute. Similarly with Apfelbaum's formulation that the ego has its own aims. One can translate the phrase to refer to such phenomena as intrinsic motivation (Hunt, 1965), the urge for competence and mastery (White, 1960; 1963; Hendrick, 1943), and the evidence of ubiquitous and autonomous curiosity, exploratory, and novelty motives.

52. It seems to me that the term "dissociation," employed by pre-psychoanalytic writers and among others, by Prince (1929a,b) and Sullivan (1947), more accurately captures the idea of disavowal and isolation from one's self-conception than the term "repression," particularly as it has come to be defined in traditional psychoanalytic theory. It is noteworthy that Klein (1976), who conceptualizes id and ego essentially as disowned versus owned, also redefines repression as "a meaning scheme that is *dissociated* (my italics) from the person's self-conception" (p. 241) and in terms of "lived meanings . . . segregated from understanding, i.e., *dissociated from the self* (Klein's italics)" (p. 251).

53. It is also, in certain respects, close to the dominant conceptualizations of such figures as Janet (1907; 1924), Charcot, Prince (1929a,b), and Breuer (1893–1895), all of whom identified dissociated and semi-autonomous clusters of aims, memories, and feelings as critical pathogenic agents in psychopathology. Further, Freud's idea of "splitting of the ego" and his contrast between splits within a single structure (in fetishism) and splits between different structures (in neurosis) is obviously one important source of similar subsequent ideas: Fairbairn's concept of "ego splits," Kernberg's (1976) notion of primitive splitting, and Kohut's contrast between defects *within* the self structure and conflicts between intact structures.

Consider Kernberg's description of primitive splitting as the primary defense in borderline conditions. Insofar as it involves a nonintegrated alternation of love and hate (and accompanying idealization and derogation), it is not so much a description of an id-ego conflict, as, in the terms of Freudian theory, an intra-id conflict—that is, a conflict between opposing id tendencies. But even this is somewhat misleading. For clinical accounts of splitting in borderline conditions make it clear that what is distinctive in splitting is failure of ego integration. That is, the borderline patient cannot, for example, integrate feelings of love and hate towards the same object (more specifically, cannot integrate loving with hating self-representations and all-good with all-bad object representations).

As noted earlier, whereas in repression there is a dominant cognitive-affect set of avowed aims, feelings, and cognitions (that is, a stable self-structure) from which certain unacceptable impulses and ideas *can* be split off, in primitive splitting there is no temporally stable and dominant cognitive-affective set of aims, feelings, and cognitions (that is, no stable self-structure) from which certain isolated impulses and ideas can be dissociated. Rather, in the latter, there are alternations of this or that prepotent cognitive-affective configuration.

54. On this particular point, I believe that Popper (1962) is correct in his criticisms of psychoanalytic theory. (Unfortunately, Popper directs his criticism to all psychoanalytic theory, as if it were a monolithic entity. For an excellent critique of Popper's somewhat indiscriminate criticisms of psychoanalytic theory, see Grünbaum, 1979; 1982). This is especially the case given the special difficulties of reliability and validity attending

interpretations regarding the latent meaning of behavior as opposed to more straightforward causal accounts focusing on antecedent conditions and underlying mechanism (for a further discussion of this issue, see Eagle, 1980).

55. See Peters (1958) for an interesting evaluation of theories which attempt to reduce behavior to a narrow set of limited motives.

56. This does not strike me as a good example of what would constitute intrapsychic conflict in traditional theory. Where is the instinctual impulse that is in conflict with ego or superego? Indeed, insofar as the patient's grandiosity serves "to deny his vulnerability and his realistic limitations," it seems to represent compensation against self-vulnerability more than defense against intrapsychic conflict.

57. Mitchell (1979) argues that this division of domains of applicability represents, in part at least, an attempt to escape the charge of heresy within the psychoanalytic community through the "strategy of preserving the drive theory metapsychological framework by establishing a diagnostic domain for orthodox concepts . . ." (p. 182). This "psychoanalytic form of ecumenicism" is declared through the "strategies of a complementarity, as in Kohut, an attempt to integrate concepts hierarchically, as in Kernberg, and the designation, by both, of a new form of psychopathology to which the formally heretical theoretical lines now apply" (p. 188).

58. There are some variations in this position. (Klein (1976), for example, rejects causal explanation as inappropriate to a *psychoanalytic* approach to human behavior, while Schafer (1976; 1978) argues that the causal mode of explanation is simply inappropriate in *any* account of human action.

59. I say "partly" correct because, as I have argued elsewhere (Eagle, 1980), I believe it can be shown that some commonly accepted clinical assumptions—for example, the ubiquitousness of sexual and aggressive wishes—were not based on induction, but were derived from broader metapsychological assumptions (see Holt, 1976).

60. Hence, I believe that it is not profitable to dismiss as not distinctively psychoanalytic (Klein, 1976) attempts to re-formulate certain aspects of metapsychology in more scientifically acceptable terms (for example, as, Peterfreund [1978] has attempted to do). For indeed, if some of what Freud attempted to accomplish with his metapsychology (which was essentially a model of mind) could be accomplished in a scientifically meaningful way, this would be an important and significant achievement, whether distinctively psychoanalytic or not.

61. Contrast the assured and definitive etiological statements in the current psychoanalytic literature with the sober conclusions reached by Kohlberg *et al.* (1972) after a careful and thoughtful review of the evidence: "Childhood emotional-disturbance symptoms are not now useful predictors. Neither is adult neurotic emotional disturbance currently predictable from childhood symptoms. Put bluntly, there is no research evidence yet available indicating that clinical analysis of the child's emotional status or dynamics leads to any more effective prognosis of adult mental health or illness than could be achieved by the man on the street who believes psychosis is hereditary and that criminality is the result of bad homes and neighborhoods in the common-sense meaning of that concept" (p. 1271).

62. Note that this is the procedure most often implemented when data derived from the clinical situation are investigated by a researcher external to that situation.

63. Another way of putting this is to ask whether psychoanalysis is to be justified because of its therapeutic efficacy or because of the truths it purportedly uncovers. As we will discuss later, Freud assumed that only interpretations which "tally with what is real" are therapeutically effective and, hence, believed that the two purposes necessarily converge.

64. The situation is not unlike some laboratory research which seems to be carried out

for its own sake and seems to concern phenomena generated largely by the laboratory itself, relatively unrelated to the larger context outside the laboratory. Although it is often called "basic research" because it has no obvious practical value, this is misleading. It is neither applied nor basic in the sense of elucidating basic processes in nature. Rather, it rightfully belongs to a third category of research which is mainly generated by the research enterprise itself and supported by a variety of motives and purposes including career pressures, status needs, etc. It seems to me that any discipline or area of activity increases the risk of stagnation and sterility when it becomes excessively involuted, too much a closed system, too turned back on itself, too much like the "bead game" depicted by Hesse (1949), and therefore, too isolated from external contributions, concerns, and purposes.

65. What I am referring to as an autonomous theory of therapy is being developed by a limited number of psychoanalytic researchers. This work is exemplified by the research of Luborsky (1953; 1967), Sampson and Weiss and their colleagues (e.g., 1977) Gill and Hoffman (1982) and Dahl (1974). All these studies have in common a well-controlled and systematic inquiry into the psychoanalytic *process*. None of them include an investigation of therapeutic *outcome* (although some of the process findings may have implications for outcome).

66. Even here one must make a number of qualifications. One can neither expect nor rely on the therapist to report or evaluate the clinical data. The few well-controlled and interesting studies which have used data from the clinical psychoanalytic situation have relied on tape recordings. Further, the evaluation and analysis of the data have been carried out by judges external to the clinical situation and have thereby permitted adequate attention to issues of control and reliability (examples of such studies include Luborsky, 1953; 1967; Horowitz *et al.*, 1975; Sampson and Weiss, 1977; Gill and Hoffman, 1982).

67. If one takes the position that historical accounts are not descriptions of what is or was the case, but merely constructions, how does one evaluate the recent obscene historical constructions to the effect that earlier accounts of the Holocaust are mainly Zionist propaganda?

68. There are noteworthy exceptions to this generalization. For example Gill, who is sympathetic to the hermeneutic position, has also conducted rigorous investigations of the psychoanalytic process himself and has urged further such work. It should be noted, however, that Gill's research is concerned mainly with process and not with the question of outcome, that is, of therapeutic effectiveness (Gill and Hoffman, 1982).

69. Whether one views psychoanalysis as a science or as a hermeneutic discipline is separate from the question of systematic and controlled studies on therapeutic outcome (as well as on the processes leading to particular outcomes). Such studies involve the use of basic experimental design characteristic of natural and social sciences. Even if psychoanalysis is seen as a hermeneutic discipline, its impact as a treatment can and should be evaluated rigorously, that is, scientifically. Hermeneutic arguments and insights, such as they are, have nothing to offer such an evaluation.

70. It seems to me that ironically, the more psychoanalytic therapy is like history—that is, exclusively concerned with reconstruction of past events and with understanding for its own sake—the more likely it is that it is too little concerned with the effectiveness of its interventions (with its technology, so to speak). As I will try to show, even within psychoanalytic therapy there is and has been confusion between therapeutic and theoretical goals and purposes.

71. If one has developed a valid and accurate fomulation of a particular kind of pathology, it does not follow that *that* formulation, if employed as an intervention and in some fashion conveyed to the patient, will be therapeutically effective. An accurate formulation, which includes an understanding of etiology and of basic processes in-

volved in the pathology, simply makes it more likely that *some* effective intervention (which may have nothing to do with psychotherapy) will be developed.

72. Bush (1978) has argued that Freud "did not believe that insight plays a major role in the process of cure" and believed that "only the irrational power of the positive transference could produce the degree of conviction and motivation needed by the ego to wage successful combat against its own defenses" (p. 12). Bush then cites the following passage from Freud to support his conclusion:

> If the patient is to fight his way through the normal conflict with the resistances which we have uncovered for him in the analysis, he is in need of a powerful stimulus which will influence the decision in the sense which we desire, leading to recovery. Otherwise it might happen that he would choose in favour of repeating the earlier outcome and would allow what had been brought up into consciousness to slip back again into repression. At this point what turns the scale in his struggle is not his intellectual insight—which is neither strong enough nor free enough for such an achievement—but simply and solely his relation to the doctor. In so far as his transference bears a 'plus' sign, it clothes the doctor with authority and is transformed into belief in his communications and explanations. In the absence of such a transference, or if it is a negative one, the patient would never even give a hearing to the doctor and his arguments (Freud 1917b, p. 445).

If Bush is correct, it would suggest that Freud, too, placed major emphasis on the therapeutic relationship and that recent apparent shifts in emphasis away from insight and on the relationship are really a further development of Freud's own views. I believe, however, that it can be shown that Bush is mistaken. For one, the bulk of Freud's comments, including his earlier referred to "tally argument," suggests that he placed great importance on insight. Secondly, a close reading of the passage cited by Bush indicates that it does not support his own interpretation. For it is clear that what Freud is writing about is the importance of positive transference in facilitating the patient's emotional acceptance of the therapist's interpretations and in preventing re-repression of what had already emerged into consciousness, that is, of material regarding which the patient had already achieved insight. Hence, Freud is emphasizing the importance of the relationship (of positive transference) in facilitating emotional insight and conviction in contrast to many current theorists who want to argue for the *direct* therapeutic effects of the relationship (through identification, "transmuting internalizations," or some other means not mediated by insight). If Bush were correct and Freud were saying that only the relationship—that is, the patient's desire to please the therapist and the "authority" of the therapist—accounts for the patient's "even giving a hearing to the doctor and his arguments" and for the patient's emotional conviction regarding the interpretations offered, Freud would essentially be acknowledging that the patient's acceptance of interpretations is entirely, or at least largely, a matter of suggestion and compliance. This seems highly unlikely insofar as Freud consistently argued against the suggestion and related hypotheses.

73. Kohut is particularly guilty of such jargon. We have already seen some examples in the discussion of his use of "hybrid concepts." An example each from his 1971 and 1977 books follows: ". . . The danger against which the ego defends itself by keeping the archaic grandiose self dissociated and/or in repression is the dedifferentiating influx of unneutralized narcissistic libido (toward which the threatened ego reacts with anxious excitement) and the intrusion of archaic images of a fragmented body-self . . ." (1971, p. 152).

In discussing Mr. M., Kohut describes him as showing "a structural defect in the area of his goals, ideals, leading secondarily to an insufficient channelling of his exhibitionistic-grandiose-creative strivings toward well-integrated, firmly internalized goals. The absence of a sufficiently organized flow of grandiose-exhibitionistic libido toward a securely internalized set of ideals . . ." (1977, p. 123).

Kohut is certainly not alone in his use of jargon. I have already indicated some examples from Mahler's (1968) writings (p. 30). I shall provide an additional one here: "Metapsychologically speaking, this seems to mean that, by the second month, the quasi-solid stimulus barrier (negative, becasue it is uncathected)—*this autistic shell* (Mahler's italics), which kept external stimuli out—begins to crack. Through the aforementioned cathectic shift toward the sensory-perceptive periphery, a protective, but also receptive and selective, positively cathected stimulus shield now begins to form and to envelop the symbiotic orbit of the mother-child dual unity . . . This eventually highly selective boundary seems to contain not only the pre-ego self representations, but also the not yet differentiated, libidinally cathected symbiotic part objects, within the mother-infant symbiotic matrix" (p. 15).

Finally, as an example of practically incomprehensible jargon, I offer a passage from a recent paper by Giovacchini (1981). In his discussion of whether one should conceptualize "the endopsychic structure that underlies the transitional phenomenon as a nurturing or functional modality" (p. 404), Giovacchini writes: "What I am emphasizing is that the vicissitudes involved in the formation of this first mental construct have an important bearing on the formation of the postsymbiotic introjects which, in turn, serve as a source of cathexis that can lead to the stabilization of a function as well as the construction of self and object representations" (pp. 411–412). (For a general discussion of jargon in psychoanalytic writing, see Leites' [1971] *The New Ego*).

74. Although Mahler does not explicitly take these positions, I believe they are implied in her formulations.

74a. For a contrary view, see Epstein, Lanza, and Skinner (1981).

75. There has been a considerable controversy in the psychoanalytic literature as to whether transitional objects are normal or pathological and whether they are to be distinguished from childhood fetishism. There is little point in reviewing this controversy here. I agree with Dickes (1978) who maintains that the transitional object is pathological and indistinguishable from fetishism when the extreme relationship to such objects involves the supplanting of the parent and when the object is used for discharge of sexual and aggressive tensions. He suggests—and I agree—that the terms *transitional phenomenon* and *transitional object* be reserved for use with the large group of children who use inanimate objects to relieve distress caused by separation.

76. It is important to clarify a point here. It is possible to interpret Winnicott's discussion of transitional objects as suggesting that cultural interests are entirely or primarily derived from the need to find symbolic substitutes for maternal security and "safe anchorage." Winnicott is not entirely clear on this matter. I am taking the position that, as argued earlier, the ultimate basis for an interest in objects is an inborn predisposition. Indeed, it is this inborn predisposition which partly explains why the child turns to the transitional object for soothing and comforting. I am suggesting further that the unfolding of this inborn predisposition serves object relational functions. Under optimal conditions the inborn predisposition to respond to objects unfolds in the development of a wide range of interests. Given this development, however, such interests come to serve object relational functions. Thus, while the development of a particular interest may develop somewhat autonomously, it can come to serve some of the psychological functions normally served by any strong cognitive-affective tie, that is, by object relations.

77. While the general proposition I am suggesting is that autonomous interests are related to early security of attachment and relative success in separation-individuation,

there are likely to be important additional factors. As noted earlier, Kohut has observed that some very disturbed people can be capable of pursuing, at least during certain periods, gratifying and creative lives. I have also noted earlier the case of a disturbed and very gifted composer whose passion for music, I believe, played a critical role in maintaining his psychological integrity. It seems to me that certain people, endowed with certain talents and sensitivities, may be able to develop particular cultural interests that can then serve as partial symbolic substitutes for early failures in security and safety. In these cases, interests may serve, at least with partial success, some of the critical psychological functions served by ordinary object relations. In this sense, they are similar to the "compensatory structures" described by Kohut (1977).

It is also possible that of two individuals with the same degree of early security of attachment and of separation-individuation, one may have been fortunate enough to have had the opportunity later in life to develop abiding interests. For example, he or she may have been exposed to the kinds of traditions, values, and intellectual challenges that stimulate the development of interests. The presence of these abiding interests may then serve important object relational functions and generally contribute to maintenance of personality integrity, particularly in situations of stress. Obviously, the social context is an important later factor in determining the likelihood that one will develop deep abiding interests.

78. The attempt to reduce behavior to the more "basic" sexual and aggressive motives is at the heart of Freud's metapsychology and represents his attempt to find uniformity and basic reality underlying diverse appearances. However, the positing of basic sexual and aggressive instincts underlying behavior is essentially a causal theory rather than a motivational formulation. That is, what is being proposed is that basic instincts are *causally generating* motives and aims which then find expression in behavior. It is analogous to the formulation of a relationship between, let us say, a hormonal system or brain mechanism and a set of desires, aims, and behaviors. In this sense, I believe Shope (1967; 1970) is correct in his observation that unconscious wish is a causal concept. As I indicated earlier, I believe Freud was essentially correct in searching for underlying variables and deeper explanation. He was incorrect in limiting his focus to the sexual and aggressive behavioral systems and unsuccessful in elucidating the processes and mechanisms linking something like endogenous somatic excitation and a personal desire or aim. But then, we all continue to be unsuccessful in fully understanding this relationship. He was also incorrect in his assumption that because a basic instinctual system exists, then *all* behavior must, directly or indirectly, be somehow related to and expressive of it.

79. Although we must have oxygen in order to survive, one would not want to say either that all behavior can be reduced to a search for oxygen or that the desire for oxygen is a necessary component in all behavior. Indeed, that desire becomes an urgent and prepotent motive only in deficiency and survival-threatening states.

80. In this regard, the situation is similar to the hypothesized relationship between emotions and cognitive processes. As Simon (1967) notes, it is generally adaptive to give high priority (in the sense of attention and cognitive processing) to items or goals to which an emotion, particularly when it is intense, is addressed or is relevant. The adaptive and survival function of such a mechanism is apparent and is likely to represent a species-wide and deeply ingrained tendency (see also Leeper, 1948; and Osgood, 1969).

81. It could be argued that because I have discussed only the "negative" case of warding off threats to self-intactness and not the "positive" case of active pursuit of self-realization or self-actualization (emphasized by theorists such as Rogers [1959; 1961] and Maslow [1954; 1968]), I have not adequately dealt with the general issue of a superordinate motive or tendency in behavior concerned with the self. First, I do not

know of any psychoanalytic theorist who posits an all-embracing self-realization motive or tendency. But, in any case, it seems to me that most, if not all, of the above arguments also apply to the case of self-realization as superordinate motive. Even if one could say that self-realization is a general tendency of the organism (assuming one knows what that means), it does not follow that it is a component motive in all behavior, and that all behavior is either motivated by self-realization or is a defensive response to thwarted self-realization. I remind the reader once again of the fact that behavior is often opaque with regard to underlying motives and, hence, it becomes possible to read into behavior those underlying motives which are in accord with one's cherished preconception of human nature. What could count as evidence for and against such an all-embracing claim regarding the general motivational tendency of behavior?

82. Obviously, there will be many people whose impulse life is so disordered and chaotic and whose self-reflective abilities are so impaired that the practical goal of treatment will be improved control. But this is a description of certain individuals, not an ineluctable fact about human nature.

83. It is Freud's *conception* of the biological (for example, drive discharge theory and its limitation to sexual and aggressive drives) which is problematic, not his belief that the biological substrate is the critical source of universal wishes and desires. It must also be noted that to say that the biological is the source of universal wishes and desires does *not* mean that all behavior is directly or indirectly in the service or motivated by these biological sources.

84. I am aware that the question of the specific nature of our human nature is, to understate the matter completely, a highly controversial one. But it is a question that cannot be ignored and must be constantly pursued.

85. This includes the possibility that the current social context is so radically different from our original "environment of evolutionary adaptedness" (Hinde, 1959) that some aspects of our human nature are no longer fitted to the environment.

86. Although not explicitly stated in this fashion, what pervades this entire discussion (as well as Freud's id-ego model) is some variation of the mind-body problem. To say that the ego must appropriate to itself portions of the id is, in certain senses of the id concept, to speak of the transformation of the biological into the psychological or at least the representation of the biological by the psychological. As I argued earlier, perhaps *the* central question with which Freud was concerned was how something like a biological instinct or, at best, something that is on the border between the mental and the physical, gets represented in one's personal experiences and aims. Perhaps this question is not essentially different from asking how something like a physiological deficiency becomes "transformed" into and represented by being thirsty. However, in the present case, we are interested in how biologically grounded but psychologically relevant basic and early needs having to do with sensuality, attachment, separation-individuation, and object-seeking propensities get represented in personal aims and desires.

87. One result of the increased turning away of psychoanalysis and psychoanalytic theory from its early emphases and spirit to the current, predominant (and, as I have argued, somewhat sterile) conception of the id-ego model is that these early emphases and insights have been taken up by splinter and somewhat simplistic movements. (For example, quite obviously primal therapy picks up from Freud's early concept of dammed up libido and from his early emphasis on catharsis and abreaction). But they most often pervert these insights by transforming them into fads and surrounding them with simple hype and outlandish notions. Unfortunately, this is to be expected in view of the fact that these emphases and insights are isolated and do not become an organic part of a larger meaningful body of theory and knowledge.

REFERENCES

Aiken, C. *Selected Poems.* New York: Meridian, 1964.

Ainsworth, M. D. Infant-mother attachment and social development: Sociali-zation as a product of reciprocal responsiveness to signals. In M. P. Richards (Ed.), *The Integration of the Child into a Social World.* Cambridge: Cambridge University Press, 1974.

Ainsworth, M. D. Attachment. In N. S. Endler & J. McV. Hunt (Eds.), *Personality and the Behavior Disorders.* (Rev. ed.). New York: John Wiley, 1984.

Ainsworth, M. D., Bell, S. M., & Stayton, D. C. Individual differences in a strange-situation behavior of one-year olds. In H. R. Schaffer (Ed.), *The Origins of Human Social Relations.* London & New York: Academic Press, 1971.

Ainsworth, M. D., & Wittig, B. A. Attachment and exploratory behavior of one-year-olds in a strange situation. In B. M. Foss (Ed.), *Determinants of Infant Behavior,* Vol. 4, London: Methuen, 1969.

Alexander, F., & French, T. M. *Psychoanalytic Therapy: Principles and Application.* New York: Ronald Press, 1946.

Apfelbaum, B. On ego psychology: A critique of the structural approach to psychoanalytic theory. *International Journal of Psychoanalysis,* 1966, *47,* 451–475.

Arendt, H. *Eichmann in Jerusalem.* New York: Viking Press, 1963.

Arlow, J. A., & Brenner, C. *Psychoanalytic Concepts and the Structural Theory.* New York: International Universities Press, 1964.

Bader, J. B., & Philipson, I. J. Narcissism and family structure: A social-historical perspective. *Psychoanalysis and Contemporary Thought,* 1980, 3, 299–328.

Bakan, D. *The Duality of Human Existence: An Essay on Psychology and Religion.* Chicago: Rand-McNally, 1966.

Bakwin, H. Psychological aspects of pediatrics. *Journal of Pediatrics,* 1949, 35, 512–521.

Balint, A. (1939). Love for the mother and mother love. In A. Balint & M. Balint, *Primary Love and Psychoanalytic Technique*. New York: Liverwright, 1965.

Balint, M. (1937). Early developmental states of the ego. Primary object love. In *Primary Love and Psychoanalytic Technique*. New York: Liverwright, 1965.

Barnett, S. A. Exploratory behavior. *British Journal of Psychology*, 1958, *49*, 289–310.

Bergin, A. E., & Lambert, M. J. The evaluation of therapeutic outcomes. In S. L. Garfield and A. E. Bergin (Eds.), *Handbook of Psychotherapy and Behavior Change*. New York: John Wiley, 1978, pp. 139–189.

Berlyne, D. E. *Conflict, Arousal, and Curiousity*. New York: McGraw-Hill, 1960.

Bettleheim, B. *The Informed Heart: Autonomy in a Mass Age*. New York: Free Press, 1960.

Bettleheim, B. *Surviving and Other Essays*. New York: Knopf, 1979.

Bettleheim, B. Reflections: Freud and the soul. *The New Yorker*, 1982, March 1, 52–93.

Bexton, W. H., Heron, W., & Scott, T. H. Effects of dcreased variations in the sensory environment. *Canadian Journal of Psychology*, 1954, *8*, 70–76.

Black, M. Review of A. R. Louch's "Explanation & Human Action." *American Journal of Psychology*, 1967, *80*, 655–656.

Blight, J. Must psychoanalysis retreat to hermeneutics? Psychoanalytic theory in the light of Popper's evolutionary epistemology. *Psychoanalysis & Contemporary Thought*, 1981, *4*, 147–206.

Bowlby, J. *Attachment & Loss, Vol. I: Attachment*. London: Hogarth Press, 1969.

Bowlby, J. *Attachment & Loss, Vol. II: Separation*. New York: Basic Books, 1973.

Bowlby, J. Symposium on Emanuel Peterfreund on Information & Systems Theory. *The Psychoanalytic Review*, 1981, *68*, 187–190.

Brandt, L. W. Process or structure? *The Psychoanalytic Review*, 1966, *53*, 50–54.

Breuer, J., & Freud, S. (1893–1898). Studies in hysteria. *Standard Edition*, Vol. 2. London: Hogarth.

Bush, M. Preliminary considerations for a psychoanalytic theory of insight: Historical perspective. *International Review of Psychoanalysis*, 1978, *5*, 1–13.

Butler, R. A. Investigative behavior. In A. M. Schrier (Ed.), *Behavior of Nonhuman Primates*. London & New York: Academic Press, 1965.

Candland, D. K., & Mason, W. A. Infant monkey heartrate: Habituation and effects of social substitutes. *Developmental Psychobiology*, 1968, *1*, 254–256.

Caston, J. I. Plan diagnosis reliability II. Studies on the effects of interventions. In J. Weiss, H. Sampson, S. Gassner, & J. Caston. Further research on the psychoanalytic process. The Psychotherapy Research Group, Dept. of

Psychiatry, Mount Zion Hospital & Medical Center, Bulletin #4, June, 1980.

Clarke, A. M., & Clarke, A. D. B. *Early Experience: Myth and Evidence.* New York: Free Press (also Harper & Row paperback), 1976.

Cofer, C. N., & Appley, M. H. *Motivation: Theory & Research.* New York: Wiley, 1963.

Cofer, C. N., & Appley, M. H. *Motivation & Emotion.* Illinois: Scott, Foresman & Co., 1972.

Cohen, E. A. *Human Behavior in the Concentration Camp.* (Transl. M. H. Braaksma) New York: Grosset & Dunlop, 1953.

Cohen, L. B., & Gelber, E. R. Infant visual memory. In L. B. Cohen and P. Salapatek (Eds.), *Infant Perception: From Sensation to Cognition, Vol. I: Basic Visual Processes.* New York: Academic Press, 1975.

Cohen, L. B., Gelber, E. R., & Lazar, M. A. Infant habituation and generalization to repeated visual stimulation. *Journal of Experimental Child Psychology,* 1971, *11*, 379–389.

Collingwood, R. G. *The Idea of History.* Oxford: Oxford University Press, 1946.

Cox, F. N., & Campbell, D. Young children in a new situation with and without their mothers. *Child Development,* 1968, *39*, 123–131.

Dahl, H. The measurement of meaning in psychoanalysis by computer analysis of verbal contexts. *Journal of the American Psychoanalytic Association,* 1974, *22*, 37–57.

Delgado, J. M. R. *Physical Control of the Mind.* New York: Harper & Row, 1969.

Deutsch, H. *Psychoanalysis of the Neuroses.* Chapter 8—Agoraphobia. (Transl. W. D. Robson-Scott) London: Hogarth, 1932.

Devore, I., & Konner, M. J. Infancy in hunter-gatherer life: An ethological perspective. In N. F. White (Ed.), *Ethology & Psychiatry.* Toronto: University of Toronto Press, 1974, pp. 113–141.

Dickes, R. Parents, transitional objects, and childhood fetishes. In S. Grolnick & L. Barkin (Eds.), *Transitional Objects.* New York: Jason Aronson, 1978.

Dilthey, W. *Meaning in History,* Ed. H. P. Rickman, London: Allen & Unwin, 1961.

Doi, Takeo. *The Anatomy of Dependence.* Tokyo: Kodansha International Ltd., 1973. (Distributed in U.S.A. through Harper & Row and in Canada by Fitzhenry & Whiteside, Ltd.).

Dollard J., & Miller, N. E. *Personality & Psychotherapy.* New York: McGraw-Hill, 1950.

Eagle, M. N. Sherwood on the logic of explanation in psychoanalysis. In B. B. Rubinstein (Ed.), *Psychoanalysis & Contemporary Science, Vol. 2.* New York: MacMillan, 1973.

Eagle, M. N. Psychoanalytic formulations of phobias. In L. Saretsky, G. D. Goldman, & D. S. Milman (Eds.), *Integrating Ego Psychology & Object Relations Theory.* Dubuque, Iowa: Kendall/Hunt Publ. Co., 1979.

Eagle, M. A critical examination of motivational explanation in psychoanalysis. *Psychoanalysis & Contemporary Thought,* 1980, *3,* 329–380. Also in Laudan, L. (Ed.): *Mind & Medicine: Explanation & Evaluation in Psychiatry & Medicine,* University of Pittsburgh series in philosophy & history of science. Los Angeles & Berkeley: University of California Press, 1983.

Eagle, M. Interests as object relations. *Psychoanalysis & Contemporary Thought,* 1981, *4,* 527–565. Also in J. Masling (Ed.)., *Empirical Studies in Psychoanalytical Theories, Vol. I.* Hillsdale, New Jersey: Lawrence Erlbaum Associates, 1982a.

Eagle, M. N. Essay review of "Object & self: A developmental approach." *Review of Psychoanalytic Books,* 1982b.

Eagle, M. N. Privileged access and the status of self-knowledge in Cartesian and Freudian conceptions of the mental. *Philosophy of the Social Sciences,* 1982c, *12,* 349–373.

Eagle, M. Psychoanalysis and modern psychodynamic theories. In N. S. Endler & J. McV. Hunt (Eds.), *Personality and the Behavior Disorders* (Revised Ed.). John Wiley, New York, 1984.

Emde, R. N., & Robinson, J. The first two months. Recent research in psychobiology. In J. D. Noshpitz (Ed.), *Basic Handbook of Child Psychiatry,* Vol. I. New York: Basic Books, 1979, pp. 72–105.

Epstein, R., Lanza, R. P., & Skinner, B. F. "Self awareness" in the pigeon. *Science,* 1981, *212,* 695–696.

Erikson, E. H. Identity and the life cycle. *Psychological Issues,* 1959, *1,* 1–171.

Erikson, E. H. *Childhood & Society,* 2nd. Ed. New York: W. W. Norton, 1963.

Fairbairn, W. R. D. *Psychoanalytic Studies of the Personality.* London: Tavistock Publications & Routledge & Kegan Paul, 1952.

Fantz, R. L. Pattern vision in young infants. *Psychological Record,* 1958, *8,* 43–47.

Fantz, R. L. Visual perception from birth as shown by pattern selectivity. In H. E. Whipple (Ed.), *New Issues in Infant Development.* Annals of the New York Academy of Science, 1965, *118,* 793–814.

Fantz, R. L., & Fagan, J. F. Visual attention to size and number of pattern details by term and pre-term infants during the first six months. *Child Development,* 1975, *46,* 3–18.

Federn, P. *Ego Psychology & the Psychoses.* New York: Imago Publishing Co., 1953.

Feldman, S. S., & Ingham, M. E. Attachment behavior: A validation study in two age groups. *Child Development,* 1975, *46,* 19–30.

Fenichel, O. Remarks on the common phobias. In *Collected Papers.* New York: W. W. Norton, 1945.

Ferenczi, S. *The Selected Papers of Sandor Ferenczi.* New York: Basic Books, 1950.

Fingarette, H. *The Self in Transformation.* New York: Harper & Row, 1963.

Fingarette, H. *Self-deception.* London: Routledge & Kegan Paul and New York: Humanities Press, 1969.

Firestein, S. *Termination in Psychoanalysis.* New York: International Universities Press, 1978.

Fletcher, R. *Instinct in Man: In the Light of Recent Work in Comparative Psychology.* New York: Schocken Books, 1966 (first published by New York: International Universities Press, 1957).

Frankl, V. *Man's Search for Meaning: An Introduction to Logotherapy.* (Transl. Ilse Lasch) Boston: Beacon Press, 1959.

Freud, A. Discussion of Dr. John Bowlby's paper. *Psychoanalytic Study of the Child,* 1960, *15,* 53–62.

Freud, A. *The Ego and the Mechanisms of Defense* (Rev. Ed.). New York: International Universities Press, 1966.

Freud, A., & Dann, S. An experiment in group upbringing. *Psychoanalytic Study of the Child,* 1951, *6,* 127–168.

Freud, S. (1893–1895). Studies on hysteria. *Standard Edition,* Vol. 2. London: Hogarth, 1955.

Freud, S. (1895). On the grounds of detaching a particular syndrome from neurasthenia under the description "anxiety neurosis." *Standard Edition,* Vol. 3. London: Hogarth, 1962.

Freud, S. (1887–1902). *The Origins of Psychoanalysis: Freud's Letters to Wilhem Fliess.* New York: Basic Books, 1954.

Freud, S. (1900). *The Interpretation of Dreams. Standard Edition,* Vols. 4 & 5. London: Hogarth, 1953.

Freud, S. (1911). Psychoanalytic notes on an autobiographical account of a case of paranoia. *Standard Edition,* Vol. 12. London: Hogarth, 1958.

Freud, S. (1912). The dynamics of transference. *Standard Edition,* Vol. 12. London: Hogarth, 1958.

Freud, S. (1914). On narcissism. *Standard Edition,* Vol. 14. London: Hogarth, 1957.

Freud, S. (1915a). Instincts and their vicissitudes. *Standard Edition,* Vol. 14. London: Hogarth, 1957.

Freud, S. (1915b). The unconscious. *Standard Edition,* Vol. 14. London: Hogarth, 1957.

Freud, S. (1916–17). *Introductory Lectures on Psychoanalysis. Standard Edition,* Vol. 16. London: Hogarth, 1963.

Freud, S. (1920). Beyond the pleasure principle. *Standard Edition,* Vol. 18. London: Hogarth, 1955.

Freud, S. (1923). *The Ego & The Id. Standard Edition,* Vol. 19. London: Hogarth, 1961.

Freud, S. (1926). Inhibitions, symptoms, and anxiety. *Standard Edition,* Vol. 20. London: Hogarth, 1959.

Freud, S. (1930). *Civilization and Its Discontents. Standard Edition,* Vol. 21. London: Hogarth, 1961.

Freud, S. (1940a). An outline of psychoanalysis. *Standard Edition,* Vol. 23. London: Hogarth, 1964.

Freud, S. (1940b). Splitting of the ego in the process of defense. *Standard Edition,* Vol. 23. London: Hogarth, 1964.

Friedman, S., Bruno, L. A., & Vietze, T. Newborn habituation to visual stimuli: A sex difference in novelty detection. *Journal of Experimental Child Psychology,* 1974, *18,* 242–251.

Fromm, E. *Man for Himself.* New York: Holt, Rinehart, & Winston, 1947.

Fromm, E. *The Sane Society.* New York: Rinehart, 1955.

Gallup, G. G. Self recognition in primates: A comparative approach to the bidirectional properties of consciousness. *American Psychologist,* 1977, *32,* 329–338.

Gallup, G. G. Self-awareness in primates. *American Scientist,* 1979, *67,* (No. 4), 417–421.

Gassner, S. Research describing the therapeutic process during the first 100 treatment hours. In J. Weiss, H. Sampson, S. Gassner, & J. Gaston. Further research on the psychoanalytic process. The Psychotherapy Research Group. Bulletin #4, Department of Psychiatry, Mount Zion Hospital & Medical Center, June 1980.

Gedo, J. E. *Beyond Interpretation.* New York: International Universities Press, 1979.

Gedo, J. E. Reflections on some current controversies in psychoanalysis. *Journal of the American Psychoanalytic Association,* 1980, *28,* 363–383.

Giere, R. *Understanding Scientific Reasoning.* New York: Holt, Rinehart & Winston, 1979.

Gill, M. M. Metapsychology is not psychology. In M. M. Gill & P. S. Holzman (Eds.), *Psychology Versus Metapsychology: Essays in Memory of George S. Klein.* International Universities Press, New York, 1976.

Gill, M. M., & Brenman, M. *Hypnosis and Related States: Psychoanalytic Studies in Regression.* New York: International Universities Press, 1959.

Gill, M. M., & Hoffman, I. Z. A method of studying the analysis of aspects of the patient's experience of the relationship in psychoanalysis and psychotherapy. *Journal of the American Psychoanalytic Association,* 1982, *30,* 137–167.

Giovacchini, P. L. Object relations, deficiency states, and the acquisition of psychic structure. In S. Tuttman *et al.* (Eds.), *Object and Self: A Developmental Approach: Essays in Honor of Edith Jacobson.* New York: International Universities Press, 1981.

Goldberg, A. Review of Kohut's "The Analysis of the Self." *Psychotherapy & Social Science Review,* 1973, *I,* 26–28.

Goldberg, A. *The Psychology of the Self: A Casebook,* International Universities Press, New York, 1978.

Goldberger, L. & Holt, R. R. Experimental interferences with reality contact: individual differences. In P. Solomon *et al. Sensory deprivation.* Cambridge, Mass.: Harvard University Press, 1961.

Goldschmidt, W. Absent eyes & idle hands: Socialization for low affect among the Sebei. *Ethos,* 1975, *3,* 157–163.

Greenson, R. R.: *The technique and practice of psychoanalysis, Vol. I,* International Universities Press, New York, 1967.

Grünbaum, A. Is Freudian psychoanalysis pseudo-scientific by Karl Popper's criterion of demarcation. *American Philosophical Quarterly,* 1979, *16,* 131–141.

Grünbaum, A.: Epistemological liabilities of the clinical appraisal of psychoanalytic theory, *Noûs,* 1980, *14,* 307–385.

Grünbaum, A. Can psychoanalytic theory be cogently tested "on the couch"? *Psychoanalysis & Contemporary Thought*, 1982, 5, (Nos. 2 & 3), 155–255; 311–436.

Guntrip, H. *Schizoid Phenomena, Object Relations and the Self*. New York: International Universities Press, 1969.

Harlow, H. F. The nature of love. *American Psychologist*, 1958, 13, 673–685.

Harlow, H. F. Syndromes resulting from maternal deprivation: maternal and peer affectional deprivation in primates. In J. H. Cullen (ed.) *Experimental behavior: a basis for the study of mental disturbances*. New York: Wiley, 1974.

Harlow, H. F. & Harlow, M. K. Social deprivation in monkeys. *Scientific American*, 1962 (No. 5) 207, 136–146.

Harlow, H. F. & Harlow, M. K. Effects of various infant-mother relationships on Rhesus monkey behaviors. In B. Foss (Ed.) *Determinants of infant behavior, Vol. 4*. London: Methuen & Co., 1969.

Harlow, H. F. & Harlow, M. K. The language of love. In T. Alloway, L. Krames, & P. Pliner (Eds.), *Communication & Affect: A Comparative Approach*. New York: Academic Press, 1972.

Harlow, H. F. & Suomi, S. J. Induced depression in monkeys. *Behavioral Biology*, 1974, 12, 273–296.

Harlow, H. F., Suomi, S. J., & Collins, M. L. Effects of permanent separation from mother on infant monkeys. *Developmental Psychology*, 1973, 9, 376–384.

Harlow, H. F. & Zimmerman, R. R. Affectional responses in the infant monkey. *Science*, 1959, 130, 421–432.

Hartmann, H. *Ego psychology & the Problem of Adaptation*. New York: International Universities Press, 1958.

Hartmann, H. *Essays on Ego Psychology: Selected Problems in Psychoanalytic Theory*. New York: International Universities Press, 1964.

Hendrick, I. The discussion of the "instinct to master." *Psychoanalytic Quarterly*, 1943, 12, 561–565.

Hermann, I. Zum Trieblebln der Primaten. *Imago*, 1933, 19, 13.

Hermann, I. Sich-Anklammern-Auf-suche-gohen. *International Zeitung für Psychoanalysis*, 1936, 22, 349–370.

Hershenson, M. Visual discrimination in the human newborn. *Journal of Comparative and Physiological Psychology*, 1964, 58, 270–276.

Hesse, H. *Magister Ludi* (transl. M. Savill). New York: F. Ungar Publ. Co., 1949.

Hinde, R. A. Behavior & speciation in birds and lower vertebrates. *Biological Review*, 1959, 34, 85–128.

Hinde, R. A. Mothers' & infants' roles: Distinguishing the questions to be asked. *Ciba Foundation Symposium*, 1975, 33, 5–13.

Hinde, R. A. & Spencer-Booth, Y. Effects of brief separation from mother on Rhesus monkeys. *Science*, 1971, 173, 111–118.

Hogan, J. A. & Abel, E. Effects of social factors in response to unfamiliar environments in Gallus gallus spadiceus. *Animal Behavior*, 1971, 19, 687–694.

Holt, R. R. Freud's mechanistic & humanistic images of man. *Psychoanalysis & Contemporary Science*, 1972, *1*, 3–24. New York: Macmillan.

Holt, R. R. Drive or wish? A reconsideration of the psychoanalytic theory of motivation. In M. M. Gill & P. S. Holzman (eds.), *Psychology versus Metapsychology: Essays in Memory of George S. Klein.* New York: International Universities Press, 1976.

Holzman, P. S. The future of psychoanalysis and its institutes. *Psychoanalytic Quarterly*, 1976, *65*, 250–273.

Home, H. G. The concept of mind. *International Journal of Psychoanalysis*, 1966, *47*, 42–49.

Horney, K. *Our Inner Conflicts.* New York: W. W. Norton, 1945.

Horowitz, L. M., Sampson, H., Siegelman, E. Y., and Wolfson, A. On the identification of warded-off mental contents: An empirical and methodological contribution. *Journal of Abnormal Psychology*, 1975, *84*, 545–558.

Hull, C. L. *Principles of Behavior.* New York: Appleton-Century-Crofts, 1943.

Hunt, J. McV. Intrinsic motivation and its role in psychological development. *Nebraska Symposium on Motivation*, Vol. 13, Ed. D. Levine. Lincoln, Nebraska: University of Nebraska Press, 1965.

Jackson, G. *Soledad Brothers: The Prison Letters of George Jackson.* New York: Coward-McCann, 1970.

Jacobson, E. *The Self & The Object World.* New York: International Universities Press, 1964.

Janet, P. *The Major Symptoms of Hysteria.* New York: Macmillan, 1907.

Janet, P. *Principles of Psychotherapy.* (transl. H. M. & E. R. Guthrie). New York: Macmillan, 1924.

Kaplan, D. M. Review of Gedo's "Beyond interpretation." *The Psychoanalytic Review*, 1981, *68*, 285–288.

Kaufman, I. C. Symposium on psychoanalysis and ethology III. Some theoretical implications from animal behavior studies for the psychoanalytic concepts of instinct, energy and drive. *International Journal of Psychoanalysis*, 1960, 318–326.

Kaufman, I. C. Mother-infant relations in monkeys and humans: A reply to Prof. Hinde. In N. F. White (ed.), *Ethology and Psychiatry.* Toronto: University of Toronto Press, 1974.

Kernberg, O. *Borderline Conditions and Pathological Narcissism.* New York: Jason Aronson, 1975.

Kernberg, O. *Object-Relations Theory and Clinical Psychoanalysis.* New York: Jason Aronson, 1976.

Kierkegaard, S. *Purity of Heart.* New York: Harper Torch Books, 1956.

Kinney, D. G. & Kagan, J. Infant attention to auditory discrepancy. *Child Development*, 1976, *47*, 155–164.

Klein, G. S. *Psychoanalytic Theory: An Exploration of Essentials.* New York: International Universities Press, 1976.

Klein, Melanie. *The Psychoanalysis of Children.* London: Hogarth, 1932.

Klein, Melanie. *Contributions to Psychoanalysis* 1921–1945. London: Hogarth, 1948.

Klein, Melanie. *Envy & Gratitude.* London: Tavistock, 1957.

Klein, Milton. On Mahler's autistic and symbiotic phases: An exposition and evaluation. *Psychoanalysis and Contemporary Thought*, 1981, *4*, 69–105.

Kohlberg, L., La Crosse, G., & Ricks, D. The predictability of adult mental health from childhood behavior. In B. B. Wolman (ed.), *Manual of Child Psychopathology*. New York: McGraw-Hill, 1972.

Kohut, H. *The Analysis of the Self*. New York: International Universities Press, 1971.

Kohut, H. *The Restoration of the Self*. New York: International Universities Press, 1977.

Kubie, L. S. *Practical & Theoretical Aspects of Psychoanalysis*, 2nd Ed. (revised). New York: International Universities Press, 1975.

Kuhn, T. *The Structure of Scientific Revolutions*. Chicago: University of Chicago Press, 1962.

Lader, M. H. & Wing, L. Physiological measures, sedative drugs, and morbid anxiety. *Institute of Psychiatry Maudsley Monographs*, No. 14. London: Oxford University Press, 1966.

Leeper, R. W. A motivational theory of emotion to replace "emotion as disorganized response." *Psychological Review*, 1948, *55*, 5–21.

Leites, N.: *The New Ego*. New York; Science House, 1971.

Levenson, E. A. Language & healing. In S. Slipp (Ed.), *Curative factors in Dynamic Psychotherapy*. New York: McGraw-Hill, 1982.

Levine, F. J. Review of "Restoration of the Self." *Journal of the Philadelphia Association for Psychoanalysis*, 1977, *4*, 238–247.

Levine, F. J. On the clinical application of Kohut's psychology of the self: Comments on some recently published case studies. *Journal of the Philadelphia Association for Psychoanalysis*, 1979, *6*, 1–19.

Loevinger, J. Three principles for a psychoanalytic psychology. *Journal of Abnormal Psychology*, 1966, *71*, 432–443.

Loewald, H. Reflections on the psychoanalytic process and its therapeutic potential. *Psychoanalytic Study of the Child*, 1979, *34*, 155–167.

Lorenz, K. *Evolution & Modification of Behavior*. Chicago: University of Chicago Press, 1965.

Lorenz, K. *On Aggression* (transl. M. K. Wilson). New York: Harcourt, Brace & World, 1966.

Luborsky, L. Intraindividual repetitive measurements (P Technique) in understanding psychotherapeutic change. In O. H. Mowrer (Ed.), *Psychotherapy: Theory & Research*. New York: Ronald, 1953, pp. 389–413.

Luborsky, L. Momentary forgetting during psychotherapy and psychoanalysis: A theory and research method. In R. R. Holt (Ed.), *Motives and Thought: Essays in Honor of David Rapaport*. New York: International Universities Press, 1967.

Mahler, M. *On Human Symbiosis and the Vicissitudes of Individuation. Vol. I: Infantile Psychosis*. New York: International Universities Press, 1968.

Mahler, M., Bergman, A. & Pine, F. *The Psychological Birth of the Human Infant: Symbiosis and Individuation*. New York: Basic Books, 1975.

Malcolm X. *The Autobiography of Malcolm X*. New York: Grove Press, 1964.

Marmor, J.: Psychoanalytic therapy as an educational process. In J. Masserman (Ed.), *Psychoanalytic Education*, Vol. 5 of *Science and Psychoanalysis*. New York: Grune & Stratton, 1962.

Marvin, R. S. An ethological-cognitive model for the alternation of mother-child attachment behavior. In T. M. Alloway, L. Kramer, & P. Pliner, (Eds.), *Advances in the Study of Communication and Affect*. New York: Plenum, 1977, pp. 25–60.

Masling, G. & Cohen, I. S. Psychotherapy, clinical evidence, and the self-fulfilling prophecy. Unpublished manuscript.

Maslow, A. H. *Motivation and Personality*. New York: Harper, 1952.

Maslow, A. H. *Toward a Psychology of Being* (2nd Ed.). Princeton: Van Nostrand, 1968.

Mason, W. A. Motivational factors in psychosocial development. In *Nebraska Symposium on Motivation*. Ed: W. J. Arnold & M. M. Page. Lincoln, Nebraska: University of Nebraska Press, 1970.

Masterson, J. *Psychotherapy of the Borderline Adult: A Developmental Approach*. New York: Brunner/Mazel, 1976.

McCall, R. B. & Nelson, W. H. Complexity, contours, and area as determinants of attention in infants. *Developmental Psychology*, 1970, *3*, 343–349.

McDougall, W. *An Introduction to Social Psychology*, 29th edition. London: Methuen, 1948.

Meissner, W. W. *Internalization in Psychoanalysis*. New York: International Universities Press, 1981.

Miller, S. C. Ego autonomy in sensory deprivation, isolation, and stress. *International Journal of Psychoanalysis*, 1962, *43*, 1–20.

Mischel, T. Psychology & explanations of human behavior. *Philosophy and Phenomenological Research*, 1963, *23*, 578–594.

Mischel, T. Pragmatic aspects of explanation. *Philosophy of Science*, 1966, *33*, 40–60.

Mitchell, S. A. Twilight of the idols: change and preservation in the writings of Heinz Kohut. *Contemporary Psychoanalysis*, 1979, *15*, 170–189.

Modell, A. The ego and the id: 50 years later. *International Journal of Psychoanalysis*, 1975, *56*, 57–68.

Moore, M. S. The nature of psychoanalytic explanation. *Psychoanalysis and Contemporary Thought*, 1980, *3*, 459–543. Also in L. Laudan (ed.), *Mind & Medicine: Explanation & Evaluation in Psychiatry & Medicine*. University of Pittsburgh series in philosophy & history of sciences. Los Angeles & Berkeley: University of California Press, 1983.

Morgenthau, H. and Person, E. The roots of narcissism. *Partisan Review*, 1978, *45*, 337–347.

Munroe, R. L. *Schools of Psychoanalytic Thought*. New York: Dryden Press, 1955.

Murray E. J.: A content-analysis method for studying psychotherapy, *Psychological Monographs*, 1956, *70*, whole no. 420.

Nardini, J. E. Survival factors in American prisoners of war. *American J. Psychiatry*, 1952, *109*, 244.

Ornstein, P. (ed.). *The Search for the Self: Selected writings of Heinz Kohut: 1950–1978.* New York: International Universities Press, 1978.

Osgood, C. E. On the whys and wherefores of E, P, and A. *Journal of Personality & Social Psychology,* 1969, *12,* 194–199.

Passman, R. H. & Erck, T. W. Visual presentation of mothers for facilitating play in children. The effects of silent films of mothers. Presented to the Society for Research in Child Development, New Orleans, March 1977.

Passman, R. H. & Weisberg, P. Mothers and blankets as agents for promoting play and exploration by young children in a novel environment: The effects of social and nonsocial attachment objects. *Developmental Psychology,* 1975, *11,* 170–177.

Patton, R. G. & Gardner, L. I. *Growth Failure in Maternal Deprivation.* Springfield, Ill.: Charles Thomas Co., 1963.

Peterfreund, E. Some critical comments on psychoanalytic conceptions of infancy. *International Journal of Psychoanalysis,* 1978, 59, 427–441.

Peters, R. S. *The concept of motivation.* London: Routledge & Kegan Paul, 1958.

Piaget, J. & Inhelder, B. *The Psychology of the Child* (transl. H. Weaver). New York: Basic Books 1969, Chapter 2, pp. 13–19.

Piaget, J. Piaget's theory. In P. B. Neubauer (Ed.), *The Process of Child Development.* New York: New American Library, 1976, Chapter 9, pp. 164–212.

Popper, K. R. *Conjectures and Refutations.* New York: Basic Books, 1962.

Popper, K. *Objective Knowledge: An Evolutionary Approach.* Oxford: Oxford University Press, 1972.

Powell, G. F., Brasel, J. A. & Hansen, G. D. Emotional deprivation and growth retardation simulating idiopathic hypopituitarism: Clinical evaluation of the syndrome. *New England Journal of Medicine.* 1967a, 276, 1271–1278.

Powell, G. F., Brasel, J. A. & Hansen, G. D. Emotional deprivation and growth retardation simulating idiopathic hypopituitarism II: Endocronologic evaluation of the syndrome. *New England Journal of Medicine,* 1976b, 276, 1279–1283.

Prince, M. *Clinical & Experimental Studies in Personality* (Revised Edition). Cambridge, Mass.: Harvard University Press, 1929a.

Prince, M. *The Unconscious* (2nd Ed.). New York: Macmillan, 1929b.

Radnitzky, G. *Contemporary Schools of Metascience.* Chicago: Henry Regnery, 1973.

Rangell, L. Contemporary issues in the theory of therapy. In H. Blum (Ed.), *Psychoanalytic Explorations of Technique: Discourse on the Theory of Therapy.* New York: International Universities Press, 1980.

Rapaport, D. (1950). On the psychoanalytic theory of thinking. In R. P. Knight & C. R. Friedman (Eds), *Psychoanalytic Psychiatry and Psychology, Clinical and Theoretical Papers.* Austen Riggs Center, Vol. I. New York: International Universities Press, 1954.

Rapaport, D. (1951). The conceptual model of psychoanalysis. In R. P. Knight

& C. R. Friedman (Eds.), *Psychoanalytic Psychiatry and Psychology, Clinical & Theoretical Papers*. Austen Rigers Center, Vol. I. New York: International Universities Press, 1954.

Rapaport, D. The theory of ego autonomy: A generalization. *Bulletin of the Menninger Clinic*, 1958, *22*, 13–35.

Reich, W. *The Function of the Orgasm* (transl. V. R. Carfagno. New York: Farrar, Straus & Giroux, 1973.

Rheingold, H. L. & Eckerman, C. O. The infant separates himself from his mother. *Science*, 1970, *168*, 78–83.

Ricoeur, P. *Freud & Philosophy: An Essay on Interpretation*. Transl. D. Savage. New Haven: Yale University Press, 1970.

Robins, L. N. *Deviant Children Grown Up: A Socio-Psychiatric Study of Sociopathic Personality*. Baltimore, Md.: Williams & Wilkins, 1966.

Robinson, P. Apologist for the superego (review of B. Bettelheim's "Surviving & other essays"). *New York Times Book Review*, 1979, April 29.

Rochlin, G. *Man's Aggression: The Defense of the Self*. Boston: Gambit, 1973.

Rogers, C. R. *Client-Centered Therapy*. Boston: Houghton Mifflin Co., 1951.

Rogers, C. R. A theory of therapy, personality, and interpersonal relationships, as developed in the client-centered framework. In S. Koch (Ed.), *Psychology: A Study of Science*, Vol. 3. New York: McGraw-Hill, 1959, pp. 184–256.

Rogers, C. R. *On Becoming a Person*. Boston: Houghton Mifflin, 1961.

Rosenblum, L. The development of social behavior in the rhesus monkey. Unpublished doctoral dissertation, University of Wisconsin, 1961.

Rosenthal, R. On the social psychology of the psychological experiment: The experimenter's hypothesis as unintended determinant of experimental results, *American Scientist* 1963, *51*, 268–283.

Rubinfine. D. Reconstruction revisited: the question of the reconstruction of mental functioning during the earliest months of life. In S. Tuttman, C. Kaye, & M. Zimmerman (eds.), *Object & Self: A Developmental Approach: Essays in Honor of Edith Jacobson*. New York: International Universities Press, 1981.

Rubinstein, B. B. On the possibility of a strictly clinical psychoanalytic theory: an essay in the philosophy of psychoanalysis. In M. M. Gill & P. S. Holzman (Eds.), *Psychology Versus Metapsychology: Psychoanalytic Essays in Memory of George S. Klein*. New York: International Universities Press, 1976.

Rubinstein, B. B. On the psychoanalytic theory of unconscious motivation and the problem of its confirmation. *Noûs*, 1980, *14*, 427–442.

Rubinstein, B. B. (1981) Person, organism, and self: their worlds and their psychoanalytically relevant relationships. Paper presented at the New York Psychoanalytic Society, January 27, 1981.

Ruff, H. A. & Birch, H. G. Infant visual fixation: The effect of concentricity, curvilinearity, and number of directions. *Journal of Experimental Child Psychology*, 1974, *17*, 460–473.

Rutter, M. Separation, loss and family relationships. In M. Rutter & L. Hersov (Eds.), *Child Psychiatry*. Oxford: Blackwell, 1976, Ch. 3.

Rycroft, C. *Psychoanalysis Observed*. London: Constable, 1966.

Sampson, H. Psychotherapy Research: Theory & findings; Research findings. Psychotherapy Research Group, Department of Psychiatry, Mount Zion Hospital & Medical Center, Bulletin #5, 1982.

Sampson, H., Weiss, J., & Caston, J. Research on the psychoanalytic process. Presentation to the opening conference on psychotherapy research, Langley Porter Institute, Psychotherapy Evaluation & Study Center, San Francisco, Calif., October 1976.

Sampson, H., & Weiss, J. Research on the psychoanalytic process: An overview 2. The Psychotherapy Research Group, Department of Psychiatry, Mount Zion Hospital & Medical Center, Bulletin #2, 1977.

Sampson, H., Weiss, J., & Gassner, S. Research on the psychoanalytic process II: A comparison of two theories of how previously warded off contents emerge in psychoanalysis. The Psychotherapy Research Group; Department of Psychiatry, Mount Zion Hospital & Medical Center. Bulletin #3, 1977.

Sampson, H., Weiss, J., Mlodnosky, I. & Hause, E. Defense analysis and the emergence of warded off mental contents. *Archives of General Psychiatry*, 1972, *26*, 524–532.

Sandler, J. & Sandler, A. M. On the development of object relationships and affects. *International Journal of Psychoanalysis*, 1978, 59, 285–296.

Sand, R. Symposium on Emanuel Peterfreund on Information & Systems Theory. *The Psychoanalytic Review*, 1981, *68*, 174–186.

Sartre, J. P. *Being and Nothingness*. (transl. Hazel Barnes). New York: Philosophical Library, 1956.

Schafer, R. *Aspects of Internalization*. New York: International Universities Press, 1968.

Schafer, R.: *A New Language for Psychoanalysis*. New Haven: Yale University Press, 1976.

Schafer, R. *Language & Insight*. New Haven: Yale University Press, 1978.

Schanberg, S. M. & Kuhn, C. M. Maternal deprivation: An animal model of psychosocial dwarfism. In E. Usdin, T. L. Sourkes, & M. B. Youdin (Eds.), *Enzymes & Neurotransmitters*. New York: John Wiley, 1980, pp. 374–393.

Scheffler, I. *Science & Subjectivity*. Indianapolis: The Bobbs-Merrill, 1967.

Sherwood, M. *The Logic of Explanation in Psychoanalysis*. New York: Academic Press, 1969.

Shope, R. K. The psychoanalytic theories of wish-fulfillment and meaning. *Inquiry*, 1967, *10*, 421–438.

Shope, R. K. Freud on conscious and unconscious intentions. *Inquiry*, 1970, *13*, 149–159.

Silver, H. K. & Finkelstein, M. Deprivation dwarfism. *Journal of Pediatrics*, 1967, *70*, 317–324.

Simon, H. A. Motivational & emotional controls of cognitions. *Psychological Review*, 1967, *74*, 29–39.

Slap, G. W. & Levine, F. J. On hybrid concepts in psychoanalysis. *Psychoanalytic Quarterly*, 1978, *67*, 499–523.

Spence, D. Narrative truth and theoretical truth. *Psychoanalytic Quarterly*, 1982, *51*, 43–69.

Spitz, R. Hospitalism: An inquiry into the genesis of psychiatric conditions in early childhood. *The Psychoanalytic Study of the Child*, Vol. 1. New York: International Universities Press, 1945, pp. 53–74.

Spitz, R. Hospitalism: A Follow-up report. *The Psychoanalytic Study of the Child*, Vol. 2. New York: International Universities Press, 1946a, pp. 113–117.

Spitz, R. Anaclitic depression: An inquiry into the genesis of psychiatric conditions in early childhood. *The Psychoanalytic Study of the Child*, Vol. 2. New York: International Universities Press, 1946b, pp. 313–342.

Spitz, R. Discussion of Dr. Bowlby's paper. *Psychoanalytic Study of the Child*, 1960, *15*, 85–94.

Steele, R. S. Psychoanalysis & hermeneutics. *International Review of Psychoanalysis*, 1979, *6*, 389–411.

Stern, D. N. The early development of schemas of self, of other, and of various experiences of "self with other." Paper presented to a symposium on "Reflection on Self Psychology" at the Boston Psychoanalytic Society & Institute, Boston, Mass., November 1980. Also in S. Kaplan (Ed.), *Reflections on self-psychology*. New York: International Universities Press, in press.

Stolorow, R. Toward a functional definition of narcissism. *International Journal of Psychoanalysis*, 1975, *56*, 179–185.

Stolorow, R. Psychoanalytic reflections on client-centered therapy in the light of modern conceptions of narcissism. *Psychotherapy: Theory, Research & Practice*, 1976, *13*, 26–29.

Stolorow, R. D. & Lachmann, F. M. *Psychoanalysis of Developmental Arrests: Theory & Treatment*. New York: International Universities Press, 1980.

Strachey, J. The nature of the therapeutic action of psychoanalysis. *International Journal of Psychoanalysis*, 1934, *15*, 127–159.

Strasman, H. D., Thaler, M. & Schein, E. H. A prisoner of war syndrome: Apathy as a response to severe stress. *American Journal of Psychiatry*, 1956, *122*, 998–1003.

Sullivan, H. S. *Conceptions of Modern Psychiatry*. New York: W. W. Norton, 1947.

Sullivan, H. S. *The Interpersonal Theory of Psychiatry*. New York: W. W. Norton, 1953.

Sullivan, H. S. *Clinical Studies in Psychiatry*. New York: W. W. Norton, 1956, Chapter 8, pp. 166–181.

Suomi, S. J., Harlow, H. F. & Domek, C. J. Effects of repetitive infant-infant separation of young monkeys. *Journal of Abnormal Psychology*, 1970, *76*, 161–172.

Thoman, E. B. & Arnold, W. J. Maternal behavior in rats. *Journal of Comparative Physiological Psychology*, 1968, *65*, 441–446.

Truax, C.: Reinforcement and nonreinforcement in Rogerian psychotherapy. *Journal of Abnormal Psychology*, 1966, *71*, 1–9.

Unamuno, M. de. *The Tragic Sense of Life in Men and in Peoples*. (trans. J. E. C. Flitch). London: Macmillan, 1931.

Volkan, W. *Primitive Internalized Object Relations: A Clinical Study of Schizoid, Borderline & Narcissistic Patients.* New York: International Universities Press, 1976.

Von Eckardt, B. On evaluating the scientific status of psychoanalysis. *Journal of Philosophy,* 1981, *78,* 570–572.

Waelder, R. *Basic Theory of Psychoanalysis.* New York: International Universities Press, 1960.

Wallerstein, R. S. Self-psychology and "Classical" psychoanalytic psychology. The nature of their relationships—a review and overview. Paper presented at the Boston Psychoanalytic Society and Institute Symposium on the Psychology of the "self," Boston, Mass., Nov. 1, 1980.

Weiss, J. Crying at the happy ending. *Psychoanalytic Review,* 1952, *39,* 388.

Weiss, J. The emergence of new themes: A contribution to the psychoanalytic theory of therapy. *International Journal of Psychoanalysis,* 1971, *52,* 459–467.

Weiss, J. Psychotherapy research: Theory and findings, Theoretical introduction. Psychotherapy Research Group, Department of Psychiatry, Mount Zion Hospital & Medical Center, Bulletin No. 5, 1982.

Weiss, J., Sampson, H., Caston, J. & Silberschatz, G. Research on the psychoanalytic process I: A comparison of two theories about analytic neutrality. The Psychotherapy Research Group, Department of Psychiatry, Mount Zion Hospital & Medical Center, Bulletin No. 3, 1977.

Weiss, J., Sampson H., Gassner, S. & Caston, J. Further research on the psychoanalytic process. The Psychotherapy Research Group, Department of Psychiatry, Mount Zion Hospital & Medical Center, Bulletin No. 4, 1980.

White, G. L. & La Barba, R. C. The effects of tactile and kinesthetic stimulation on neonatal development in the premature infant. *Journal of Developmental Psychobiology,* 1976, *9,* 569–577.

White, R. W. Competence & psychosexual stages of development. In M. R. Jones (ed.), *Nebraska Symposium on Motivation.* Lincoln, Nebraska: University of Nebraska Press, 1960.

White, R. W. Ego & reality in psychoanalytic theory. *Psychological Issues,* 1963, *3,* (monograph No. 11).

White, R. W. *Lives in Progress.* New York: Holt, Rinehart & Winston, 1966.

Wilson, W. R. & Rajecki, D. W. Effects of the presence of familiar objects on the tendency of domestic chicks to peck in a novel situation. *Revue du Comportement Animal,* 1974, *8,* 95–102.

Winnicott, D. W. *Collected papers: Through Pediatrics to Psychoanalysis.* New York: Basic Books, 1958.

Winnicott, D. W. *The Maturational Processes and the Facilitating Environment.* New York: International Universities Press, 1965.

Yourcenar, M. *Hadrian's Memoirs.* New York: Farrar, Straus & Young, 1965.

Index

Abel, E., 26
"Absolute perfection" (Kohut), 50–51, 60–61, 219–220
Acknowledgment, role of, in validation of interpretation, 177–181
"Action language," 148
Adequacy, sense of, vs. narcissism, 60–61
Adult (mature) dependence in ego development, 77, 185
  (See also Self-cohesiveness; Separation-individuation process)
Adult narcissism vs. infant narcissism, 139
Adult pathology and infant behavior, incompatibility of analogies between, 69, 137–139, 155–157, 220
"Adultomorphization" of infancy, 69, 137–139, 155–157, 220
Affective reactions in developmental defects, 129–130
Aggressive instincts and behavior, 29, 132
  and anxiety, 45, 109–110
  interactional characteristics of, 118
  misapplication of, 37, 40
  and personality development, 197–198
  as reaction to deprivation, 76
  (See also Id instincts)
Agoraphobia, 33–34, 176–177, 215
  sources of, 113
Aiken, C., 209
Aim(s):
  cognitive-affective, 126
  empirical vs. theoretical approach to, 125–126

Aim(s) (*Cont.*):
  personal, transformation of universal needs into, 207–208
  superordinate, self-cohesiveness as, 130–131, 199–202
  therapeutic vs. theoretical, 154
Ainsworth, M. D., 27
Alexander, F., 12, 104, 221
Ambitions, development of:
  and mirroring and idealization, 52–53, 57
  and self-cohesiveness, 54–55
Anaclitic model of attachment, 10–11, 13–14
Anatomy of Dependence, The (Doi), 187
Annihilation, sense of:
  and agoraphobia, 33–34
  and intensity of instincts, 32–33
Anti-libidinal ego, 77, 84
Anxiety:
  castration, 45, 46, 109, 110, 141–142
  chronic, 112
  crime-punishment model of, 45, 109–110
  degrees of, 44–45
  disintegration vs. neurotic, 40, 44–47
  (See also Disintegration anxiety)
  and excessive excitation, 45–46, 110–112, 216–217
  and instinct, relationship between, 45, 112
  intense, 112–113
  Kohut's conception of, 44–47

About the Author

Morris N. Eagle is Professor and Chairman of the Department of Psychology, York University, Downsview, Ontario, Canada. He received his Ph.D. in clinical psychology at New York University. He has served on the faculty of New York University's Research Center for Mental Health, as Director of the Clinical Psychology program and as Chairman of the Graduate Psychology Department at Yeshiva University.

Dr. Eagle has been a Visiting Scholar at Cambridge University and the University of California at Berkeley, as well as Visiting Professor at the University of Pittsburgh's Western Psychiatric Institute and Senior Fellow at the University's Center for the Philosophy of Science.

In addition to his duties at York University, Dr. Eagle maintains a part-time private practice in psychoanalytically oriented psychotherapy. He has published more than 50 papers and chapters in professional journals and books, including *American Journal of Psychology, Journal of Experimental Psychology, Philosophy of the Social Sciences, Psychoanalysis and Contemporary Thought, The Psychoanalytic Review,* and *Science.*